THE END OF MORALITY

According to the moral error theorist, all moral judgments are mistaken. The world just doesn't contain the properties and relations necessary for these judgments to be true. But what should we actually do if we decided that we are in this radical and unsettling predicament—that morality is just a widespread and heartfelt illusion? One suggestion is to eliminate all talk and thought of morality (abolitionism). Another is to carry on believing it anyway (conservationism). And yet another is to treat morality as a kind of convenient fiction (fictionalism). We tend to think of moral thinking as valuable and useful (e.g., for motivating cooperative behavior), but we can also recognize that it can be harmful (e.g., hindering compromise) and even disastrous (e.g., inspiring support for militaristic propaganda). Would we be better off or worse off if we stopped basing decisions on moral considerations?

This is a collection of twelve brand new chapters focused on a critical examination of the options available to the moral error theorist. After a general introduction outlining the topic, explaining key terminology, and offering suggestions for further reading, the chapters address questions like:

- Is it true that the more that people are motivated by moral concerns, the more likely it is that society will be elitist, authoritarian, and dishonest?
- Is an appeal to moral values a useful tool for helping resolve conflicts, or does it actually exacerbate conflicts?
- Would it even be possible to abolish morality from our thinking?
- If we were to accept a moral error theory, would it be feasible to carry on believing in morality in everyday contexts?
- Might moral discourse be usefully modeled on familiar metaphorical language, where we can convey useful and important truths by uttering falsehoods?

- Does moral thinking support or undermine a commitment to feminist goals?
- What role do moral judgments play in addressing important decisions affecting climate change?

The End of Morality: Taking Moral Abolitionism Seriously is the first book to thoroughly address these and other questions, systematically investigating the harms and benefits of moral thought and considering what the world might be like without morality.

Richard Garner is Professor Emeritus of Philosophy at Ohio State University, USA. He is the author of *Beyond Morality* (1994). He has written articles on meta-ethics, the philosophy of language, and Chinese philosophy.

Richard Joyce is a Professor of Philosophy at Victoria University of Wellington, New Zealand. He is author of *The Myth of Morality* (2001), *The Evolution of Morality* (2006), and *Essays in Moral Skepticism* (2016), as well as numerous articles and book chapters on metaethics and moral psychology. He is also the editor of *The Routledge Handbook of Evolution and Philosophy* (2018).

THE END OF MORALITY

Taking Moral Abolitionism Seriously

Edited by Richard Garner and Richard Joyce

Routledge
Taylor & Francis Group

NEW YORK AND LONDON

First published 2019
by Routledge
52 Vanderbilt Avenue, New York, NY 10017

and by Routledge
2 Park Square, Milton Park, Abingdon, Oxon, OX14 4RN

Routledge is an imprint of the Taylor & Francis Group, an informa business

© 2019 Taylor & Francis

Library of Congress Cataloging-in-Publication Data
A catalog record for this title has been requested

ISBN: 978-0-8153-5859-6 (hbk)
ISBN: 978-0-8153-5860-2 (pbk)
ISBN: 978-1-351-12215-3 (ebk)

Typeset in Bembo
by Swales & Willis Ltd, Exeter, Devon, UK

Printed and bound in Great Britain by
TJ International Ltd, Padstow, Cornwall

CONTENTS

CONTRIBUTORS

Russell Blackford is a Conjoint Senior Lecturer in the School of Humanities and Social Science, University of Newcastle (Australia). He is co-editor (with Udo Schuklenk) of *50 Voices of Disbelief: Why We Are Atheists* and (with Damien Broderick) of *Intelligence Unbound: The Future of Uploaded and Machine Minds*. He is co-author (with Schuklenk) of *50 Great Myths About Atheism*, and author of *Freedom of Religion and the Secular State* and *Humanity Enhanced: Genetic Choice and the Challenge for Liberal Democracies*.

Björn Eriksson, a Lecturer at the Department of Philosophy at Stockholm University, works in normative ethics, metaethics, and the philosophy of social science. Notable contributions include "Utilitarianism for sinners" (*American Philosophical Quarterly*, 1997) and "Understanding narrative explanation" (*Croatian Journal of Philosophy*, 2005). He is currently working on a project he calls "Moral Practice in a Worthless World."

Richard Garner is Professor Emeritus of Philosophy at Ohio State University. He is the author of *Beyond Morality* (Echo Point Books & Media, 1994, 2014). He has written articles on metaethics, the philosophy of language, and Chinese philosophy. Two relevant recent articles are "Abolishing morality" (Joyce & Kirchin (eds.), 2010) and "Morality: The final delusion?" (*Philosophy Now*, 2011).

Ian Hinckfuss ("Hinck") was a lecturer at the University of Queensland (Australia) from 1966, until his death in 1997 (aged 65). He worked in logic, metaphysics, philosophy of language, and philosophy of science. He is author of *The Existence of Space and Time* (Oxford University Press, 1974). He was politically active, and passionately interested in peace studies and conflict resolution. His views on morality were radical, and he had some trouble publishing his manuscript on metaethics under its working title *To Hell With Morality*, but eventually Richard

Sylvan agreed to publish it as part of his "Discussion Papers in Environmental Philosophy" series at the Australian National University, though under the sadly subdued title *The Moral Society: Its Structure and Effects*.

Jessica Isserow is a lecturer at the University of Leeds. Her primary research interests are in metaethics, moral psychology, and normative ethics. Her doctoral project focused upon the "what next?" question for moral discourse, which concerns the best choice of action given the truth of a moral error theory. Her articles include "On having bad persons as friends" (*Philosophical Studies*), "Moral worth and doing the right thing by accident" (*Australasian Journal of Philosophy*), "Evolutionary hypotheses and moral skepticism" (*Erkenntnis*), and (*with Colin Klein*) "Hypocrisy and moral authority" (*Journal of Ethics and Social Philosophy*).

Richard Joyce is a Professor of Philosophy at Victoria University of Wellington (New Zealand). He is author of *The Myth of Morality* (Cambridge University Press, 2001), *The Evolution of Morality* (MIT Press, 2006), and *Essays in Moral Skepticism* (Oxford University Press, 2016). He is co-editor of *A World Without Values* (Springer, 2010) and *Cooperation and Its Evolution* (MIT Press, 2013), editor of *The Routledge Handbook of Evolution and Philosophy* (Routledge, 2017), as well as author of numerous articles and book chapters on metaethics and moral psychology.

Joel Marks is Professor Emeritus of Philosophy at the University of New Haven and a Bioethics Center Scholar at Yale University. In addition to writing hundreds of columns and articles, Marks is the editor of two books on emotion: *The Ways of Desire: New Essays in Philosophical Psychology on the Concept of Wanting* and (with Roger T. Ames) *Emotions in Asian Thought: A Dialogue in Comparative Philosophy*. He is also the author of a trilogy of books on amorality: *Ethics Without Morals: A Defense of Amorality*, *It's Just a Feeling: The Philosophy of Desirism*, and *Bad Faith: A Philosophical Memoir*.

Hans-Georg Moeller is Professor of Philosophy at the University of Macau. His research focuses on Chinese and comparative philosophy and on social and political thought. He is the author of *The Philosophy of the Daodejing*, *The Moral Fool: A Case for Amorality*, and *The Radical Luhmann* (all published by Columbia University Press). He has authored many other academic books and articles.

Jonas Olson is Professor of Practical Philosophy at Stockholm University. His main research interests are metaethics and the history of moral philosophy. He has published "Getting real about moral fictionalism" in *Oxford Studies in Metaethics, Vol. 6* (2011). He is the author of *Moral Error Theory: History, Critique, Defence* (Oxford University Press, 2014) and co-editor (with Iwao Hirose) of *The Oxford Handbook of Value Theory* (Oxford University Press, 2015).

Nicolas Olsson Yaouzis has just finished a post-doc project (in which he "demystified ideology") at the Institute for Advanced Studies at University College London. Currently, when he is not teaching at the Department of Philosophy at

Stockholm University, he is thinking and writing on political philosophy, philosophy of the social sciences, and the philosophy of video games. His articles include "'That is just what they want you to believe': A modest defence of Marxist paranoia" (*European Journal of Philosophy*) and "An evolutionary dynamic of revolutions" (*Public Choice*).

Thomas Pölzler is a Post-Doc at the Philosophy Department of the University of Graz, Austria. His main areas of research are metaethics and moral psychology. Further research interests include the philosophy of Albert Camus, intergenerational justice, and environmental ethics. He is author of *Moral Reality and the Empirical Sciences* (Routledge, 2018).

Jordan Howard Sobel (1929–2010) was a Professor of Philosophy at the University of Toronto. His research interests covered ethics, decision theory, logic, and philosophy of religion. He is author of *Taking Chances: Essays on Rational Choice* (Cambridge University Press, 1994), *Puzzles for the Will* (University of Toronto Press, 1998), *Logic and Theism: Arguments for and Against Beliefs in God* (Cambridge University Press, 2004), and *Walls and Vaults: A Natural Science of Morals* (Wiley, 2011).

Caroline West is Senior Lecturer in Philosophy at the University of Sydney (Australia). Her research interests span metaphysics (especially personal identity), metaethics, political philosophy, philosophy of wellbeing, and feminist philosophy. She has published widely in academic and popular journals. Her publications in the area of metaethics include "Business as usual? The error theory, internalism, and the function of morality" (Joyce & Kirchin [eds.], 2010) and (with Daniel Nolan and Greg Restall) "Moral fictionalism versus the rest" (*Australasian Journal of Philosophy*).

INTRODUCTION

Moral Skepticism and the "What Next?" Question

Sometimes—quite often, in fact—we discover that we've all been horribly massively mistaken about things. We were wrong about the Earth being at the center of the universe, we were wrong about men being smarter than women, we were wrong in thinking that the body contains four humors, and (I'll go out on a limb here) we were wrong about human affairs being observed and judged by an all-powerful invisible being.

What if we were mistaken about *morality*, too? I don't mean mistaken about the *content* of morality—we're all familiar with the idea of someone's judging that one course of action is morally right when really that action is morally wrong (or vice versa). I mean mistaken about the very idea of there being moral requirements and moral values in the first place. Maybe *nothing* is morally right or wrong, morally good or bad, morally praiseworthy or blameworthy; maybe there's no such thing as a moral virtue or vice, or moral desert, or moral responsibility. Maybe the whole conceptual scheme is just horribly massively mistaken.

Most people find this idea unsettling, to say the least. Some find it dangerous. And many find the very act of advocating the idea itself morally wrong (though it should hardly come as a surprise that the act of denying morality will be considered a moral transgression; one would expect the system to be self-vindicating).

Philosophers have always been aware of the prospect that there is something inherently fishy about morality, and down through the centuries copious amounts of ink have been spilled trying to prove otherwise. The results have been, I think it's fair to say, underwhelming. No consensus has ever emerged concerning the nature of moral truth or how we have access to it; every attempt ever offered seems vulnerable to pretty obvious objections. It is far from apparent that in over 2,000 years there has even been anything deserving of the name "progress" concerning our grasp of the nature of morality. Yet the struggle persists; cottage industries in moral philosophy flourish and wither; the arguments and counter-arguments continue without pause.

This book does not aim to contribute much to those arguments. What it concerns, rather, is the "What next?" question. Suppose, if only for the sake of argument, that we *were* to decide that morality is horribly massively mistaken. What would happen next? The usual thought is that we'd be in some manner substantially *worse off*: that our collaborative society would be threatened, that our motivation to cooperate would be diminished, that no one could be trusted, that perhaps the whole point of living would be lost. It all sounds very grim—at least until one realizes that there's not a shred of solid evidence that any of it is true.

Similar apocalyptic anxieties have been voiced before and found to be baseless—most obviously when the question was raised as to what would happen if most of us ceased to be religious. Those of a theistic inclination found it enormously challenging to imagine how society could possibly function in a civilized manner without the underpinning of religious belief. (Many continue to find it challenging.) "Established religion," wrote the Victorian historian James Anthony Froude, "is the sanction of moral obligation, . . . it creates a fear of doing wrong, and a sense of responsibility for doing it, . . . it is teaching men to be brave and upright, and honest and just, . . . noble-minded, careless of their selfish interests" (1883: 155). To raise doubts about religion, he concluded, "is a direct injury to the general welfare" (ibid.). But it turns out that the secular society that Froude so feared seems to operate at least as well as its religious predecessor. Atheists still find it in themselves to be trustworthy, they still cooperate, and they often even still find life meaningful.[1] How is this possible? The answer is obvious: because, typically, our reasons for acting in these prosocial ways are *over-determined*. Believing that the gods command us to keep our promises was not the only reason people had for doing so; it wasn't even necessarily the strongest reason. So, when that theistic reason fell by the wayside, other secular reasons remained to keep us flying straight. Even if there's no god to command promise-keeping, the atheist tells herself, it's still the morally right thing to do.

It's possible that the same pattern of over-determined reasons holds for morality. Perhaps, even without the backing of morality, people will still find it in themselves to be trustworthy, cooperative, and to find life meaningful. Even if one comes to the conclusion that there's no *moral obligation* to keep promises, for example, there are still good practical reasons for doing so.

In order to see that this is plausible, suppose that it were not the case—suppose that the only reason we had for keeping promises (to stick with that example) was a sense of moral obligation to do so. Then one couldn't declare that it is *pragmatically good* or *useful* that morality encourages us to keep our promises; one could make only the internal claim that it's *morally good* that morality encourages us to keep promises. Most believers in morality, however, will be keen to maintain that the question "What's good/useful about morality?" can receive an answer that makes reference to some framework of *external* values. (After all, mere internal self-vindication is hardly satisfying; even contemptible normative systems can pat themselves on the back.) And as soon as it's allowed that there is something practically good about morality's urging us to perform and refrain from various actions, it follows that there are more than moral reasons for doing so.

One thing that is apt to cause misunderstanding here is the unfamiliarity of stepping out of the moral framework altogether, for within that framework the declaration that there's no moral obligation to do X will be taken to indicate that one believes that refraining from X must be morally permissible. So someone who says "Nobody is morally obligated to keep promises" will ordinarily be taken to be expressing a *tolerance* toward promise-breaking—a tolerance to which most people will object. But this is, as I say, a misunderstanding. If one is doubtful of morality *altogether*, then the implication from "X is not morally obligatory" to "Refraining from X is morally permissible" breaks down: one no more believes that refraining from X is morally permissible than one believes that X is obligatory. (In an analogous way, when the atheist rejects the claim that God forbids stealing, he or she does not thereby embrace the claim that God allows stealing.) And therefore the connection to tolerance is severed, too. Just as one does not need a nod from God in order to be passionately opposed to something, nor does one's passionate opposition require *moral* backing. Our reasons to be passionately opposed or passionately in favor of things are often over-determined.

The view under discussion—that morality is horribly massively mistaken—is called the "moral error theory"—coined by John Mackie in 1977. The moral error theorist takes an attitude toward morality analogous to the one that the atheist takes toward religion: the world simply isn't furnished with the objects, properties, or relations necessary to render any of the discourse true. This is a view that this book does not much argue for but takes as its point of departure. Our focus is on the question "If we were to become moral error theorists, then what should we do with morality?"

At the center of this book is the theory known as "moral abolitionism," which is the view that, generally speaking, we'd be better off without moral thinking. One might be forgiven for thinking that this position follows automatically on the heels of the error theory, for surely if we conclude that some conceptual scheme is fundamentally broken, then we should just do away with it—as we've done away with talk of bodily humors, say. But in fact the two positions can be peeled apart. For a start, one might accept that there *are* such things as moral obligations, moral desert, moral responsibility, etc., but maintain that constantly thinking and talking in these terms—basing our decisions on these concepts—is, in practical terms, counter-productive, and we'd be better off if we stopped. And the reverse is also possible: one might argue that even if there are no moral obligations, etc., it serves our pragmatic purposes best if we carry on talking and thinking in moral terms. Therefore, even if one has accepted the moral error theory, further arguments are needed to establish abolitionism. This book is dedicated to the scrutiny of that task.

Before introducing the chapters and the structure of the collection, I will take some time to briefly sketch out the "point of departure" (i.e., the moral error theory) in a bit more detail. On what grounds might one think that all of morality is horribly massively mistaken—that none of it is true? In the course of this introduction I will also identify some key metaethical positions that may help readers orient themselves in subsequent discussions: noncognitivism, naturalism, constructivism, realism, skepticism, fictionalism, and conservationism. (I shan't burden the text with general citations to these positions, but refer the reader to a "further reading" section that follows this introductory chapter.)

Let's begin by reflecting further on the analogy of religion—where the reasons for doubt may be more familiar. There is no master argument that leads people to believe that religion represents a false description of the world; I suppose that fairly common considerations run along the following lines. The atheist knows of no phenomenon that requires a theistic explanation; the very features of a god (along with associated accoutrements such as an afterlife, miracles, etc.) seem sufficiently extraordinary to require particularly strong evidence; some of those features (e.g., creating the universe) seem potentially incoherent; it isn't clear by what means people would have access to theistic facts (the atheist likely endorses an epistemology wherein appeals to *faith* are looked upon with deep suspicion); the multitude of non-equivalent religions in the world and throughout history (the respective believers of which are confident that they are right and the others wrong) sets off alarm bells; and the atheist probably thinks that there is a good naturalistic explanation of the origin and persistence of religious belief—in sociological, psychological, and perhaps evolutionary terms—according to which the whole framework is an illusion (though possibly a socially useful one).

Though all of these considerations can be beefed up into more rigorous arguments, I suspect that most actual atheists find them sufficiently plausible even in this sketchy form that their disbelief is grounded in nothing much more complicated. The atheist need not claim to *know* that there are no gods; it is enough that the considerations are deemed strong enough that *disbelief* is reasonable. And my point is not that these arguments are sound (though I happen to believe at least some of them are); my point is just to sketch out the familiar kinds of reasoning that lead ordinary people to come to believe that an extremely widespread way of thinking—one which is deeply important to billions of people, one which lies at the heart of every historical culture we know of—is utterly mistaken.

The moral error theorist is an altogether less familiar creature than the atheist, but in all likelihood is moved by similar considerations against morality. The error theorist knows of no phenomenon whose explanation requires moral facts; the very features of moral properties seem sufficiently extraordinary to require particularly strong evidence; some of those features (e.g., free will) seem potentially incoherent; it isn't clear by what means people would have access to moral facts (the error theorist likely endorses an epistemology wherein appeals to *moral intuition* are looked on with deep suspicion); the multitude of non-equivalent moral systems in the world and throughout history (the respective believers of which are confident that they are right and the others wrong) sets off alarm bells; and the error theorist probably thinks that there is a good naturalistic explanation of the origin and persistence of moral belief—in sociological, psychological, and perhaps evolutionary terms—according to which the whole framework is an illusion (though possibly a socially useful one).

Again: some of these considerations can be beefed up into more rigorous arguments, but an ordinary person may be a confident error theorist while resting his or her disbelief on just these rough grounds. And again: my claim isn't that these are uncontroversial arguments—on the contrary, any of them will provoke howls of protest. My point is just to draw attention to the fact that although moral thinking is widespread and considered of deep importance—to the point that many will find the idea of doubting it simply unspeakable and unthinkable—in fact the kind of grounds that one might have for concluding that morality is utterly mistaken are not so very unfamiliar.

Some will object to the analogy. Religion, they will say, necessarily involves a reference to *things*—albeit invisible and supernatural things—like gods and heaven, and therefore it is possible for us to be mistaken if it turns out that the world lacks these things. But morality (they will say) is different, because it doesn't involve reference to *things*; so when we say "Promise-keeping is morally good" (for example), we are not really asserting anything about the world (in the way that we are if we say "God loves you"); therefore, regardless of what is or isn't in the world, it simply isn't possible for moral judgments to be *mistaken*.

It is true that religion deals in objects (e.g., gods), events (e.g., miracles), and places (e.g., heaven) more than morality does. Morality deals more in *properties* (e.g., being blameworthy) and *relations* (e.g., X's having an obligation to Y). But this doesn't show that the latter is somehow immune from error in a way that the former is not, since mistakenly thinking that something instantiates a property (when in fact it does not) is no more unusual or puzzling than being mistaken about the existence of an object, event, or place.

There is, however, a longstanding view that denies that moral judgments do involve the ascribing of properties or relations—that maintains that moral judgments are not really in the business of making assertions at all, in which case moral discourse would be by its very nature exempt from the kind of mistake of which the error theorist accuses it. This is the noncognitivist view. Assuming that noncognitivism about religion is implausible—assuming, that is, that religious language typically is in the business of making assertions about the nature of reality—then the moral noncognitivist would argue that the analogy that I've been pushing, between moral error theory and atheism, is misguided. Atheism (it will be said) is at least a *coherent* position, since if religious discourse involves assertions, then it might involve *false* assertions; but if moral discourse doesn't

even involve assertions, then it cannot involve false assertions. So, for example, if we consider one of the aforementioned reasons that might lead someone to sympathize with the error theory—that we know of no phenomenon whose explanation requires moral facts—the response will be that this is based on a misunderstanding: that moral judgments do not refer to moral facts, that the very idea of "moral facts" is flawed, and hence that it's misguided to expect any phenomena to have such an explanation.

The error theorist therefore must maintain that the noncognitivist is mistaken (i.e., error theory is a form of cognitivism). Noncognitivism has many potential problems, and I won't run through them here. But let's once more consider the religion analogy. A moment ago, the assumption was made that noncognitivism about religion is implausible. The intuitive basis of this assumption is that it seems farfetched to claim that there is no such thing as religious belief or assertion. There is probably no other discourse that so explicitly prizes *belief*! Could it be that no one has ever believed in God, that no one has ever asserted that God exists, that all the people who adamantly claim that they do believe in God are deluded about themselves? It seems hardly credible. It is one thing to be deluded about the nature of the world (a commonplace condition); it is quite another to be utterly deluded about the nature of one's own mental states (which is not to say, of course, that one is an infallible judge of one's own mental states).[2]

But once we reflect on the implausibility of religious noncognitivism, the prospects of *moral* noncognitivism appear to fade, too. Could it be that no one has ever believed that what the Nazis did was morally wrong, that no one has ever asserted that what they did was morally wrong, that all the people who adamantly claim that they do believe that what the Nazis did was morally wrong are deluded about themselves? It seems reasonable to think that the answer to these questions is probably "no." This, in any event, is what the error theorist thinks. We appear to treat many moral claims as if they are assertions, as if they do express beliefs—and the error theorist sides with appearances here.

If the noncognitivist is mistaken—if moral judgments are what they appear to be: assertions—then the next question to ask is "What would the world have to be like in order for these assertions [some of them, at least] to be true?" Since what a standard moral judgment does is ascribe a property to something (say: ascribe the property of *wrongness* to the action *stealing*), then we are really asking about the nature of moral properties. Here there is no shortage of different and competing answers, and my goal on this occasion is just to provide a very broad sketch.

The fundamental distinction in which we are interested here is between answers that have the result that moral assertions are sometimes true and those that have the result that they are never true. Consider analogous questions concerning what it takes for someone to be a witch. One account might say that witches are women who revere Satan and who practice rituals in an attempt to win his favor. A competing account might say that witches are women who communicate with Satan and who practice rituals that sometimes do win his favor. The variation in wording is slight but makes all the difference: according to the former account there may well actually *be* witches, since all it requires is certain attitudes and attempts; whereas according to the latter account there presumably aren't any witches, since it requires actually being in causal contact with Satan, who (going back out on my limb here) doesn't exist.

One might say that this would be "just a verbal dispute"—and I suppose it is, but admitting so isn't to denigrate the importance of the disagreement. It would be particularly important if there were a law that all witches are to be executed, for example. On the other hand, we can envisage a dispute that is more than verbal. Suppose two people agreed upon the second definition of "witch." One of these people might accept a worldview that includes supernatural beings like Satan, while the other does not. And so, according to the former, assertions of the form "She's a witch" might be true, while according to the latter no such assertions will be true. Thus we see that to be an error theorist about witches involves two components: a conceptual claim (concerning what the word "witch" means) and an ontological claim (concerning what the world is like).[3]

This imaginary dispute over the existence of witches boils down to whether there is an essential component to the concept *witch* that fails to fit within the naturalistic world order. The same is true of the dispute over the morality. The error theorist is, in all likelihood, a *methodological naturalist*: accepting into her global ontology only things that can be integrated into the scientific worldview. Since she maintains that moral properties are essentially imbued with characteristics that don't fit comfortably into this worldview, she rejects their existence. She is therefore no *moral* naturalist.

Moral naturalism comes in two flavors: constructivist and realist. The constructivist thinks that moral properties are constituted by certain attitudes and conventions. (Think, by analogy, of the property of *being illegal*.) The realist thinks that moral properties are mind-independent (in a sense that actually proves difficult to nail down[4]): moral facts are there to be discovered, not invented. Both the constructivist and the realist believe in moral facts, but they disagree about the nature of those facts. The error theorist need disagree with no part of the naturalistic constructivist's or naturalistic realist's *ontological* views, but she thinks that these naturalists make *conceptual* errors about morality: they misidentify or underestimate what a proper use of moral discourse commits speakers to.

There need be no single reason why moral properties cannot be naturalistic, any more than there is a single reason why *God* cannot be naturalistic. For example, the error theorist might think that the central moral concepts of *blameworthiness* and *praiseworthiness* depend on an idea of actions performed autonomously, but that the latter notion of *free will* isn't naturalistically defensible. (Needless to say, there is much to argue over there.) Or the error theorist might think that moral properties are imbued with a certain kind of practical authority: that moral requirements aren't considered simply as ways of satisfying our desires,

but often place demands on us regardless of our desires. (After all, one cannot evade morality just by saying "Yeah, but I don't care about that"—even if that is entirely truthful.) These categorical demands, moreover, seem imbued with more force than can be provided by the rules of any human institution—since, again, a person might reasonably ignore institutional requirements if he doesn't care and can avoid any negative repercussions. The error theorist may find no place for such institution-transcending desire-independent requirements within a naturalistic worldview. (Again: there is much to argue about there, of course.) In short, the error theorist believes that morality consists (conceptually) of types of demand and value that no combination of naturalistic properties alone can accommodate.

In contrast to the naturalist, the moral *non-naturalist* maintains that moral properties exist but that it is a mistake to expect them to be able to be integrated into the scientific worldview. Again, we can recognize constructivist and realist flavors. The view that moral properties depend on the decrees or preferences of a supernatural being could be categorized as a version of non-naturalistic constructivism. As for non-naturalistic realism, consider the following thoughts that might be said to do a decent job of capturing a package of common inchoate folk beliefs:

> Of course it's morally wrong to imprison people just because of the color of their skin. It would be wrong for you to do this even if you didn't care and could get away with it; and it's morally wrong regardless of whether everyone accepts that it's wrong—its wrongness isn't something we just make up. But, no, of course one wouldn't expect this wrongness to be something that science can demonstrate or investigate. We don't need science to tell us that it's wrong; any decent person *just knows* that it's wrong.

The error theorist may well hold that non-naturalism has gotten things right at the conceptual level: it has correctly identified what an ordinary use of moral discourse commits speakers to. But she thinks that non-naturalism makes *ontological* errors about what the world is like. If we take the above lines as capturing folk platitudes surrounding the concept of *moral wrongness*, then (the error theorist thinks) there simply isn't any property in the world answering to that concept. Any version of non-naturalism will, obviously, offend against any principle of methodological naturalism to which the error theorist has a standing commitment.

We have seen, then, that the error theorist's argument is a combination of a conceptual clam and an ontological claim, but it is worth stressing that neither claim considered alone has the label "error theory" stamped on it. The conceptual claim is one that moral non-naturalists may also want to endorse, and the ontological claim is one that is attractive to moral naturalists. We can, thus, interpret the error theorist as pinching a premise from each camp and combining them to come to a skeptical conclusion to which both will emphatically object.

[A word on the word "skeptical." Moral skepticism is the view that there is no such thing as moral knowledge. If we think of knowledge as *justified true belief*, then there are three forms of moral skepticism, two of which we have now encountered. The noncognitivist denies that moral judgments consist of beliefs, and therefore noncognitivism is a form of moral skepticism. The error theorist denies that moral beliefs are ever true, and therefore is also a type of moral skeptic. The third kind of moral skeptic denies that moral beliefs are justified. (Note that an unjustified belief may nevertheless be objectively true, so moral skepticism is compatible with moral realism.)]

This book takes the error-theoretic view of morality as its point of departure. With the exception of the first chapter, by Jordan Howard Sobel, there isn't much attention paid to establishing this skeptical position; rather, we are focused on the "What should happen next?" question.

Earlier in this introduction I suggested that one answer to this question—abolitionism—has a kind of default status: it seems natural to assume that if we come to the conclusion that some topic or way of talking is just false, then we should pretty much drop it. Of course, nobody is recommending a complete moratorium on even uttering moral words. The abolitionist doesn't object to people saying "Moral wrongness doesn't exist" or saying "Many people believe that breaking a promise is morally wrong," or even saying "Breaking promises really is morally wrong" as a line in a play (for example).[5] What these three examples have in common is that the speaker doesn't commit herself to the existence of moral wrongness, and therefore makes no error about the nature of the world. But it's probably fair to describe these uses as "peripheral." For all those more standard uses—where people use moral language *to make moral judgments*—the abolitionists recommend that we cease. Instead, they propose that our assertions, beliefs, decisions, and negotiations should involve a candid and truthful engagement with what we need and want.

The abolitionist faces competition from the fictionalist, who looks at some of these non-committing uses of moral language that the abolitionist allows, and wonders whether they might be extended more generally, such that a lot more moral language can remain than the abolitionist envisages. The fictionalist might take a particular interest in the third example: of how the context of being in a play (i.e., being involved in a fiction) removes assertoric force from one's speech, allowing one to say essentially anything without epistemic error. When, for example, an actor playing the lead in Orwell's *1984* writes "$2 + 2 = 5$," no one later lambasts him for his foolishness, for everyone knows that the actor never asserted this.[6] The fictionalist thinks that so long as we employ similar commitment-removing devices in our speech, we could carry on using moral language in many of the standard contexts that we currently do. The fictionalist is an error theorist about our current moral discourse, wherein things like "Breaking promises is morally wrong" are *asserted*; but if we were to alter our practices, such that we no longer asserted these claims, then the resulting moral discourse would no longer be in error.

But why would anyone want to do this? On the face of it, carrying on with a way of talking which we believe to be false, even if we transform it into a kind of non-committing fictional talk (perhaps *especially* if we thus transform it), seems an odd thing to want to do. The fictionalist's answer is that maintaining moral discourse, even as something similar to a fiction, is in some manner *useful*. This, then, is an important battleground for the fictionalist and the abolitionist. The abolitionist emphasizes the *harm* that morality has wrought and claims that therefore we should do away with it; the fictionalist stresses its *benefits* and claims that therefore we should keep it. Both parties recognize that this is, at bottom, an empirical dispute.

If, though, these theoretical decisions are to be decided on the basis of a cost-benefit analysis, then the possibility should be recognized that the course of action with the greatest net benefit might be that of simply carrying on *believing* in morality—even if these beliefs would be false and, moreover, the speaker accepts that they're false. This is the recommendation from the conservationist. The conservationist joins with the fictionalist (and against the abolitionist) in thinking that morality is, on balance, a useful practice. But the conservationist is doubtful whether the non-doxastic attitude recommended by the fictionalist can deliver the practical goods. Surely (the conservationist thinks), in order for us to get the benefits of morality, we need to *believe* in what we're saying. And so the conservationist proposes that, even if we come to accept the moral error theory (even if we believe that nothing is morally wrong, for example), when engaged in everyday decision-making we should pay no attention to this belief but instead carry on with our regular moral beliefs (believing, for example, that breaking promises is morally wrong).

This book is a collection of chapters focused largely on the cost-benefit analysis of what we should do with moral discourse were we to become moral error theorists. Each of the three positions just outlined—abolitionism, fictionalism, and conservationism—is, in its own way, an uncomfortable one, and none could fairly be described as "popular." Yet the debate warrants sensitive and charitable attention, to which it is the ambition of this volume to contribute.

The collection is divided into four parts of three chapters each. Part I ("Background Thinking") consists of chapters by Jordan Howard Sobel, Ian Hinckfuss, and Hans-Georg Moeller. The piece by Sobel is being published posthumously; it is extracts from an unfinished book-length manuscript which covers many of the broad moves of metaethics in the 20th century. It is unusual in this collection insofar as much of Sobel's energy is spent clarifying and arguing for our "point of departure"—moral error theory, with a particular focus on Mackie—and for this reason it makes a fitting opening to the collection. Sobel's thoughts eventually turn toward the "What next?" question, where he outlines some options without taking a strong stand. Hinckfuss's piece is also presented posthumously; it is excerpts from a book published in 1987 (but never widely disseminated). In many ways, Hinckfuss's arguments set the agenda for subsequent discussion—his was the first unashamed unambiguous no-holds-barred attack on the institution of morality. For this reason we are quite pleased to reinstate the title that he originally intended for his book, but was prevented from using: *To Hell With Morality*. Moeller provides some fascinating historical scene-setting: discussing amorality in the context of ancient Chinese philosophy and revealing unexpected connections with modern social theorist Niklas Luhmann. Moeller's chapter is noteworthy for the rich threads it ties together around the topic of moral skepticism, including (*inter alia*) examination of a passage from *Huckleberry Finn*, discussion of the medieval carnival, and even the analysis of a mundane German joke.

Part II of this collection ("The Case for Abolitionism") consists of a trio of chapters that all firmly advocate the abolitionist view—by Russell Blackford, Richard Garner, and Joel Marks—all of whom have in the past published books arguing for this view. Very broadly speaking, all three chapters pursue the same strategy—they situate abolitionism within contemporary metaethics, they criticize alternative options, and they stress the harm that moral thinking has done and does—but, of course, each author does this in his own nuanced way. All three are confident that we could get by perfectly well without the conceptual framework of morality—indeed, could probably get by a good deal *better*—and they paint complementary pictures of what life without morality might look like.

Part III ("Alternatives to Abolitionism") consists of a pair of chapters arguing in favor of conservationism, and one chapter arguing for moral fictionalism—two positions that currently represent the main alternatives to abolitionism for the moral error theorist. The chapter by Björn Eriksson and Jonas Olson ends up arguing for a qualified kind of conservationism that they call "negotiationism," which is designed to allow for a degree of flexibility in the extent to which a person conceives of a decision in moralistic terms, tailoring his or her response to the situation. In her chapter, Jessica Isserow offers a critique of abolitionism, arguing that, rather than jettisoning morality entirely, our practical ends would be better served by maintaining it with care and vigilance. In the third chapter of this section, I present the case for moral fictionalism, arguing that those who attack it (including abolitionists) often have a skewed view of what the position entails.

Part IV, the final part of this book ("Moral Skepticism: Case Studies"), critically examines the practical role that moralized thinking plays in some particular areas of real debate. Such empirically oriented discussions are invaluable to the metaethical dispute we are concerned with, the discussion of which all too often consists of "plausible speculation" sorely in need of evidential grounding. Nicolas Olsson Yaouzis's chapter examines contemporary debates about the nature of social justice. He argues that moralized political beliefs encourage the persistence of a status quo that serves the interests of the powerful, and that political activists have nothing to fear, and much to gain, by abolishing moral considerations from their arguments. Caroline West takes a contrary view when discussing feminism, arguing that the aspirations of those committed to feminist ideals are well served by the availability of a moral framework and would be badly undermined if we abolished it. Thomas Pölzler examines the debate over climate change, and comes to the conclusion that the "moralization" of this debate has neither the obviously harmful effects that the abolitionists would predict, nor the obviously beneficial effects that the conservationists and fictionalists might suppose. Pölzler's chapter, thus, sounds a cautionary note for those engaged in this debate: human psychology is often more complicated, and more odd, than our speculative and simple metaethical theories accommodate.

The two editors of this collection have divided the labor. Richard Garner conceived of the book and invited contributors; Richard Joyce edited the contributions and wrote this introduction. We thank both the Research School of the Social Sciences (Australian National University) for permission to reprint excerpts from Hinckfuss's 1987 work, and the literary executor of Sobel's estate for permission to print excerpts of his unpublished manuscript. Thanks also to Max Leiva for permission to use the cover image.

Richard Joyce

Notes

1 For empirical evidence that non-religious people are no less moral than religious people, see Zuckerman 2009; Hofmann et al. 2014. At the societal level, there is no discernible positive correlation between crime and a lack of religiosity; if anything, evidence indicates a negative correlation (Paul 2005; Jensen 2006).
2 Despite my pessimistic tone, noncognitivism about religion has had its defenders. See Santayana 1906; Braithwaite 1955; Randall 1958.
3 Two components, that is, in addition to requiring cognitivism about "witch discourse."
4 See Joyce 2015; Tropman 2018.
5 The abolitionist need not object even to someone's saying "Abolitionism is utterly false and moral realism is definitely true!" *if it's a line in a play*—that is, so long as the speaker isn't *asserting* this proposition. (It's hard to imagine that it would be a good play, though.)
6 Maybe the *character* (Winston) asserted it, but that's a different matter entirely. The fictionalist advice may conceivably be construed roughly as "Become like an actor engaging with a fiction," but not as "Become like a character within a fiction."

References

Braithwaite, R. B. 1955, *An Empiricist's View of the Nature of Religious Belief.* Cambridge: Cambridge University Press.
Froude, J. A. 1883. *Short Studies on Great Subjects, Fourth Series.* New York: Charles Scribner's Sons.
Hofmann, W., Wisneski, D., Brandt, M., & Skitka, L. 2014. "Morality in everyday life." *Science* 345: 1340–1343.

Jensen, G. 2006. "Religious cosmologies and homicide rates among nations." *Journal of Religion and Society* 8: 1–13.

Joyce, R. 2015. "Moral anti-realism." In E. Zalta (ed.), *The Stanford Encyclopedia of Philosophy*. Available at https://plato.stanford.edu/archives/win2016/entries/moral-anti-realism.

Mackie, J. L. 1977. *Ethics: Inventing Right and Wrong*. New York: Penguin.

Paul, G. 2005. "Cross-national correlations of quantifiable societal health with popular religiosity and secularism in the prosperous democracies." *Journal of Religion and Society* 7: 1–17.

Randall, J. H. 1958. *The Role of Knowledge in Western Religion*. Boston: Starr King Press.

Santayana, G. 1906. *The Life of Reason, Vol. 3: Reason in Religion*. London: Archibald Constable.

Tropman, E. 2018. "Formulating moral objectivity." *Philosophia*. Available at https://doi-org.helicon.vuw.ac.nz/10.1007/s11406-017-9942-9.

Zuckerman, P. 2009. "Atheism, secularity, and well-being: How the findings of social science counter negative stereotypes and assumptions." *Sociology Compass* 3: 949–971.

Further reading

Moral Error Theory

Joyce, R. 2001. *The Myth of Morality*. Cambridge: Cambridge University Press.

Joyce, R. & Kirchin, S. (eds.), 2010. *A World Without Values: Essays on John Mackie's Moral Error Theory*. Dordrecht: Springer.

Mackie, J. L. 1977. *Ethics: Inventing Right and Wrong*. New York: Penguin.

Olson, J. 2014. *Moral Error Theory: History, Critique, Defence*. Oxford: Oxford University Press.

Noncognitivism

Bedke, M. 2017. "Cognitivism and non-cognitivism." In D. Plunkett & T. McPherson (eds.), *Routledge Handbook of Metaethics*. New York: Routledge. 292–307.

Blackburn, S. 1998. *Ruling Passions*. Oxford: Oxford University Press.

Miller, A. 2010. "Noncognitivism." In J. Skorupski (ed.), *Routledge Companion to Ethics*. New York: Routledge. 321–334.

Schroeder, M. 2010. *Noncognitivism in Ethics*. London: Routledge.

Realism

Brink, D. 1989. *Moral Realism and the Foundations of Ethics*. Cambridge: Cambridge University Press.

Enoch, D. 2011. *Taking Morality Seriously: A Defense of Robust Realism*. Oxford: Oxford University Press.

McGrath, S. 2011. "Skepticism about moral expertise as a puzzle for moral realism." *Journal of Philosophy* 108: 111–137.

Smith, M. 1994. *The Moral Problem*. Oxford: Blackwell.

Constructivism

Bagnoli, C. (ed.). 2013. *Constructivism in Ethics*. Cambridge: Cambridge University Press.

Barry, M. 2017. "Constructivism." In D. Plunkett & T. McPherson (eds.), *Routledge Handbook of Metaethics*. New York: Routledge. 385–401.

Lillehammer, H. 2011. "Constructivism and the error theory." In C. Miller (ed.), *Continuum Companion to Ethics*. London: Continuum. 55–76.

Street, S. 2010. "What is constructivism in ethics and metaethics?" *Philosophy Compass* 5: 363–384.

Abolitionism

Campbell, E. 2014. "Breakdown of moral judgment." *Ethics* 124: 447–480.

Garner, R. 1993. *Beyond Morality*. Philadelphia: Temple University Press.

Ingram, S. 2015. "After moral error theory, after moral realism." *Southern Journal of Philosophy* 53: 227–248.

Marks, J. 2013. *Ethics without Morals: In Defence of Amorality*. New York: Routledge.

Conservationism

Cuneo, T. & Christy, S. 2011. "The myth of moral fictionalism." In M. Brady (ed.), *New Waves in Metaethics*. New York: Palgrave Macmillan. 85–102.

Jaquet, F. & Naar, H. 2016. "Moral beliefs for the error theorist?" *Ethical Theory and Moral Practice* 19: 193–207.

Olson, J. 2011. "Getting real about moral fictionalism." In R. Shafer-Landau (ed.), *Oxford Studies in Metaethics, Vol. 6*. New York: Oxford University Press. 182–204.

Suikkanen, J. 2013. "Moral error theory and the belief problem." In R. Shafer-Landau (ed.), *Oxford Studies in Metaethics, Vol. 8*. New York: Oxford University Press. 168–194.

Fictionalism

Hussain, N. 2012. "Error theory and fictionalism." In J. Skorupski (ed.), *Routledge Companion to Ethics*. London: Routledge. 335–345.

Joyce, R. 2017. "Fictionalism in metaethics." In D. Plunkett & T. McPherson (eds.), *Routledge Handbook of Metaethics*. New York: Routledge. 72–86.

Kalderon, M. 2005. *Moral Fictionalism*. Oxford: Oxford University Press.

Nolan, D., Restall, G., & West, C. 2005. "Moral fictionalism versus the rest." *Australasian Journal of Philosophy* 83: 307–330.

PART I
Background Thinking

1

GOOD AND GOLD

Jordan Howard Sobel

Editors' Note

Jordan Howard Sobel (1929–2010) was, at the time of his death, working on a book-length manuscript entitled *Good and Gold: A Judgmental History of Metaethics From G. E. Moore Through J. L. Mackie.* We are happy here to publish substantial excerpts. While the title "Good and Gold" is a sensible one for Sobel's whole project, it is clearly somewhat misplaced when applied only to this selection; nevertheless, we prefer to leave it as he intended.[1]

1 Introduction

This chapter is mainly about J. L. Mackie's projectivist error theory of the concepts and realities of ethics (Mackie 1977, 1980, 1982). The theory is in part that "the realities of the concepts" do not answer to them: this is the error part. It is for the rest that in moral thought and discourse we project what are, in reality, subjective sentiments to "make up" objective moral properties and conditions: this is the projectivist or objectificationist part. Ordinary moral views and statements in which these would-be properties and conditions are ascribed are in error, which is not to say that these views and statements are all false.[2] Consequent to the particular error common to them all, ordinary moral views and statements are none of them true or false. They are, of course, *grammatically* truth-apt, and may be true in the superassertability-sense of Crispin Wright (1996). They are also truth-apt in the sense of Frank Jackson (1998): they do purport to represent things as being a certain way. But as a matter of philosophical fact, given failure of presuppositions of the reality of their subjects, ordinary moral views are none of them true, nor are any of them false. So goes Mackie's projectivist error theory. [. . .]

This theory has three pillars. The first is that the realism common to ethical intuitionisms regarding "moral values" is true of the *concepts* of moral thought and talk. The second is that this realism is not true of the *realities* of this thought and talk. And the third is that the realities of this thought and talk are subjective sentiments and interpersonal demands, the projection and objectification of which are in the interest of humanity, in that they facilitate the enhancement of these sentiments, since it is in the interest of humanity that they be strong.

2 Intuitionist Realism Is Correct as a Theory of the *Concepts* of Ordinary Moral Thought and Talk

> Intuitionism has long been out of favour, and it is indeed easy to point out its implausibilities. What is not so often stressed, but is more important, is that the central thesis of intuitionism is one to which any objectivist view of values is in the end committed: intuitionism merely makes palatably plain what other forms of objectivism wrap up.
>
> *(Mackie 1977: 38)*

According to Mackie, ordinary moral thought and talk is in itself largely as intuitionists say it is. They are right as far as the *semantics, logic*, and *concepts* of moral thought and talk. They say of it nothing but "platitudes" made precise and sometimes unfamiliar by being dressed out in philosophic terms ("*a priori*," "synthetic"), and terms used with particular philosophic edges ("entails," "necessary"). There are many arguments for the power of the *conceptual* analysis run out by the intuitionist. Mackie organizes his own support for intuitionist realism as a good theory of the concepts of morality, and the "platitudes" surrounding them, by playing off principal alternatives in modern metaethics: naturalism and noncognitivism. Major weaknesses of these approaches to the concepts and semantics of ordinary moral thought and talk are strengths of the intuitionists' line.

According to Mackie, moral judgments presuppose that there are *objective values*, that there are *objectively prescriptive* qualities. Simple moral judgments purport to ascribe them to things, deny them of things, and so on.

> We do think of goodness [for example] as a supposedly objective ought-to-be-ness. In calling something good we do commonly imply that it is intrinsically and objectively required or marked out for existence, irrespective of whether any person, human or divine, or any group or society of persons, requires or demands or prescribes or admires it.
>
> *(Mackie 1982: 238)*

Not only philosophers think of values as "at once prescriptive and objective," as "external, extra-mental realities" which when known and appreciated do not "merely tell men what to do but will ensure that they do it" (Mackie 1977: 23). Ideas of values "at once prescriptive and objective" (1977: 23) are to be found not only in Plato. They are implicit in, they are part and parcel of (Mackie maintains), all ordinary distinctively moral thought and talk. They are central to the *meanings* of special words for this thought and talk: *moral concepts* are of such realities, such values. [. . .³]

3 Intuitionist Realism Is Incorrect as a Theory of the *Realities* of Ordinary Moral Thought and Talk

The first sentence of *Ethics*, after its preface, expresses its manifesto: "There are no objective values" (1977: 15).

Intuitionists are wrong about the *realities* of morality. And so are most people, though there are some, including some "outlaws and thieves" (1977: 10), who may have seen the light. If they have not clear consciences, but *no* consciences, this could be because they see that there is nothing moral. But such characters are rare. Most people are mistaken and encouraged by our ordinary moral concepts and ordinary moral thought and talk to take moral matters seriously.

But all of this is mistake-ridden, and centrally: it is *of the essence* of moral thought and talk to say that there are objective values. It is a general presupposition of all ordinary moral judgments that there are instantiable properties of objective value—which is to say that there can be objectively valuable things, or (in equivalent theoretical terms) that there are objectively valuable things in some possible worlds. This is the error Mackie finds in ethics. When he says there are no objective values, he is not saying merely that nothing is *actually* morally good, bad, right, wrong, and so on ("not merely"?!). He is saying that, as a matter of metaphysical fact, nothing is *possibly* morally good, bad, right, wrong, and so on.

It is not merely that, for example, there are *no objectively wrong actions*, but that there is no such thing as *objective wrongness* (cf. Mackie 1982: 115). It is certainly not merely that no kinds of action are actually objectively wrong, or wrong in *this* world, though some are wrong in other possible worlds. For the objective wrongness of a *kind* of action would supervene on its nature. And though (contrary to Swinburne 1976) "the logical character of this supervenience" would not be analytic (1982: 115),⁴ it would be necessary, so that if a kind of action were objectively wrong in *any* possible world, it would be actually objectively wrong in every world, and variations in what would be objectively wrong are not so much as *possible*. Mackie's nihilism runs not only against there being particular actions and things that are objectively right or wrong, or good or bad; it runs not only against there being kinds of actions and things that instantiate these properties; it runs against these properties themselves of objective rightness and wrongness (objective ought-to-be-doneness, and ought-not-to-be-doneness), of objective good and bad (ought-to-be-ness and ought-not-to-be-ness). [. . .]

4 Reading Mackie's Argument in Bayesian Terms

Mackie has negative reasons and positive reasons against ontological intuitionism. He opposes this theory somewhat as someone might (and as Mackie does) oppose the hypothesis that there is an Intelligent Designer of enormous power who is largely responsible for the variety and details of forms of life.

Negatively, a person can be impressed by features of living things that are apparently pointless and useless, and thus puzzling on the Intelligent Design hypothesis: nothing like the quite useless human appendix will be found in a well-made watch or computer. And a person can be impressed by how different a designer of forms of life would need to be from designers of which we have uncontested experience, and how different and mysterious it would be in its work. For this designer would evidently be *incorporeal*, since otherwise there would be the mystery of how it has gone all these years without being seen, or involved in collisions with things seen. Given this, it would have set about its great work of shaping species simple and complex, assembling genes, "tweaking" DNA, and so on (I am out of my depth!), with "no hands," simply by the power of thought and will.

Positively, a person opposed to *that* hypothesis may be comfortable in his opposition because he has in hand another hypothesis that would explain the phenomena of forms of life simple and complex, especially those details that challenge designer hypotheses. There is, he might reflect, Darwin's hypothesis of random variation and natural selection over billions of years *sans* intelligent intervention and free of deep mysteries of process and agency. There is, he might think, an alternative hypothesis to Intelligent Design that would have had "in the beginning"—i.e., before assimilation of the evidence of life, its history and diversity, now in hand—greater *initial plausibility* (that is, in terms of Bayesian confirmation theory, a greater prior probability), and which would have made the total evidence now in hand more likely (that is, in terms of Bayesian confirmation theory again, he might think that this alternative hypothesis will have had a *greater likelihood* for the now-in-hand evidence, or that this evidence would have been more likely) (cf. Sobel 2004, ch. 7.)

Mackie (1946: 77) writes that he pretends not "to be advancing any particularly new ideas" but to be offering a "re-statement of them" that reveals "how they may be brought together and interrelated" in a manner "radically destructive of all common views of morality." I am offering to contribute to this project by casting the ideas Mackie's advances in his 1977 book in terms of Bayesian "priors" for possible explanations of evidence, and "likelihoods" of this evidence on these explanations, i.e., for a Bayesian assessment that favors error theories (particularly Mackiean) over realistic theories (particularly intuitionist) of morality. I make this offer though there is no indication that Mackie was thinking in Bayesian terms when he first formulated his argument (1946: 77–86) and very little that he had it even somewhat in mind when he reformulated it in 1977.

I make it because: (i) it is clear that from the start he intended an argument from many "considerations" to an "in all probability conclusion":

> In this paper I do not pretend to be advancing any particularly new ideas . . . But I think I am justified in offering this re-statement of them, because it is seldom realised how they may be brought together and inter-related, or how radically destructive they are of all common views of morality, when this is done."
>
> *(Mackie 1946: 77)*

> None of these considerations is conclusive, but each has weight: together they move the moral sceptic (who is often of a scientific and inductive turn of mind . . .) to conclude that in all probability we do not recognise moral facts, but merely have feelings of approval and disapproval.
>
> *(1946: 80)*

> [I]n fact all the evidence suggests that not only are moral judgments derived from feelings, but there are no objective moral facts: the feelings are *all* that exists.
>
> *(1946: 86)*

(ii) In my opinion, bringing together and interrelating "all the evidence and con-siderations" of chapter 1 of Mackie's 1977 book, in terms of Bayesian "priors and likelihoods" assessment of a projective/objectifying error theory and an intui-tionist theory of objective moral values, enhances the argument of this chapter for the former "in all probability" over the latter.

Further to Bayesian *priors* and *likelihoods* of an hypothesis h in relation to evi-dence e: What would have been unconditional probability Pr(h), before this evidence was in hand, is *the prior of h*; and what would then have been the condi-tional probability Pr(e|h) = Pr(h & e)|Pr(h), is *the likelihood of h*. In this scheme, what would then have been the conditional probability Pr(h|e) is *the posterior of h*. It is a theorem of standard probability theory that if hypotheses h and h' are probabilistically exclusive, Pr(h & h') = 0, and probabilistically jointly exhaustive, Pr(h ∨ h') = 1, then:

$$Pr(h \mid e) \; = \; \frac{Pr(h)Pr(e \mid h)}{Pr(h)Pr(e \mid h) \; + \; Pr(h')Pr(e \mid h')}$$

and similarly (of course):

$$Pr(h' \mid e) \; = \; \frac{Pr(h')Pr(e \mid h')}{Pr(h')Pr(e \mid h') \; + \; Pr(h)Pr(e \mid h)}$$

so that:

$$\Pr(h\,|\,e) > \Pr(h'\,|\,e) \textit{ if and only if } \Pr(h)\Pr(e\,|\,h) > \Pr(h')\Pr(e\,|\,h')$$

Indeed, this equivalence of inequalities obtains for evidence e and alternative hypotheses h and h' whether or not these hypotheses are probabilistically exclusive and jointly exhaustive alternatives, since it is a theorem of standard probability theory that, for any probability function Pr, and propositions p and q,

$$\Pr(q\,|\,p) \;=\; \frac{\Pr(q)\Pr(p\,|\,q)}{\Pr(p)}$$

This is a consequence of the so-called definition of conditional probability, and the principle that probabilities of logically equivalent propositions are equal.

A Darwinist would find that to his mind both the priors and likelihoods, in relation to relevant evidence now known, of *his* hypothesis would have been, in the beginning, before this evidence was known,[5] superior to those of the Intelligent Design hypothesis. (A Darwinist *would* find this so, wouldn't he?!) From this it follows—assuming that to his mind these hypotheses are probabilistically exclusive and exhaustive—that the posterior of his hypothesis would have been then superior to that of Intelligent Design: this follows for him on "two counts" by the displayed form of Bayes's Theorem.

Not incidentally, these "posteriors"—the conditionals probabilities, Pr(Darwinism|NwKnwnEv) and Pr(IntDesign|NwKnwnEv) on the now known evidence *before this evidence was known*—are *equal* to our Darwinist's *present* unconditional probabilities Pr'(Darwinism) and Pr'(IntDesign)—*assuming no change in the relevance of this evidence for these hypotheses*—that is, assuming "rigidity" for them in the sense that what would have been his probabilities for the hypotheses conditional on this evidence *then* (before this evidence was known) are equal to his present probabilities for these hypotheses conditional on this evidence *now* (when it is known)—i.e., Pr(Darwinism|NwKnwnEv) = Pr'(Darwinism|NwKnwnEv) and Pr(IntDesign |NwKnwnEv) = Pr'(IntDesign|NwKnwnEv).

Why those equalities, given this assumption? Because (i) the unconditional probability of the now known evidence, Pr(NwKnwnEv), is *now* 1, and (ii), in general, for any probability function Pr and propositions p and q, such that Pr(p) > 0, $\Pr(q\,|\,p) = \Pr(p\ \&\ q)\,|\,\Pr(p)$: the so-called definition of conditional probability. From (i) and (ii), and a few elementary principles of probability theory, it follows that if Pr(p) = 1, then Pr(q|p) = Pr(q). Here is how. First comes (iii) if Pr(p) = 1, then $\Pr(q\,|\,p) = \Pr(p\ \&\ q)\,|\,\Pr(p) = \Pr(p\ \&\ q)$ (from (ii) and some algebra and logic). Also (iv) for any p and q, $\Pr(q) = \Pr(p\ \&\ q) + \Pr(\sim p\ \&\ q)$: total probability. And (v) for any p, $\Pr(\sim p) = 1 - \Pr(p)$: probabilities of negations.

So (vii) if $Pr(p) = 1$, then $Pr(\sim p) = 0$ (from (v)). Now, as mentioned in the previous paragraph, it is a principle of probability theory that probabilities of logical equivalents are equal. So (vii) $Pr(q \& \sim p) = Pr(\sim p \& q)$. So (viii) if $Pr(p) = 1$, then $Pr(\sim p \& q) = 0$ (from (vii) and (iv) and some algebra and logic given that probabilities are non-negative.) So (ix) if $Pr(p) = 1$, then $Pr(p \& q) = Pr(q)$ (from (iv) and (viii)). Therefore (x) if $Pr(p) = 1$, then $Pr(q \mid p) = Pr(q)$ (from (iii) and (ix)). QED. [. . .[6]]

5 Projectivism Is the Correct Theory of the Realities of Ordinary Moral Thought and Talk

Intuitionism is a special case of common-sense realism, the general idea of which is that "what you see is what you get." Implicit, however, is always the idea that the *best explanation* of "what you see" is that things (whatever sorts of "things" are addressed in a common-sense realism) *are as you see them*. This is, in the case in hand, the phenomena of moral thought and talk. Included are concepts of a range of would-be realities, moral qualities and modalities, and facts involving these. The best explanation of these phenomena, a moral realist must claim, runs in terms of there *being* such realities, and of their applications being as if the moral realm constituted thereby were made for us.

The moral realist of course thinks that he tells an essential part of the best, the most illuminating and edifying, story of the phenomena of moral thought and talk *as found*. How might his story go? Perhaps like this:

> There are ethical realities of right and wrong, and good and bad, that are "intrinsically reason-giving [instantiations] of properties" (Wright 1996: 1). They are realities that are necessarily motivating when apprehended and considered. Morality, as constituted by these realities, is *for* humanity. *Justice*, realized in the characters of its members, is essential for the maintenance of societies in which humans can interact to mutual advantage, without which interaction they can survive only with difficulty—life outside society is, for a man, "solitary, brutish, and short," wrote Thomas Hobbes. We are communal animals. *Benevolence*, realized in considerable measure, is essential to the flourishing of human communities. It was therefore likely, if not necessary, that human beings should have evolved with capacities to notice the realities of morality, to form ideas of them, and to think and talk about them as we do, and thus to be influenced by them. And it was likely that human cultures should have evolved, and should continue to evolve, to more or more complete and mature embodiments of morality's objective principles.

In this story, ethical realities enter as "theoretical entities" somewhat analogous to the particles of the physics. The hypothesis of their reality is (intuitionists can be allowed implicitly to claim) the bedrock of a best explanation of how we come think and talk as if there were objectively real properties of right and wrong, and good and bad.

Mackie proposes, on the contrary, that the realities presupposed by our moral talk and thought are fictions, but—and now comes the essential point of his alternative antirealist theory—they are a very useful fiction for humanity. Were a person transported to early days, long before there were human beings, and asked to consider the likely psychological nature of human beings, he would, with an eye to their usefulness to the species, have predicted that selection would produce for it a nature that facilitated the making up of these fictional value-properties, and their acceptance as real. Mackie's projectivism says how this has taken place. It provides, he says, a better account of the phenomena: his view is that "our best science" finds no explanatory use for the "queer, intrinsically reason-giving properties" of the intuitionist.

As I said, there is according to Mackie a theory other than intuitionist onto-logical realism that explains better what he holds is the truth of intuitionist conceptual realism and the phenomena of moral talk and thought that it accu-rately summarizes. This other theory explains better why there is just this thought and talk, without granting it the possibility of representative truth.[7]

Mackie finds the main lines of this theory in the work of that most subtle phi-losopher of human nature and social living, David Hume. Now come passages in which Mackie's details, and elaborates, the theory that he finds in Hume.

> Although the only hard fact of the matter is that the speaker and others have or would have certain sentiments . . . we tend to project these senti-ments onto the actions or characters that arouse them . . . so that we think of those actions and characters as possessing, objectively and intrinsically, certain distinctively moral features; but these features are fictitious. Since these fictitious features are projections of sentiments which are intrinsi-cally action-guiding, these features too are naturally thought of as intrinsically action-guiding. Since the system of sentiments includes a social demand that certain things be done or not done, the fictitious features are taken to involve corresponding requirements and necessities . . . This projection or objectifi-cation is not just a trick of individual psychology [though it is this in Hume's view, as far as it is made explicit (Sobel)] . . . [T]here is a system in which the sentiments of each person both modify and reinforce those of others; the supposedly objective moral features both aid and reflect this communication of sentiments, and the whole system of thought of which objectification, the false belief in the fictitious features, is a contributing part, flourishes partly because . . . it serves a social function.
>
> (Mackie 1980: 70)

It [i.e., Hume's projective error theory] seems to be the only explanation which will accommodate together (i) the fact that moral statements are regularly treated, both syntactically and conversationally, as being capable of being simply true or false—and true or false through and through, even in their distinctively moral aspect, not just with regard to a pre-moral core—(ii) the way in which these statements are taken to be intrinsically action-guiding, not only contingently upon the hearer's having certain desires or inclinations, that is, to state categorical imperatives, and (iii) the thesis, for which Hume has argued forcefully, that the essential fact of the matter, which underlies moral judgments . . . is that people have various sentiments, or rather that there are interpersonal systems of sentiments.

(Mackie 1980: 71)

Moral and evaluative thinking arises from human sentiments and purposes; it involves systems of attitudes developed particularly by interactions between people in societies, and the concept of intrinsic requiredness results from a projection of these attitudes upon their objects, by an abstraction of the requiring from the persons—or institutions built out of persons—that really do the requiring. This Humean style of explanation of our concept of goodness or objective requiredness is much more acceptable than the rival view that things or states of affairs actually have such objective requiredness.

(Mackie 1982: 239)

According to the error theoretic account, by a complex of processes, from what are "interpersonal systems of sentiments" (Mackie 1980: 71), nothing more, have been raised objective values—"a new creation" (Hume [1751] 2006: 89)—that are perceived and felt to make objectively authoritative demands for the very sentiments out of which they have been raised. "But why?" Because all this is *useful* for humanity, facilitating as it does talking up shared sentiments that it is useful for us should be strong—sentiments, for example, that approve of veracity, honesty, and benevolence. This is not to say there is no downside to our dispositions to the fictions of morality, but only that "all in all" they have been good for the species.

Mackie can claim with considerable plausibility (to many minds[8]) that something like Hume's theory provides a *better* account than that of intuitionism of the phenomena, including most prominently that we have the concepts we have of objective values, and that we engage in thought and talk that presupposes the possible instantiations of the concepts. This hypothesis is, he can argue, superior in two ways, though there is textual evidence only for his sense for the first of these ways: namely, that of its intrinsic plausibility in which dimension the hypothesis of objective moral values is stressed.

An advantage in terms of what would "beforehand" have been the initial or intrinsic plausibility enjoyed by error theory is that does not include the posit of objective values, and of nascent capacities to notice these, that natural selective processes could favor and nurture. It instead affirms the nascent dispositions (i) to approve and disapprove, to demand and condemn, in ways useful to our lives by way of their influence on our behavior, (ii) to project onto their objects—as if they were objective qualities—sentiments of approval and disapproval, and (iii) that perceptions (whether or not veridical) of objectively authoritative values attaching to objects of approval and disapproval subjectively validate and thereby enhance our sentiments, making their expression *more* useful for our lives—that is, that we have come by natural selective processes to have sentiments for and against things, dispositions to demand that others share these sentiments, dispositions to project our sentiments, and to depersonalize and objectify demands we experience, thereby to create illusions of objective values.

Error theory explains *better* why we have concepts of objective values, and engage in thought and talk that presupposes their reality, than does the intuitionists' hypothesis that says that objective values are real. It explains this better, in part, as said, because it is not burdened by the most improbable and very hard to believe in reality of what would be very queer properties and modalities. It has this advantage in terms of its "beforehand" initial plausibility. Also, this Humean account has certain advantages in terms of the likelihoods, on the assumption "beforehand" of its truth, of the phenomena surrounding our concepts of objective value, for, while intuitionism may make as likely the fact that we have these concepts, it is challenged by certain other facts about them.

For one batch, there are the facts of cultural relativity. Assuming, before one knew of these facts, the truth of error theory, one would *expect* the use of these concepts in a culture to be supportive of the ways of living of this culture, and so would expect cultural differences in their uses, *unless* one expected cultures would not differ in their ways of living. The likelihood of cultural differences in applications of these concepts, even if not great on the assumption of error theory, should be, to most minds, greater than it is according to intuitionism, which needs to labor in order so much as to accommodate facts of these differences without putting them down to the sub-hypothesis that they are due to "perceptions, most of them seriously inadequate and badly distorted, of objective values" (Mackie 1977: 37), and in the process of this labor to suffer diminishment of its initial plausibility.

For another batch, there are facts of *bias* reflected in generally confident applications of our concepts of objective value; there is extensive evidence of bias favoring *us*—that is, favoring human beings. That we predicate "wrong" of lies and promise-breaking serves conditions in which we can count on others to tell the truth and keep promises they have made, and so share information and enter into arrangements for acting in each case to mutual advantage. These prominent applications of "wrong" are nothing to oysters and flies, and are very little if anything to dogs and cats. For another manifestation of bias, consider that it is a likely universal that in every culture when it is a choice whether to drive a runaway tram into a crowd of people or a gaggle of geese, there is a uniquely moral choice.

The bias displayed in confident and uncontroversial applications of our moral concepts, the bias to us, to humankind, is what one expects before knowledge of it, on the assumption that the Mackie/Hume theory is true of these concepts. For on this theory the *extensions* of these concepts have *evolved* for us. What can intuitionism say of patterns of bias and moral speciesism? It is, according to this theory, *as if* morality were made for us, though on an intuitionist view that is no more possible than that arithmetic, which is similarly a system of eternal necessary truths, was made *for us*, which is to say: it is impossible. What luck for humanity that the moral edifice happens to tilt so in our favor! This system of moral truths could, it seems, have been species neutral. Or, if skewed, arranged just as well in the favor of the buffalo, the oak, or the oyster. For surely "the life of man is of no greater importance to the universe than that of an oyster" (Hume [1777] 1998: 319). And yet it is a "truth universally acknowledged *by us*" that the life of a man is vastly more important than that of an oyster, which are, you know, best eaten *alive*! [. . .]

"If God did not exist," says Voltaire, "it would be necessary to invent him." Intuitionists should be prepared to say "If objective values did not exist, we would have to invent them," for intuitionists believe that *it is a good thing for us* that there are objective values instantiated as they are in an objective moral realm. This is, I have implied, at the heart of their best explanation of why we have concepts of objective values. So they should believe that if they were not to exist, we would have invented them and this realm for them to inhabit: they should believe, in that case, that social and rational beings such as us would have, in the fullness of time, evolved psychologies for illusions of objective values deployed in morality designed to facilitate our social lives, and to favor us over all other creatures great and small. Intuitionists should be prepared to concede this to Mackie and Hume; it is a point at which the explanations of their theories intersect. But on reflection they could not be *happy* with this concession, for they would see coming this invitation:

> Let us then say that we *did* invent them, in the sense that Mackie and Hume say that we have done—that is, let us say that we have evolved to have concepts of them with extensions suited to our social needs. In this manner we return to a theory that explains, *without* positing objective values, all that can be explained *with* them, and explains it *better*. We reach, given this difference, a theory that should be of much greater "beforehand" intrinsic plausibility than an intuitionist theory tweaked (as it would need to be) to predict the hardly deniable bias of morality towards humanity. Error theory, since (to most minds) superior in intrinsic plausibility as well as in likelihoods for the phenomena of moral concepts and judgments, is (to most minds) a better theory of this phenomena, and we should say that since objective values do not exist, processes of evolutionary selection *have* invented them for us. [. . .]

6 Is it Possible to Hold Strong Views While Believing That They Are Simply Attitudes?

> A man can hold strong moral views . . . while believing that they were simply attitudes and policies with regard to conduct that he and other people held.
>
> *(Mackie 1977: 16)*

There is no problem with a person's holding "strong views" that he thinks are simply attitudes and ways he happens to feel. The problem with the above quotation is entirely in the word "moral," for Mackie thinks (and is by no means alone in thinking) that to have in mind a strong moral view is *not* to have in mind simply an attitude, but to have acceptingly in mind a proposition that presupposes an objectively authoritative prescriptive reality coincident with having in mind a *moral* attitude. The problem is how Mackie can think that a person can have such views in mind, strong moral views, while mistaking them for attitudes, nothing more: according to his theory, moral views are *not* simply attitudes, nothing more, and could hardly be mistaken for them.

Consider what would be a misunderstanding in roughly the other direction. In our prayers for some future conduct, we *wish* for it. Could someone rehearse a fervent prayer for future conduct, while thinking that what he was doing was merely *expecting* that conduct? Surely not. It is imaginable, just, that a person might, in linguistic confusion, have in mind for "would that" the sense of "will that," and so use words that are properly for prayers to express instead expectations. He could believe this about his optative utterances, and be right, but he can hardly pray believing that what he is doing is simply *anticipating*. Indeed, he could hardly pray and think he was simply *wishing*.

Again, one could hardly *believe* that it is raining, while thinking that one is not believing but, say, *hoping* that it is raining. Indeed, one could hardly believe that it is raining, while thinking that one is *wishfully thinking* that it is raining. Similarly, surely, for *holding strong views* while thinking they are merely strong personal attitudes: similarly, surely, at least if Mackie is right about the semantics and concepts of these views, and they are most definitely *not* merely strong personal attitudes. Might someone, attending to his *belief* that God exists—that is, reflecting on his state of mind when he is thinking that God exists—mistake what he has in mind for a mere *longing* that God exists. Or *vice versa*?!

Of linguistic vehicles for moral views, Mackie writes:

> Any analysis of the meanings of moral terms which omits this claim to objective, intrinsic, prescriptivity is to that extent incomplete.
>
> *(Mackie 1977: 35)*

> [T]he meaning of moral statements is approximately as suggested above . . . [i.e.,] Moral statements typically say that such a quality ["this

objective quality"] is found in a certain action (etc.); they are capable of being simply true or false.

(Mackie 1980: 71–72)

A person who holds a moral view thinks that something—some action, person, character—has a certain quality. And *at least* a person who holds a *strong* moral view can leave nothing out of it and must, Mackie maintains, experience that quality objectively and intrinsically prescriptive for an attitudinal response, and so not separable from this. There is no way in which a person, while actively rehearsing a strong moral view, could so mistake his state of mind as to think it was one of *simply* being for or against, nothing more. There is, for contrast, no difficulty with a philosopher's actively rehearsing strong moral views when "in the street," and at other times, say "in the seminar," believing all sorts of false things about strong moral views including those of his own. It is bringing together at more or less one time *first-order strong moral views* with some false *second-order views about them* that is impossible.

What Mackie should have said is that it is *impossible* to think, for example, that it is wrong to inflict unwanted pain just for the fun of it, while thinking that this moral thought is simply an attitude. What he could have added is that one can hold *strong views or positions*—that one can be, for example, *very much against* the infliction of unwanted pain just for the fun of it—"while believing that they were simply attitudes and policies with regard to conduct that he and other people held" (Mackie 1977: 16). There is no problem with *views or positions* being understood as being simply non-propositional attitudes for and against. The problem is only with strong moral views, which are in Mackie's view (and in truth, I would say) *propositional* attitudes. I do not understand what Mackie could have had in mind for the lead sentence of this section.

7 On the Possibility of Mackiean Moralists

Now comes for consideration a person who holds Mackie's second-order philosophical view about his first-order moral views. He holds amongst others the view that no first-order moral view is true. This person can have first-order moral views as long as he lives a somewhat double life and does not always remember, think about, and apply to his own thoughts his second-order philosophical views of first-order moral views. He can have first-order moral views, but he will need to distance these from his second-order views, for the latter—his second-order views about first-order moral views, including his own—*threaten* these views. For his philosophy, whether or not it is correct, *excludes*, while he has it in mind, his having in mind as well what he considers to be a first-order moral view of his, unless he fails to apply his philosophy to this view, which a person could hardly fail to do. [. . .]

In light of Mackie's familiarity with his philosophy and his acuity, one may wonder how he managed to have views that he considered to be moral beliefs.

It is true that "the lack of objective values is not a good reason for abandoning subjective concern or for ceasing to want anything" (Mackie 1977: 34). However, believing that there are no objective values should "tend" to the abandonment first-order moral views, if you think that every such view is a belief in a proposition that presupposes that there are objective values and so in a proposition that is not true. Mackie could have found words of Russell which he quotes appropriate to his own case:

> Certainly there *seems* to be something more. Suppose, for example, that some one were to advocate the introduction of bullfighting in this country. In opposing the proposal, I should *feel*, not only that I was expressing my desires, but that my desires in the matter are *right*, whatever that may mean.
> *(Russell, quoted in Mackie 1977: 34)*

"But how," Mackie could have wondered, "knowing the error of this feeling, can I ever give private voice to them? How can I *think* in these words ('I am *right* to be against bullfighting') knowing what they mean, for I know that what they mean is *not true*?!"

Suppose that Mackie realizes that he does sometimes think in such words. An answer to his puzzle could be: "As comes naturally and easily from habits of a life-time, you let slip from your mind, for moments around that moral feeling, your philosophy of it." Mackie cannot, consistently with his philosophy of them, think, when he is rehearsing them, that his attitudes concerning bullfighting and flaying human beings alive for the sport of it are *objectively right*. Mackie can have his "moral convictions and lose them too" (Dworkin 1996: 94), *though not at once*. It is impossible at one time both to have and lose anything. But there is no logical or psychological problem with *sometimes* having in mind moral convictions—for example, "on the street" and in forums of debate over public policy, when one does not have in mind one's philosophy of them—while one does not have in mind and could not sustain those same convictions at other times—for example, in seminars, when one's philosophy of them is very much in mind.

Bernard Williams says that Mackie "did not suppose that when this error was exposed, everyday moral convictions would properly be weakened or opened to doubt" (Williams 1985: 204). Williams doubts that Mackie was right about this. I very *much* doubt it. William writes:

> If all this is so, it is not easy to combine the two claims [the claims that moral convictions, because of the error of their presuppositions, are not true, and the claims of moral convictions] . . . Mackie's theory, and any like it, leaves a real problem of what should happen when we know it to be true.
> *(1985: 212, 213)*

What should happen in the sense of "what *probably will* happen" is, however, not a big problem. When a person is persuaded that Mackie's theory is true, he can be expected to retain something of the *enthusiasm* of his "old convictions," but not all of it. But I do not think, as Williams seems to think, that Mackie would disagree with this, though he might wish that it were not true, for he seems to have taken seriously the possibility that his philosophy of morals not merely "might be thought dangerous" (Mackie 1977: 239), but *be* dangerous.[9]

8 Is This a Dangerous Philosophy?

> In so far as the objectification of moral values and obligations is not only a natural but also a useful fiction, it might be thought dangerous, and in any case unnecessary, to expose it as a fiction. This is disputable.
>
> *(Mackie 1977: 239)*

Yes, but Mackie does not overtly dispute it before showing by the act of publishing that in his opinion there was little danger in his exposing the fiction. He would not think that this was *at all* dangerous, if he thought that morality, complete with its fictions, is on balance no longer a good thing, which he allowed is a possibility: he raises the question whether "morality does more harm than good," but adds that a "thorough discussion . . . would be beyond the scope of this book" (Mackie 1980: 154, 156). Pending that discussion, he seems to have thought that morality *may well* be, as it must have been, on balance a good thing for humanity. And yet he is now famous for exposing its error.

Hume, in the second part of the conclusion to his second *Enquiry*, when he is about "to consider our interested *obligation* to [virtue and moral rectitude], and to inquire whether every man, who has any regard to his own happiness and welfare, will not best find his account in the practice of every moral duty" (Hume [1751] 2006: 79), implies that he would not raise this issue if he were not confident of the positive result that, yes, it is in everyone's personal interest that he be virtuous and dutiful. He implies that were the truth otherwise he would keep it to himself.

> And though the philosophical truth of any proposition by no means depends on its tendency to promote the interests of society; yet a man has but a bad grace who delivers a theory, however true, which, he must confess, leads to a practice dangerous and pernicious. Why rake into corners of nature which spread a nuisance all around? Why dig up the pestilence from the pit in which it is buried?
>
> *(Hume [1751] 2006: 79)*

Mackie believes that "the whole system of thought of which objectification, the false belief in the fictitious features, is a contributing part, flourishes partly because it serves a social function" (Mackie 1980: 71). He was, I think, always of the opinion that, for the social good of this system of thought, "we had better believe it" (Dworkin 1996). Presumably Mackie's judgment was that, though his publishing was likely to do society some harm, this did not bring his act to the level of perniciousness, and that the risk of this harm was balanced by the likely benefits of the truth for his readers. There is no evidence that Mackie agonized over the question to publish or not to publish. [. . .]

9 What Is an Adherent of This Philosophy to Do?

"Strictly speaking," says David Lewis, "Mackie is right: genuine values would have to meet an impossible condition, so it is an error to think there are any" (Lewis 1989: 136–137). True, says Mark Johnston, who offers his response-dependent account of value, which "abandon[s] definitional descriptive reductionism about value" (Johnston 1989: 168) in favor of "a partly revisionary account" (170) "designed to eliminate precisely this error" (171)—i.e., the "projective or hyper-objectifying error" (170) of "the idea of value as 'the objectively prescriptive,' an idea which Mackie successfully stigmatized as an error at the heart of our thought about value" (171).

Suppose that one agrees, as I do, with Mackie, Lewis, Johnston, and not a few others, regarding the state of moral thought and talk. What is one to make of the intelligence that there is at its core something rotten? How is one personally to deal with this in conversations outside the classroom? Lewis surveys options.

> You can bang the drum about how philosophy has uncovered a terrible secret: there are no values! (Shock horror: no such thing as simultaneity! Nobody ever whistled while he worked!) You can shout it from the house-tops—browbeating is oppression, the truth shall make you free. Or you can think it better for public safety to keep quiet and hope people will go on as before. Or you can declare that there are no values, but that nevertheless it is legitimate—and not just expedient—for us to carry on with value-talk, since we can make it all go smoothly if we just give the name value to claimants that don't quite deserve it. This would be a sort of quasi-realism, not the same as Blackburn's quasi-realism. Or you can think it an empty question whether there are values: say what you please, speak strictly or loosely. When it comes to deserving a name, there's better and worse but who's to say how good is good enough? Or you can think it clear that the imperfect deservers of the name are good enough, but only just, and say that although there are values we are still terribly wrong about them. Or you can calmly say that value . . . is not quite as some of us sometimes thought. [Or, to augment Lewis's menu, you can obfuscate to conceal the truth, and of course you can lie about it.] What to make of the situation is mainly a matter of temperament.
>
> *(Lewis 1989: 137)*

"Myself," Lewis concludes, "I prefer the calm and conservative responses. But so far as the analysis of value goes [so far as *philosophy* goes], they're all much of a muchness" (137).

As for me, I vacillate between radical responses. Always in philosophic discourse, believing that ordinary moral thought and talk are essentially implicated in errors of objective values, when the issue comes up I denounce them. Almost always in unphilosophic practical discourse, while choosing words carefully in order not strictly to be implicated in them, I do not challenge with a display of my amoralism. Never, in such unphilosophical discourse, do I denounce the errors of participating moralists.[10] And sometimes, though less and less often, I notice myself trafficking in them, when thinking and talking about things that matter to me and that I am very much for or against.

Notes

1 *Editors*: We have drawn from both a 2006 and 2009 version of Sobel's manuscript. Much has been left out here, so please note that ellipses sometimes mark the omission of *pages* of discussion. When the omission is relatively small—a few words or a footnote (many of which have been left out)—in the interests of readability we haven't always included an ellipsis mark. We have also simplified the numbering of the sections for the purposes of this chapter.

2 This is not a possible view, since, for example, that pleasure is good and that pleasure is not good (expressed when "good" is used in the sense relevant to ethics) are moral judgments. If one of these judgments is true, then the other is false.

3 *Editors*: Omitted here is (inter alia) Sobel's discussion of Mackie's case against both naturalism and noncognitivism.

4 Mackie offers for this point the following argument: "Objective wrongness, if there is such a thing, is intrinsically prescriptive or action-guiding, it in itself gives or constitutes a reason for not doing the wrong action . . . independent of that agent's desires or purposes. But the natural features on which the moral ones supervene cannot be *intrinsically* action-guiding or reason-giving in this way. Supervenience, then, must be a synthetic connection" (Mackie 1982: 115).

5 The orienting clause gestures to a response to "the problem of old evidence," which is elaborated in Sobel 2004 (ch. 7, section 4.3). (See also Earman 1992: ch. 5.)

6 *Editors*: Omitted here is (inter alia) Sobel's discussion of Mackie's well-known arguments from relativity and queerness.

7 I go to Darwin to complete the argument for the projective error of morality. The argument to come is that the moral error theory explains certain phenomena of morality—that we have and use moral concepts in the ways we do—better than moral realism, phenomena for which every theory of morality "owes us an account," phenomena that challenge alike the particular theories before us of error and intuitionistic realism. Richard Joyce makes a very different connection between Darwinian theory and moral error theory. He goes to Darwin to fulfill an obligation. As an error theorist he thinks he "owes us an account of why we have been led to commit such a fundamental, systematic mistake . . . the answer is simple: natural selection" (Joyce 2001: 135).

8 The parenthetical qualification reflects that I do not believe in objective probabilities, to which I add objective *plausibilities*. I do not know whether Hume and Mackie share this skepticism.

9 Joyce says that we can go on using the language of morality after having seen the error of it, and that probably it would serve our interests to do so, engaging in moral discourse non-assertorically (Joyce 2001: 200–201) without believing in it. We can engage

in it usefully without embracing the fiction of it. "[M]orality can continue to furnish significant benefit, both at a societal and an individual level, even when it is has the role of a fiction" (205), which, he adds, is not to say that once a community had seen the error of it, they can get *all* of the benefits that had accrued to them from the old, erroneous, real thing. He argues only that fictive moral discourse is better than no moral discourse at all, and that it is not only better but that it can furnish *significant* benefits. Joyce does not, however, assess the benefits of believed morality that would be lost, by this philosophically enlightened community, even if they continued to use moral discourse to the best effects then possible. And so he does not deal with the question whether, all considered, it might best to call off the philosophic debate and leave the pestilence well buried in the pit.

10 While I cannot agree with Wittgenstein that moral thought "is a document of a tendency of the human mind which I personally cannot help respecting deeply," I do think that belief in objective moral values (as belief in God) can be *important* in the lives of those who hold it—that it can be a central belief by which they live, and for this reason "I would not on my life ridicule it" (Wittgenstein 1965: 12).

References

Dworkin, R. 1996. "Objectivity and truth: You'd better believe it." *Philosophy and Public Affairs* 25: 87–139.

Earman, J. 1992. *Bayes or Bust? A Critical Examination of Bayesian Confirmation Theory.* Cambridge, MA: MIT Press.

Hume, D. [1751] 2006. *An Enquiry Concerning the Principles of Morals.* Oxford: Clarendon.

Hume, D. [1777] 1998. *Selected Essays.* Oxford: Oxford University Press.

Jackson, F. 1998. *From Metaphysics to Ethics: A Defence of Conceptual Analysis.* Oxford: Clarendon.

Johnston, M. 1989. "Dispositional theories of value." *Proceedings of the Aristotelian Society* (suppl. vol.) 63: 139–174.

Joyce, R. 2001. *The Myth of Morality.* Cambridge: Cambridge University Press.

Lewis, D. 1989. "Dispositional theories of value." *Proceedings of the Aristotelian Society* (suppl. vol.) 63: 113–137.

Mackie, J. L. 1946. "A refutation of morals." *Australasian Journal of Psychology and Philosophy* 24: 77–90.

Mackie, J. L. 1977. *Ethics: Inventing Right and Wrong.* London: Penguin.

Mackie, J. L. 1980. *Hume's Moral Theory.* London: Routledge.

Mackie, J. L. 1982. *The Miracle of Theism.* Oxford: Clarendon Press.

Sobel, J. H. 2004. *Logic and Theism: Arguments For and Against Beliefs in God.* Cambridge: Cambridge University Press.

Swinburne, R. 1976. "The objectivity of morality." *Philosophy* 51: 5–20.

Williams, B. 1985. "Ethics and the fabric of the world." In T. Honderich (ed.), *Morality and Objectivity: A Tribute to J. L. Mackie.* London: Routledge & Kegan Paul. 203–214.

Wittgenstein, L. 1965 "Lecture on ethics." *Philosophical Review* 74: 3–12.

Wright, C. 1996. "Truth in ethics." In B. Hooker (ed.), *Truth in Ethics.* Oxford: Blackwell. 1–18.

2

TO HELL WITH MORALITY

Ian Hinckfuss

Editors' Note

Hinckfuss (1932–1997) published *The Moral Society: Its Structure and Effects* in 1987, as part of a series produced by the Australian National University. It consists of five chapters and, while running to almost 50,000 words, has an incomplete feel to it. Here we republish substantial excerpts from the work, including the Introduction, which provides an overview of the whole project, and large portions of Chapters 2, 3, and 4. (Note: We have retained the original labeling of sections, hence their numbering is noncontinuous. When only a few words are omitted, in the interests of readability we haven't always included an ellipsis mark.) We are also happy to reinstate the provocative title that Hinckfuss originally intended for his book.

Introduction

There is a widespread belief that if most people were to abide by their moral beliefs, then life would be much more satisfying for almost everybody than it would be if most people were not bothered about morality at all.

In opposition to this position, it is suggested here that the more that people are motivated by moral concerns, the more likely it is that their society will be elitist, authoritarian and dishonest, that they will have scant respect for most of its members, that they will be relatively inefficient in engendering human happiness, self-esteem or satisfaction, that they will be relatively inefficient in the resolution of conflicts, and that their moralising will exacerbate conflicts, often with physical violence or even war as a result.

The arguments which will be offered for this position are unlikely to be conclusive. The issue falls within the realm of moral sociology, and the fact is that there is very little solid sociological evidence available for or against the position.

My motive for presenting my views on the matter as best I can is not simply the desire to correct a widespread false belief. Many widespread false beliefs would be relatively harmless. But this one, if I am right, is not. I am concerned enough for others to try to warn them of the dangers of morality. Even if the evidence for such danger is below par, a warning is not irrelevant to such concern if the dangers are great. This book will have served a purpose if it stimulates some of its readers into a genuine investigation of their own beliefs concerning morality.

Here is a synopsis of what is to follow.

Chapter 1 is about the meaning of moral terms. Though the meaning of moral terms clearly varies from some people to others, I argue that the meaning of moral terms delineated here is traditional and in conformity with most common practice. That view is that morality is not relative to persons or societies; that if some particular act (as opposed to a type of act) is morally good or bad or right or obligatory, it is absolutely so. The view is also that the moral worth of people and their behaviour is an objective matter that is not to be determined by subjective feelings about those people or their behaviour.

Thus, I argue in particular that "morality" does not usually mean what some people name, or rather, I would say, misname personal morality, that is, the ways in which some individual person would like everybody, including herself or himself, to behave. On the contrary, it will be allowed that some person could want everyone to behave in a way which was, perhaps unbeknown to that person, immoral.

I argue also that "morality" does not usually mean what sort of behaviour is acceptable or unacceptable to a society, that is, what I shall call the mores of a society. It will be allowed that when William Wilberforce and other reformers argued that the mores of their society were immoral, they were not contradicting themselves.

By the same token, when people talk about what is and is not moral, they are not to be taken as talking merely about the moral beliefs of a society or individual; nor merely about how things appear morally to a society or individual. It will be allowed that moral beliefs can be false; and that appearances, including moral appearances, can be deceptive.

More controversially, I shall argue that if there were any knowledge of moral obligation, it would have its primary source in an intuitive apprehension of a moral quality by some person using a faculty that most people call "conscience"; in other words, that morality has an intuitionist epistemology. Neither purely logical considerations nor these combined with sense experience can be a primary source of moral knowledge.

In Chapter 2, I present my view of the structure of the moral society and its method of self-perpetuation. I suggest that the faculty of moral conscience is a myth and that moral obligations are myths also. There are no moral obligations to be known, and, even if there were, we are not possessed of the intuitive apparatus needed to apprehend them.

Since there are no moral obligations, there is nothing whose existence would entail the existence of moral obligations. So there are no moral virtues, vices, sins, morally good, bad or evil people, acts, or products of such acts, or goods that we are morally obliged to promote, or evils that we are morally obliged to avoid or eradicate.

The morality of a society is stipulatively defined as the extent of the occurrence throughout society of:

(a) the belief in moral obligations, vices, moral virtue, sins and morally good or bad acts or morally good or bad people, and
(b) the wish to conform behaviour to these moral beliefs.

I shall claim, and these are sociological conjectures, that:

(a) Many, if not most, societies today are highly moral in the sense just outlined.
(b) Within moral societies, the desire in moral agents to act morally and to have others acting morally is instilled by using reward and punishment in childhood. Some moral beliefs will be instilled in the process.
(c) Moral agents may also accept moral beliefs from those whom the agent regards as moral authorities—parents, teachers, ministers of religion, et cetera.
(d) There is a rough social ordering of moral authority within the moral society for the purposes of moral indoctrination and the application of rewards and punishments for moral success and failure.
(e) Those at or near the top of the moral hierarchy may sometimes modify their systems of moral belief by mistaking their personal desires about behaviour for moral insights.
(f) One's place in the moral ordering is a function of, among other things, one's self-esteem, and this, in turn, is a function of the extent to which rewards have exceeded punishments or vice versa in one's moral conditioning.

In Chapter 3, the sociological effects of morality's perpetuation mechanisms are discussed. It is argued that the moral society will have a tendency to be elitist, authoritarian and inegalitarian. Its members may have unnecessary burdens of ego competition and guilt. Where there is conflict between conflicting moral leaderships, the chances of physical violence and warfare are enhanced.

Chapter 4 critically examines various ideas about how morality or systems akin to morality may be used to maximise satisfaction. It is concluded that there is no evidence to suggest that morality as an institution within human society is of any such use.

Chapter 5 examines the possibilities for empirically testing the theories outlined in Chapters 2 and 3.

[. . .]

Chapter 2: The Moral Society: Its Structure and Preservation

2.2 The Perpetuation of Morality: Some Implausible Views

Few who are reading this will disagree that they live in a moral society. Few will disagree that the society that they live in is elitist, authoritarian, intellectually dishonest in its social decisions, lacking in esteem for most of its members, inefficient in the resolution of conflicts, inefficient in maximising human happiness, satisfaction or self-esteem, and, because of the threat of war with other societies, physically dangerous. Again, few will disagree that most, if not all, moral societies bear these rather dislikeable qualities.

The fact that all moral societies bear these qualities is no evidence for the theory that morality tends to generate these aspects of society. Perhaps any amoral society would bear these qualities also. Perhaps these qualities of societies are brought about by "human nature" and societies would bear these qualities in greater degree were it not for the ameliorating effects of morality.

Many would argue that these qualities arise in a society because of its immoral nature. They would claim that if the society were moral (as opposed to immoral) as well as moral (as opposed to amoral), then all such distasteful qualities would vanish.

An alternative and contrary claim is that, as a sociological matter of fact, the way morality perpetuates itself within a society is causally sufficient for the perpetuation and aggravation of these aspects of society. It is the purpose of this essay to present this conjecture in such a light as to make it plausible enough to be at least worthy of more thorough investigation.

What do we know about the way morality within society perpetuates itself? Let us begin by examining a fairly common explanation for the perpetuation of morality, namely that morality brings obvious advantages to all the individual members of a society—or at least a large proportion of them. Hence most members of a moral society will make it their business to perpetuate the system for the sake of these obvious advantages—or so goes the argument.

Why would people believe, if indeed they do, that the morality of others is generally an advantage to themselves or at least to most people? It does not seem plausible that direct empirical evidence generates their confidence in the advantages of morality. Most of us have never lived in an amoral society to compare it with what we have. [. . .]

Many writers assume that there is no problem for the altruistic agent in providing a reason to be moral. They assume that the agent will perceive that moral behaviour will always coincide with altruistic behaviour. That assumption would be valid if the only beliefs in moral obligations implied that one ought always to behave as if one were kindly disposed to all other people. But it is clearly false that all moral beliefs are of this kind. Some people have beliefs in their moral duty to their god, their sovereign, their country or their political ideals and such morality could (and frequently does) run counter to such altruistic inclinations such people have.

If any such person were strongly altruistic, or had any other strong motivations that ran counter to their moral inclinations, both the question "Why should I be moral?" and the question "Why should I want anyone else to be moral?" would be of considerable significance.

However, for many people with a conflict between moral and non-moral motivations, the moral motivations would be overriding. For such people the idea that they should not be moral seems absurd. The question "Why should I be moral?" has for them the false presupposition that being moral is not an end in itself—that it is merely a means to some other end. Their response to this question would be to deny this presupposition rather than to attempt to provide the requested explanation.

Yet there is no logical necessity about the overriding nature of the supposed moral obligations of these people. So the question still remains: why are these people so motivated? Why do they prefer that they and others be morally good and not bad? If it is neither through observation nor rational calculation that people come to prefer the moral society, how does it come about that they do?

Fear of the unknown could be an explanation except for the fact that few people have ever reflected at length on the matter. They take it for granted, quite correctly, that society is moral (as opposed to amoral) and any suggestion that they might reconsider their preferences in favour of an amoral society is rejected with the immediacy of a knee-jerk reflex. But if only a handful of eccentric philosophers have ever considered the matter at length, it seems hardly likely that these considerations should have provided a motivation or a mechanism for the perpetuation of morality. We must look, therefore, for a mechanism which does not involve a continual rational choice by large numbers of people.

Most people would agree that it is in early childhood, when the moral concepts are being learnt, when the child lives in an environment of continual moral injunction, that these pro-attitudes to morality are instilled. In the following three sections, I sketch a theory concerning the development of pro-attitudes to morality and the perpetuation of morality as an institution. There is no claim for originality in what follows and the account is doubtless an oversimplification of all the psychological and sociological complexities involved. The account is presented as a first approximation which, hopefully, is accurate enough to support the consequences which I believe to follow from it.

2.3 The Moral Upbringing

In our society most children have many of their actions rewarded by smiles, hugs, sweet foods or other gifts in association with words which translate into "good" or one of its cognates. They are told that they are good or that they have done well. Other actions are punished with frowns, withdrawals, angry shouts or physical violence accompanied by words which translate into "bad" or one of its cognates. The child is told that it is naughty, that it has failed in its duty or that it has sinned.

The end result of this training is a person who wants to be good and who has an aversion to being bad. When people reach this psychological condition, they will usually have quite a few beliefs about which sort of acts are good and which bad. It little matters for the perpetuation and operation of the moral society as a moral society what these moral beliefs are. What does matter is that these morally trained people are now in a position to be morally propagandised by those whom they regard as their "betters," that is, those who they feel know more about what is right and what is wrong than they do. [. . .]

The moralisation process is more than a mere socialisation process. Moralising tends to generate people whose concern to be good and to avoid being bad overrides their other concerns—including any concerns to satisfy the wishes of themselves and others, where these are inconsistent with their moral introjections.

Of course, if the moral nihilist is right in believing that there are no moral obligations, such moralising also gives the child a false view of the world as one in which moral goodness and badness are exemplified. In any case, the resulting self-image of the child could turn out to be that of a morally bad person—and the morally trained child is very anxious not to be morally bad. That would certainly be psychologically disturbing.

Morally trained people of all ages look for moral guidance in the same way as morally trained children do. They look for and receive injunctions from their elders, priests, newspaper editors, television commentators, radio announcers, doctors, lawyers, magistrates, university lecturers, union organisers, people in uniform or perhaps even their mates down at the public house. Almost all people will be candidates for moral leadership provided that they bear themselves with sufficient pride and dignity and self-esteem to encourage the respect and confidence of their followers.

2.4 The Moral Hierarchy

The occurrence of moral leadership generates a moral hierarchy—a hierarchy of authority in matters moral. At the pinnacle will be those whose moral injunctions spread furthest: the controllers of the mass media, be that the pulpit, the press, radio or television. Some of these leaders may not be known to the majority of the population, but it matters only that they are known and respected by the succeeding tier of the elite.

Often, too, the heroines and heroes of society, the leading politicians or journalists, may at best be puppets well removed from the centres of power. Even though they may believe themselves to be autonomous and uninfluenced, their positions as mouthpieces in the moral society may rest in the hands of relatively unknown people who nevertheless have sufficient influence at an appropriate level to control the occupation of those positions, if not the charismatic occupiers themselves.

This is not to deny the possibility of a society's hero or heroine being at the peak of a moral hierarchy. Nor is it to deny that there may be tensions, even dangerous conflicts, between members of a moral elite vying for prestige and its accompanying power. Nor is it to deny that there may be value-laden ideological feedback via various societal structures from the common people to the controllers and operators of the mass media. It is being suggested, however, that the more moral a society is, the more it is that power and moral authority are to be equated. How would this hierarchy of moral authority arise, and how would it be perpetuated?

Remember that our morally well-brought-up people desperately want to do what is right. Hence they will be anxious to know what is right and what is wrong. Let us assume for the moment that the moral nihilist is right—that there is no moral right or wrong and that there are no moral obligations. Our moral agents, of course, will not be acting on this assumption. They will believe that there are moral obligations to be known. They will not be able to see or otherwise sense or rationally calculate these obligations. There will not be any moral obligations to see, sense or calculate. Neither will they be able to deduce their nonexistent moral obligations from any truths that they have come to know. Hume's is–ought gap will be there if only because it is invalid to deduce falsehood from truth.

Now when there is something we wish to know and we do not know how to discover the truth for ourselves, we usually look for an authority on the matter. There are physicists, medicos, lawyers and accountants who not only have knowledge of physics, medicine, law and tax dodging, but who are trained to discover truths in these areas for themselves. Their ways of coming to know what they know are often a mystery to we lay people, but we trust in their expertise. So likewise, the moral lay person, not knowing the answer to his or her moral dilemma, nor knowing any way of finding out for himself or herself, may seek out an authority in whose moral expertise he or she feels confident. The authority, in turn, may sometimes feel the need to appeal to a still higher authority and so on.

If this were the only explanation of moral belief, it would lead to an infinite regress of moral authorities, in which case the moral society could not exist. So, if moral nihilism and hence moral scepticism were correct, there must be at least one other mechanism for the production of beliefs in moral values and obligations.

David Hume has given us an insight into the mechanism required in his *Treatise of Human Nature*. Hume claimed that morality "consists not in any relations that are the objects of science;" and "that it consists not in any matter of fact, which can be discovered by the understanding." He says:

Take any action allowed to be vicious; wilful murder for instance. Examine it in all lights, and see if you can find that matter of fact, or real existence, which you call vice. In whichever way you take it, you find only certain passions, motives, volitions, and thoughts. There is no other matter of fact in the case. The vice entirely escapes you, as long as you consider the object. You never can find it, till you turn your reflection into your own breast, and find a sentiment of disapprobation, which arises in you, towards this action. Here is a matter of fact; but it is the object of feeling, not of reason. It lies in yourself, not the object.[1]

Thus Hume is claiming that belief in objective moral values is a mistake. The mistake can occur if one takes one's personal sentiments for perceptions of objective reality.

Some have taken this idea of Hume's to be an argument in favour of naturalism. Hector Monro writes:

According to the non-naturalist natural qualities give rise to the non-natural quality of goodness which gives rise to feelings of approval in human beings.

Now, the naturalist will ask, is the middle step here really necessary? Why not just say that the natural qualities of things produce feelings of approval in human beings and that we use moral terms to express these feelings. This would give us an explanation of the facts of morality without invoking any dubious entities.[2]

Although the naturalist's attempt to avoid explanations involving the dubious non-natural qualities is along the right tracks, the explanation offered by Monro for moral sentiments is dissatisfying in three ways. First, it is consistent with a lack of non-natural qualities that many people may nevertheless believe in such qualities (if not by that description) and may therefore use moral terms in order to state those beliefs. Second, the approval these people feel for some natural qualities may not be quite so directly a function of those qualities as the naturalist explanation would have us believe. Such approvals are likely to be tempered, or even drastically altered, by the moral agent's beliefs in non-natural qualities and the attitudes she or he has been conditioned to bear towards things with such qualities. Third, the subjectivist-naturalist account of moral feelings fails to explain the existence and role of a glaringly evident feature of the moral society, namely the moral elite or what P. W. Musgrave in his book *The Moral Curriculum* calls "the agents of respectability," whose identification, as Musgrave points out, is of major importance in the sociological study of morality.[3]

Furthermore, there is a way in which it may be moderately reasonable for moral agents to take their personal sentiments as an indication of objective moral fact, if not of the direct result of the application of their moral conscience. Let me explain.

Moral people who believe themselves to be less than virtuous are those who endure the annoyance, if not the psychological stress, of having some of their natural tendencies inconsistent with what they believe their moral obligations to be. Good people, virtuous people, would be those whose natural tendencies and whose moral obligations are in accord. Of course, if there were no moral obligations there would be no good or virtuous people. However, insofar as any people believe themselves to be virtuous, they are able to equate their natural preferences and inclinations with what is morally acceptable, and such injunctions that they wish everyone to abide by they can equate with moral obligations. Thus they can believe themselves to have a sound moral judgement or a good conscience and can feel confident enough in their moral beliefs to pass on their moral judgements to others. Sometimes, perhaps often, this confidence in their own valuations and their lack of confidence in other people's valuations, combined with a fear that society is headed down the morally wrong tracks, taking them and their loved ones with it, can lead them to give their moral advice whether solicited or not. This, I conjecture, is the mechanism behind the priests and their pulpits, the newspaper editors and their editorials, the politicians and their platforms, the propagandists and their mass media.

How then does the moral society generate its pharisees, its magistrates, its priests and cardinals, its charismatic leaders—its moral elite? Several mechanisms could be responsible, but I shall describe one which seems plausible. Again, the needed training takes place at an early age.

Children will vary in the way they react to condemnation and praise, and the quantities of condemnation and of praise will vary from child to child. One child will be held up to others as an example—good or bad—thus giving some children a moral boost at the expense of others. The children who receive most moral boosts from their parents or guardians are likely to believe what they are continually told, namely that they are very good. These will be the children who succeed in pleasing their moral mentors most. Other children get the inverse treatment and go into adulthood with an inferiority complex and a tendency to seek continual moral guidance and leadership from their "betters." Most people end up somewhere on the spectrum in between.

But those who are convinced of their own goodness will be those most likely to become the moral leaders of society. In fact, such moral self-confidence is a necessary condition for entry into the moral elite. For with such self-confidence, it is easy to believe that what one wishes for oneself is moray permissible, and how one wants others to behave is morally obligatory. A good person will not want what is wrong.

2.5 Moral Deserts

The moral training of children involves reward and punishment for being what their moral superiors regard as good and bad respectively. But the training does not end at childhood. It extends throughout life. If adults stop worrying about doing their duty, they may cease to train their children to do so and the moral society may fall rapidly into disrepair. This may sound like Malcolm Muggeridge or Mary Whitehouse, but in this case they would be correct. They may be right, too, if they believed that Western society is already some way along the road to moral dissolution.

However, to return to my point, if morality is to keep going, the moral carrot and stick must be displayed or applied continually to most people throughout their lives. The punishments include frowns, snubs, deprivation of income, deprivation of possessions, imprisonment and physical violence. The rewards include smiles, honours, property, economic security, power and privilege. This is the system of moral deserts. Again, it is the trainers, not the trainees, who determine who deserves what.

Further, many of those low on the moral scale seem to be content or even eager to see that the privileged elite, loaded as they are with wealth and power, are rewarded still further. This is because they will be trained to assent to the proposition that people should get what they deserve—and of course better people deserve more.

According to the gospels, Christ taught that it was easier for a camel to get through the eye of a needle than for a rich man to enter the kingdom of heaven. That sort of talk would have been enough to bring ruin to any nicely established moral hierarchy. But despite the message of the gospels, the Christian church soon found that it, too, had to embrace economic inequalities if it was to flourish as a strong moral system.

Of course, economic reward is not the only possible reward, but to a moral trainer the advantage of economic or material rewards is that they show in a much more permanent way than the more ephemeral smiles or ego-strokes, and thus the trainee can be held up as an example and an incentive to others.

But there is another reason which could influence the moral trainers to keep up some sort of system of deserts, economic or otherwise. Being higher up the moral pyramid, they are believed to "deserve" more than would otherwise be their "fair" share. They have a vested interest in morality and its system of deserts and the perpetuation of both. So their propaganda is heavily laden with their views on the "importance" of morality with the presupposition, often made explicit, that in making any decision moral considerations outweigh any other considerations.

To sum up, it is conjectured that the moral society perpetuates itself in the following way: Moral trainers apply the doctrine of deserts to condition most of the populace into being moral. The training program generates a moral elite who have a vested interest in preserving the system and whose rewards include the power to see that the training program is preserved. [. . .]

Chapter 3: The Consequences of Morality

3.4 Moral Denigration and Guilt

The majority of objects in any pyramid are at or near its base, and similarly the majority of members of a moral society have relatively low status in that society. Moral denigration for the bulk of society is the other side of the coin to the honours bestowed on the elite minority.

Nietzsche, in *On the Genealogy of Morals* (first essay, section 2) captures the mechanism:

> [It] was the "good" themselves, that is to say the noble, mighty, highly placed and high-minded who decreed themselves and their actions to be good, i.e. belonging to the highest rank, in contradistinction to all that was base, low-minded and plebeian . . .
>
> The origin of the opposites good and bad is to be found in the pathos of nobility and distance, representing the dominant temper of a higher, ruling class in relation to a lower, dependent one.

If we replace the past tense of Nietzsche's genealogy with the present tense of the mechanism of perpetuation, we change doubtful origins into a plausible sociology.

Nietzsche also conjectured that the terminology referring to social classes is etymologically related to moral terminology. Doubtless there are etymological facts of many languages which demonstrate that association of the upper classes with goodness and the lower classes with baseness has been a continuing feature of moral societies. But what is more interesting for our present purposes is the double meaning that so many of our social class words exhibit. Thus, "noble" means both being a person of high rank or title and also being of lofty and exalted character. The words "high," "elevated," "lofty" can be used to describe both social status and moral character. The same applies to "low," "common," "ordinary," "vulgar," "churlish," and "plebeian" to describe the base of the moral society's pyramid. Again, the political right wing is that which supports the upper classes against the demands of the lower classes. One further example is a word used in the heading for this section—the word "denigration." This means "the blackening of character" and has common etymological roots with "negro." Little wonder that black-skinned people have been such a rarity in the upper strata of English-speaking societies.

Clearly the moral elite have all the advantages and the lower classes all the disadvantages when it comes to fallacies of equivocation. But it is important to realise that these double meanings do not arise by chance. To the extent that a society is a moral society, the lower classes are regarded as morally inferior to the upper classes, the nobles are supposed to be noble, the churls churlish, common people common, ordinary people ordinary, and plebeians plebeian. The snobbery inherent in the moral society seems to extend to the very language used to describe it.

Someone may ask why we should worry if most people regard themselves as morally inferior. After all, most people regard themselves and are regarded as inferior at mathematics, tennis, karate, athletics, nuclear physics, medicine and motor car maintenance, but this usually does not worry people. So why worry about their sense of moral inferiority? The reason is that in the moral society people are trained to want above all to be good and noble and to want to be other than vulgar, ignoble and low. Yet the structure of the society destines the majority of them to be regarded as failures in that regard. The situation is similar to the old-fashioned present-day competitive education systems within which most children receive a training which urges academic excellence upon them but nevertheless guarantees that only a small minority will make the grade. The majority end their educational career with an inferiority complex with respect to their academic abilities.

At the extreme lower end of the moral pecking order would be those who, believing themselves to be bad if not vile, lose all hope of what they think of as moral betterment and in their despair feel they might as well get what enjoyment and satisfaction they can out of doing what they think is bad. In this way (though perhaps not only in this way) the phenomena of juvenile gangs, vandalism and what commonly passes for criminality could be generated. At higher levels on the social scale, the moral inferiority complex could be characterised by ego-competition, including continual attempts to denigrate the character of others, in order to achieve a higher place in the moral pecking order than would otherwise be believed to be possible.

Moral and evaluative language would provide a useful tool for this exercise, not only because of the inbuilt snobbery of moral language, but also because almost any describable human behaviour and almost any human characteristic can be described in two ways—derogatively or euphemistically. People who try to boost their ego or image at the expense of others continually make use of this moral parsing, as Bertrand Russell once called it. Table 2.1 shows just a few examples.

TABLE 2.1 Positive and negative descriptions: self vs. other

I . . .	You . . .
am discreet	are deceitful
am different	are abnormal
am normal	are common
am a rough diamond	are churlish

To return to our theme, even where a sense of moral inferiority is not accompanied by perversions and ego competition, the feeling of continual moral failure, the feeling that for all one's efforts one is still morally inferior, will be a saddening thing for those who bear it.

An associated sadness that morality can render even to those who feel fairly content with their moral status is the feeling of guilt, the feeling of remorse at having done something that they believe to be morally wrong

People who are amoral may experience regret. They may regret having done something with a consequence they disliked and which they did not foresee, or which they did foresee but did not care about at the time of the act. But they cannot have regrets at having done something wrong. They either do not care about what is right and what is wrong, or they do not believe that there are such things as right or wrong acts. Thus, insofar as a society is amoral, there is no possibility of feelings of guilt, guilt complexes or moral inferiority complexes with all the sadness, madness and suffering that these feelings and complexes entail.

3.5 Economic Inequality and Revolution

In section 2.5, it was explained how the way was wide open for either subconscious or deliberate but morally sanctioned exploitation of the rest of society by the moral elite. But there are limits to the extent to which the gullible can be fooled by the confidence trickster, and likewise there are limits to which there can be an unequal distribution of wealth before someone comes up with the idea that perhaps the wealthy are giving themselves more than they deserve.

These are dangerous revolutionary thoughts because it is thought to be ignoble to take more than one's just deserts. The revolutionary, therefore, is in effect crying "Imposter!" and such imposters deserve to be parted from their power and possessions, if not their lives—or so would go the revolutionary injunctions.

The moral society at this stage may divide like an amoeba, with the rebels attached to a revolutionary moral leadership and the remainder remaining "loyal." The situation is then physically dangerous, with the moral leadership of each side denigrating the other with a strong possibility of civil war.

The danger of rebellion is mitigated by the recently invented so-called "democratic" elections of the Presbyterian style. This device is efficient in yielding the minimal change in the power structure to satisfy the feelings of injustice within the community, at least to the point where the great majority feel that the fruits of rebellion would not outweigh the dangers of the rebellion itself. The rebellious minority, however, continue to be irked by what they see as the injustices of the usurpers of social power and decry the elections as a "liberal" device for the retention of the status quo. In this they are right, but where they are wrong is in thinking that the revolution for which they strive would make any fundamental difference to the structure of society.

If the story told in sections 2.3 to 2.5 is somewhere near the truth, such a revolution would merely alter the membership of the power elite and perhaps redistribute rewards and sanctions. Large-scale economic inequality would remain as long as the doctrine of moral desert was retained. But if this were discarded, the perpetuation mechanism of morality would be lost and morality itself would rapidly become nonexistent. This is the bloodless but much more significant revolution that I, for one, would welcome. [. . .]

Chapter 4: The Alleged Usefulness of Morality

4.1 Introduction

It has been suggested in the last chapter that morality as an institution within society brings undesired consequences for many people at many times. It would not follow from that, however, that it would be imprudent to sustain the moral institution. It may have other effects which we desire strongly enough to make it worthwhile for us to put up with the effects we dislike. Negatively valued consequences are never a sufficient condition for the rational rejection of anything any more than positively valued consequences are a sufficient condition for acceptance. A rational person will think about both costs and benefits.

Many people since the times of ancient Greece have conjectured that morality is manmade and is there for some purpose beneficial to all. Included in this tradition are Protagoras, Hobbes, Hume and, more recently, Warnock, Mackie, and Rawls. Hobbes claimed that man has motivations which are primarily self-interested and that, in a state of nature, that is, without an artificial morality imposed by a sovereign, man would lead a life that was solitary, poor, nasty, brutish and short, in a continual war of all against all. Hume, Warnock and Mackie do not have quite as dim a view of natural man as this, but nevertheless they teach us that the function of morality is to mitigate the bad effects of the limitations on man's generosity and sympathy. The idea is that morality takes society a little closer to what it would be, if, contrary to fact, we were able to sympathise with all the people whom our actions were likely to affect, instead of just those who are nearest and dearest to us.

One of the questions that arises concerning the point, purpose or function of morality is "Who is it whose purposes we have in mind, if anybody's?" The authors mentioned above would say "everybody." But is it plausible that, for any given person, the moral society is likely to yield that person more satisfaction than an amoral society? We have in sections 2.5 and 3.5 talked of the vested interests of the moral elite in the moral society. But what does morality do for the lower classes besides degrading and impoverishing them? Few would enjoy these consequences. What consequences of being a moral agent in a moral society might they enjoy? It is true that there could be, or indeed actually are, many cases when an invocation of moral attitudes is conducive to maximal satisfaction—even for those having low status in society. But that is not the point at issue. One could say as much for the use of draconic legislation, carelessness and war. We do not for that reason seek to enshrine these things as social institutions—on the contrary. The question here is not whether the moral institution has on some occasions a useful effect. It is whether it is worth preserving, given the sum total of its effects on and within society. [. . .]

4.2 Is Morality of Any Use in Conflict Resolution?

Conflict is not always distasteful to people. Competition is enjoyed by sadists and egomaniacs who have the ability to win most of the time, as well as masochists who do not. Even ordinary people enjoy a bit of a tussle now and then. But conflict can very often be annoying, to say the least. When people are pulling against one another, neither may get anywhere. If they cooperate, both may get what they want quickly. Conflict can be a frustration when it comes to satisfying desire.

However, conflicts can be resolved without satisfaction. A duel may resolve a conflict, but may leave one person dead and the other maimed for life. Both parties could have received more satisfaction from life if the conflict had been left unresolved. So the question is not whether conflicts can be resolved more readily using morality, but rather whether the use of morality leads to optimal satisfaction of the disputing parties. I argue in this section that morality may not be as effective in this regard as commonly supposed and, indeed, may be a positive hindrance to this end.

For moral considerations to be effective in resolving a dispute in any way at all, satisfactory or otherwise, all parties must agree on what their moral values and obligations are, about how this good has or has not more weight than that, about which obligation overrides which in which circumstances or, failing initial agreement on these issues, all parties must possess a common moral leadership. Where these conditions fail to obtain, the dispute may develop into mutual denigration leading to one of the disputants feeling morally justified in ignoring the desires of the other party. They may even feel obliged to treat their opponent harshly, by resorting to sanctions including physical violence or even death. In this way a moral agent could have an increased, not a lessened, motive for treating his opponent like a natural disaster.

Of course, there is no guarantee that moral agents in conflict will choose the same moral leadership or share the same moral ideals. Hence we have the situation in Ireland (unresolved after 400 years of bloody conflict); the situation in the Lebanon (unresolved after about 800 years of conflict between Christian and Muslim); the Palestinian Arabs versus the Zionists; the Vietnamese versus the Khmer, the Chinese, the French and the Americans; all the wars of religion and all the blood-letting of the two world wars.

Think of any one of these conflicts and think of how the situation would have been if, by a miracle, moral thought could have been eradicated from the minds of all the agents involved. I, for one, find it difficult to conceive of how the conflicts would have proceeded. There would be no sense of duty, no sense of loyalty, no patriotism, no feeling morally obliged to fight for a cause, no sense that the people one is trying to kill or subjugate are less worthy of survival or freedom than oneself or anyone else.

There could be war without morality. But moral propaganda eases the task of those with control of the mass media to get almost all the nation determined to attack, plunder, slaughter and subjugate another group of people. Cooperation has a pleasant sound to it. But people can cooperate to do many things which disgust or endanger others. It would not seem to be unreasonable, then, to conjecture that moral disagreement tends to exacerbate conflict.

Let us turn now to the less bellicose situation in which the contenders agree on their moral values or agree to abide by the moral rulings of some member of the moral elite whom they both respect. Let us assume they are both moral agents who want above all to do whatever is right. Then the conflict may be quickly and amicably resolved. But will it be resolved in a way that maximises satisfaction?

It may be so resolved if the guiding moral principles enjoin an attempt to maximise satisfaction, that is, if the guiding moral principles are utilitarian. However, there is no guarantee that the guiding moral principles will be utilitarian, and in general they are not likely to be utilitarian if one of the disputants thinks that she or he would be better satisfied by some other principle which could be intuited to be overriding in the circumstance.

That way of putting the point may be interpreted as overly cynical. Let me put the point another way. Most systems of moral beliefs are rule-inconsistent. That is to say, although the beliefs may not be inconsistent with one another, taken as a set they may be inconsistent with the facts concerning the prevailing circumstances. For example, a polygamist who has been converted to Christianity and its attendant morality has to choose between what he believes to be the sin of continuing his polygamist ways and what he believes to be the sin of failing to honour family commitments. Now, although it may seem reasonable to conjecture that many if not most moral agents would have a utilitarian strand or two among their moral beliefs, it seems reasonable to conjecture that most would have non-utilitarian strands also. Further, it often seems to be the case that it is these strands—the property ethic, the doctrine of deserts, familial duties, patriotic duties and other in-group duties—that become emphasised in just the sort of conflicts we are considering. In any case, one certainly cannot rely on any sort of utilitarian ethic being overriding to all parties in a dispute between moral agents.

Of course, it remains true that the utilitarian ethic may prevail in the situation and that accordingly the dispute will be settled with a maximum likelihood of optimal satisfaction. But given the multitude of alternative moral principles that could prevail instead, one would be unwise to encourage a moral input to conflict resolution on the basis of the mere possibility of utilitarianism prevailing. One might just as well encourage those who wished to go north to proceed in the direction they are facing—whatever that may be. After all, it's possible that they could be facing north.

If moral desires are an artificiality, the non-moral desires at the root of the conflict may well be left completely dissatisfied by the arbitration. The mere fact that morality can in some cases result in a quick resolution of conflict in no way entails that the resolution involves an optimal satisfaction of desire any more than a non-amicable resolution would do. Indeed, the moral arbitrator may even rule that both sides have a moral obligation to fight it out. It is not very long ago that men in Europe felt morally obliged to defend their honour by duelling. Even within the twentieth century, Hitler's bellicose morality enjoined conflict between races. But even where the moral elite are opposed to conflict between their disciples, their rulings will probably be contrary to what would otherwise satisfy one of the parties, and often the ruling will be dissatisfying to both parties, except for the artificial satisfaction that both may enjoy in doing what they falsely believe is the right thing to do.

Again, it may be objected that there could be and, indeed, are many cases when the invocation of moral attitudes and considerations yields a maximum of satisfaction in the resolution of a conflict. Again, the reply is that that is not at issue. The question is whether the institution is worth preserving given the likelihood or otherwise of moral invocations having greater costs than benefits overall. It is simply invalid to argue that an institution is worth preserving on the basis that its invocation is often beneficial. Its invocation may even more often be disastrous.

4.3 The Alternative: Conflict Resolution Without Morality

If it turns out that moralising is ill-conducive to rational conflict resolution, should we look for some other tool to do the job done by morality?

At this stage, this question may remind one of the person who suggests to the man who is hitting his mouth with a brick that he stops. "What is the alternative?" the masochist asks as if stopping were not enough—as if something else were required.

No one to my knowledge, least of all myself, has ever suggested that doing without morality would be a positive cure for all the stresses, strains and conflicts within society. The proposal is that doing without it is doing without something that is likely to cause more stress and strain than it alleviates.

If morality is ill-conducive to satisfaction in situations of conflict, and if morality has the disadvantages to society as outlined in chapter 3, then using morality as a device for the resolution of conflicts is like using a brick as a toothpick. If you want to be rid of the fibre between your teeth and you do not want broken teeth, then throw the brick away, and think of how you can rid yourself of the fibre without it. Likewise, if you want to minimise conflict and you do not want widespread denigration, guilt complexes, elitism, authoritarianism, economic inequality, insecurity and war, then throw morality away and think about how best you can resolve conflict without it.

Notes

1 *A Treatise of Human Nature* 3.1.1.
2 Monro, D. H. (1967), *Empiricism and Ethics* (Cambridge: Cambridge University Press), 80–81.
3 Musgrave, P. (1978), *The Moral Curriculum: A Sociological Analysis* (London: Methuen), 14.

3

MORAL FOOLISHNESS EXPLAINED

Hans-Georg Moeller

1 Introduction

Moral foolishness is a form of "negative ethics" advocating moral restraint.[1] It is the opposite of moral smartness: moral fools do not aspire to improve their moral reasoning, to refine their moral sentiment, or to become more effective in moral communication. To the contrary, they encourage amorality or moral disengagement, and prefer not to distinguish morally between good and bad.

Moral fools avoid moral engagement because it can easily become moral *over*-engagement, and thus it can become "sick." As a theoretical activity, defending moral foolishness consists, to a large part, in analyzing and describing the social, psychological, and philosophical ills of morality or of the cultivation of moral smartness. It gives an account of moral pathologies and thereby cautions against morality. Positively speaking, such an account can be understood as a contribution to moral hygiene. Moral fools try to build up immune systems that can protect them, and others, against moral infections.

In the present age, moral communication has become ubiquitous (once again). In academic philosophy, where jobs are otherwise hard to come by, ethicists are still in demand. Accordingly, there is a flood of publications in moral philosophy (including the present one). Not only politicians and doctors, but also bankers and businesspeople, are nowadays expected and thus trained to express themselves ethically. And even advertisements often highlight the moral quality (such as eco-friendliness) of the products they try to sell. The omnipresence of morality may give the impression that amoral positions are, at best, odd exceptions at the fringes of intellectual history. A closer look, however, reveals that this is not the case. The "moral revival" of our times obscures a wide spectrum of negative ethics, including defenses of amorality, and, indeed, theories of moral foolishness.[2]

In this chapter though, I will not trace the history of negative ethics in world philosophy, though it is long and more varied than one might imagine. Rather, on a much smaller scale, I will present an account of two main historical and theoretical sources for moral foolishness. These two sources are ancient Chinese Daoism and Niklas Luhmann's (1927–1998) social systems theory.[3]

It needs to be stressed that the word "fool" not only connotes idiocy or being stupid; it also denotes a jester. In medieval times, such fools were "employed to amuse a monarch or noble, usually by telling jokes, singing comical songs, or performing tricks."[4] Thus, a moral fool can also be someone who ridicules and performs tricks on morality and moralists. In this—very important, but often neglected—sense, Daoist philosophers and Luhmann were "moral fools" too. In recognition of this form of amorality, I will conclude this chapter with some remarks pointing towards the connection between moral foolishness and humor and irony.

2 "There is no disorder worse": On Daoist Moral Foolishness

In order to understand and appreciate the Daoist notion of moral foolishness, it is crucial to be aware of its larger philosophical context. Cosmologically speaking, Daoism represents a decidedly non-anthropocentric position. The cosmos as such is believed to be an orderly and regular *natural process* or "way"—referred to as *dao* 道, from which Daoism (*dao jia* 道家) derives its name—which operates in self-sustaining and self-reproductive circularity. Rather than having any privileged natural role or function, humankind is embedded in encompassing natural contexts that determine the conditions of its survival. Humans are not in a position to impose their rules as "masters of the earth," but have to follow the non-human regularities of the earth and of *dao*.

Central to Daoist non-anthropocentrism are, I believe, its epistemological aspects. The *Daodejing* (道德經) proclaims what may be called a "negative cultivation" of human knowledge. The text not only famously dismisses the correspondence of *dao* to the "names" (*ming* 名) of human language (as, for instance, in chapters 1 and 37), but, more concretely, advocates a minimization of knowledge claims: "To know not-knowing is the highest" (*zhi bu zhi shang* 知不知 上, chapter 71).[5] It proposes an engagement in a paradoxical process of learning. Chapter 48 says: "One who engages in learning increases daily. One who hears of the *dao* diminishes daily" (*wei xue ri yi, wei dao ri sun* 為學日益，為道日損). I understand this not as a total dismissal of any knowledge, but read it in a quite Socratic fashion as the advice to minimize one's insistence on knowing things that one does not really know or cannot know at all—or the advice to be smarter at being foolish.

These lines of the *Daodejing* can be understood as variations of one of the core topics of this text; namely, the "emptying of the heart-mind"—as expressed in the "Daoist imperative" in chapter 3: "Empty your heart-mind!" (*xu qi xin* 虛其心).

Chapter 20 of the *Daodejing* illustrates this topic with poetic imagery. Here, the ruler, while taking part in a public festivity and mingling with the population, is described as resembling "an infant that does not yet smile" (*yinger zhi wei hai* 嬰兒之未孩) and as having "the heart-mind of an idiot" (*yu ren zhi xin* 愚人之心). This imagery can be read as suggesting that Daoist sages rid themselves of the intellectual, cultural, and emotional prejudices that they have acquired through socialization so that they will be able to attain what the Chinese philosopher Feng Youlan has called "a-posteriori non-knowledge" (*hou de de wu zhi* 後得的無知).[6]

The topic of the "emptying of the heart," and thus of negative epistemological cultivation, is further elaborated in the *Zhuangzi* (莊子). One famous passage of the philosophically central *Qi Wu Lun* (齊物論) chapter (2.11),[7] has been understood as expressing a Daoist "relativism" or "skepticism."[8] I believe, however, that this passage is not really concerned with such matters, but rather indicative of a Daoist cultivation of equanimity. Here it is in A. C. Graham's translation (2001: 58):

> When a human sleeps in the damp his waist hurts and he gets stiff in the joints; is that so of the loach? When he sits in a tree he shivers and shakes; is that so of the ape? Which of these three knows the right place to live? Humans eat the flesh of hay-fed and grain-fed beasts, deer eat the grass, centipedes relish snakes, owls and crows crave mice; which of the four has a proper sense of taste? Gibbons are sought by baboons as mates, elaphures like the company of deer, loaches play with fish. Mao Qiang and Lady Li were beautiful in the eyes of man; but when the fish saw them they plunged deep, when the birds saw them they flew high, when the deer saw them they broke into a run. Which of these four knows what is truly beautiful in the world?

I think that a closer observation of the passage reveals that it neither defends the respective relative validity and merits of differing knowledge claims, nor skeptically encourages us to question the validity of whatever we hold to be true. In fact, I think if we take a good look at the imagery and the humor of the passage, it is rather obvious that it neither defends nor questions any knowledge claims. Actually, the passage undermines the specifically human tendency to operate in a "mode of knowledge." Rather than defending or questioning specific forms of human knowledge, it ridicules with foolish or "idiotic irony"[9] the human attitude of looking at everything in terms of right or wrong. Humans not only live in places fitting human needs, eat food fitting the human appetite, and mate with partners they are attracted by, but, unlike animals, they often unnecessarily, and potentially unhealthily, conceive of all these (most basic) aspects of their natural form of life in terms of "knowledge" about how to live—and they then go on to promote them as the "right" or "proper" way to live. In this way, they become unable to achieve equanimity.

Once one assumes a "mode of knowledge," one is prone to (a) try to impose what one knows onto others, and (b) quarrel with others who claim to know things differently or "better" or "truly." The above passage mockingly illustrates a major difference between animals and humans: Animals live how they live without claiming to know how to live. They never engage in arguments about the respective merits of their habitat, they never try to convince other animals to change their diet in accordance with any "eating ideology," and they also never skeptically question whether the partners they mate with are really right for them. Humans, on the other hand, tend towards such quarrels and replace the art of living with the dubious art of "*knowing* how to live"—which may then threaten social harmony, since it easily leads to "relativist" conflicts or skeptical indecision.

With the above passage, the *Zhuangzi* illustrates a problem of human knowledge claims. In the text, this problem is addressed in a rhetorical question by the fictitious Daoist character Wang Ni: "How do I know that what I call knowing is not not-knowing? How do I know that what I call not-knowing is not knowing?" (Graham 2001: 58). Evidently, rather than skeptically or relatively qualifying human knowledge claims in the various manners found in the Western philosophical tradition, this passage occurs in the context of a Daoist plea for the not-knowing "empty" or "idiotic" or "infant-like" heart-mind of a fool. Such a heart-mind does not subject itself to established discourses that impose specific value-centered interpretations and does not replace actual experience with a judgmental attitude. Speaking in postmodernist terms, it tries to distance itself from reigning "master narratives."

Daoist negative epistemological cultivation entails the advocacy of a paradoxical smart foolishness. An empty heart-mind refrains from evaluative human-centered knowledge claims, and this is particularly so with respect to knowledge claims regarding the distinction between good and bad—and the all-too-human distinction between good and evil. Thus, Wang Ni concludes his comparison between judgmental humans who argue about the right way of life and animals that do not by saying: "The grounds of benevolence and righteousness and the paths of right and wrong are utterly confusing. How would I know to dispute them!?"[10] Again, Wang Ni is not interested in defending any relativist or skeptical position here, but rather points out that he does not want to engage in any argumentation about matters of right and wrong or good and bad. "Benevolence and righteousness" (*ren yi* 仁義) are central Confucian moral values, and thus this *pars pro toto* expression denotes (Confucian) moral discourse in general. In a similar way, the expression "right and wrong" (*shi fei* 是非) is used to denote the philosophical debates among the various schools of thought of the time. Wang Ni, the Daoist, thereby declares his abstinence from the "petty" arguments among the philosophers, and, particularly, his refusal to take part in their moral discourse. For him, the human practice of judging good and bad is objectionable since it opens up a path he'd rather not go down. He will not even begin to engage in the project of cultivating moral disputation skills but instead will remain morally foolish.

Two forms of distinguishing between good and bad are considered as particularly pernicious in the *Zhuangzi*: first, the distinction between good and bad luck, and, second, the moral distinction between good and bad. To think and talk in terms of these distinctions may easily preoccupy an individual or a group and lead to unease, constant worry, and friction. Both distinctions are considered as especially prone to causing *stress*. In ancient China, divination or, more precisely, *fortune telling*, was widely practiced. Quite tellingly, the first of the ancient Chinese "Five Canonical Scriptures" is the divination manual *Yi Jing* 易经 or *Book of Changes*. And the interest in such matters has hardly lessened in contemporary Chinese everyday culture. From a Daoist perspective, the interpretation of whatever happens as either auspicious or inauspicious (for humans) blinds one's perception. Every event then becomes something different—it is not only what it is, but either something threatening or promising. The tendency to interpret whatever happens in life as good or bad luck consumes our intellectual attention and, simultaneously, shifts our focus from the present to an unknown future. In this way, it not only creates unnecessary hopes or worries, but also spoils our capacity to experience. Instead of cultivating such superfluous quasi-knowledge about good and bad, Daoism recommends cultivating foolishness. The *Zhuangzi* says that the Daoist sage remains "unperturbed by good or bad luck" (17.7). And, commenting on the *Daodejing*, it uses once more the image of the infant to illustrate this state of mind (23.6):

> "Can you become like an infant?"[11] The infant moves without knowing what it does. It goes without knowing where it gets to.[12] Its body is like the branch of a rotten tree, and its heart-mind is like dead ashes.[13] In this state, it meets neither bad luck nor good luck. When there is neither bad luck nor good luck, how can there be human misery?

In its historical context, the image of the infant may well have been understood quite literally as an ideal example of an unperturbed mental and physical state that Daoist cultivation sought to emulate and that would result in an elimination of human misery. This does not disallow, however, a more metaphorical reading of this passage as advocating perceptual immediacy through the avoidance of good/bad evaluations in order to increase mental and physical health.

Even more harmful than the preoccupation with the distinction between good and bad luck is, for the Daoists, the concern with the moral distinction between good and bad. The pathology of moral discourse is a major theme in both the *Daodejing* and the *Zhuangzi*, and it is a focal point of the Daoist criticism of Confucius. Both texts, by frequently "deconstructing" the Confucian moral vocabulary, clearly indicate that Confucian moral teachings were already pervasive at the time of their composition. Thus, not completely unlike amoral positions today, both texts contradict the ethical "mainstream" of their era.

Chapter 6 of the *Zhuangzi* contains a short dialogue depicting a prospective student seeking instruction from a Daoist master (6.8). When the prospective student tells the master that he had previously been learning Confucian morality (i.e., "benevolence and righteousness, and right and wrong"), the Daoist master strictly rejects him, because he has thus already been "tattooed" with Confucian morality which also "cut off his nose." Tattooing and cutting off the nose were not only punishments for criminals in China, but also indicate irreversible distortions of the body and the loss of sensitivity. Thus the imagery of this short dialogue nicely summarizes what, according to Daoism, engagement in moral reasoning and behavior does to humans: it turns them into crooks, afflicts them with incurable harm, and makes them senseless. The story also exemplifies that it is hopeless to engage with people who are "infected" by morality. Rather than trying to argue with them, persuade them, or convert them, it is better, if only for the sake of remaining sane, to stay away from them. The reaction of the Daoist master in this case is reminiscent of Nietzsche's outcry in the *Genealogy of Morality* (3.14): "We need good air! good air! In any case: Away from the proximity to all the insane asylums and infirmaries of culture!"

A sequence of four chapters in the *Zhuangzi* (chapters 8–11) deals extensively with the pathology of morality. Right at the beginning of chapter 8, morality is compared with webbed toes, a sixth finger, an obstinate wart, and a dangling wen (Graham 2001: 200). Just as these additions do nothing to improve our physical abilities and powers, moral distinctions do nothing to improve our mental and social skills. They do not contribute to the art of life. However, as the text says (8.1), "someone with webbed toes will weep when they are ripped apart and someone with a sixth finger will scream when it is bitten off" (Graham 2001: 201). The "deconstruction" of firmly established moral habits will not please moralists— and this is another reason for amoralists to keep their distance from them, in the interest of their own safety.

Chapter 9 of the *Zhuangzi* ironically describes the "civilization" of humankind by the invention of morality as a process of corruption. It begins with an allegory of a legendary horse trainer who, by taming and grooming them, makes the horses lose their natural abilities. Eventually, he kills a good percentage of the horses under his care. The imposition of the Confucian moral codes on society, it is argued, disturbs natural human relations and introduces hypocrisy as well as, ultimately, social division and conflict.

Chapter 10 includes a famous narrative about robber Zhi, a legendary personification of evil in ancient China, whose notoriety was comparable to that of Osama Bin Laden in our times. The chapter has robber Zhi explain that he, too, acts only in accordance with generally accepted morality (10.1): "Being first man in is courage. Being last man out is righteousness. Knowing whether or not you can bring it off is wisdom. Giving everyone fair shares is benevolence" (Graham 2001: 209). The point of this story is, again, not to point out any moral "relativism" ("One person's terrorist is another person's freedom fighter"), but rather that moral communication can embellish whatever one does and provide it with a supposedly "higher" meaning or interpretation. Moral language is used to super-impose a secondary "code" on social behavior. Once moral language is introduced, the moral interpretation of an act "perverts" the act by translating it into something else. Moral language is a tool that enables us to construct a significance of an act which then replaces the act. Daoist philosophy tries to avoid falling into the habit of pretending to "know" the moral significance of behavior in such a fashion.

Chapter 11 (11.2) says: "How do I know that Zeng and Shi are not the whistling arrows which signal the attack of tyrant Jie and robber Zhi?" (Graham 2001: 213). Tyrant Jie is, just as robber Zhi, an emblematic arch-villain, and Zeng and Shi are emblematic moral exemplars. The "inventions" of moral heroes and moral language create not only righteousness, but also self-righteousness. Once morality is embraced, it is only "logical" to identify oneself with the moral and not with the immoral side of the distinction. Moral communication thus serves as a tool for adopting the moral "high ground." Typically, the same moral values are embraced by the moral exemplars and villains alike. Moral language leads to self-aggrandizement and moral vanity, which, in extreme cases, can turn into a catastrophic moral frenzy. It is better not to make use of this kind of semantics since, in the words of the *Zhuangzi* (14.6), "Benevolence and righteousness torment our heart-minds and keep them restless; there is no disorder worse" (Graham 2001: 129).

As these examples from the *Zhuangzi* show, ancient Daoist philosophy addresses the pathology of morality in various ways. In fact, the cultivation of an amoral way of life seems to be central to the Daoist pursuit of an encompassing equanimity and comprehensive mental and physical health. However, the Daoist texts do not formulate a systematic theory of amorality or lengthy elaborate argu-ments on the "rightness" of amoral claims. They speak, mostly, in images and allegories or in poetic verse and formulaic pronouncements. Historically, texts like the *Daodejing* and the *Zhuangzi* prove that, at least in early China, a counter-tradition to elaborate moral communication (in the form of, e.g., Confucian texts) existed basically as long as this communication itself.

It is up to contemporary interpreters of these texts to apply them to a revival of amoral communication today. The Daoist classics certainly show a keen sense of the paradoxes involved in the attempt to improve society by training people to think and talk in moral terms. As such, they can provide their readers today with an education in the art of suspicion against moral discourse; they can shape an awareness of amoral alternatives to otherwise often unchallenged moral pre-sumptions; and while not yet constituting a proper theory of amorality, they can help one to change one's perspective on morality by no longer conceiving of it as some sort of natural ingredient of life, but rather as a contingent form of com-munication whose benefits are by no means clear. In this way, they can be read as an unlikely ancient preparation for a current systematic account of morality as a form of potentially pathological communication—as found in the social theory of Niklas Luhmann.

3 "A highly contagious substance": Luhmann on Moral Communication

Like ancient Chinese Daoist philosophers, the contemporary German social theorist Niklas Luhmann identifies morality as pathological: "In normal everyday interaction, after all, morality is not needed anyway; it is always a symptom of the occurrence of pathologies" (Luhmann 2000: 79). In order to understand Luhmann's diagnosis of morality as a (potential) social illness—and how this diagnosis leads to an advocacy of moral foolishness—it is important to acknowledge Luhmann's specific understanding of morality and how it relates to his general theory of society.

Interestingly enough, Luhmann, the social theorist, does not share any of the standard philosophical and "commonsense" understandings of morality. For him, morality is not a quality of a person, an act, or a principle, but rather a specific *type of communication*. When, for instance, theoretically reflecting on a father's moral admonishment of his son, or a priest's moral sermon to his congregation, Luhmann is not interested in finding out if the principles underlying their remarks are correct, but in how they communicate and how this way of communication functions. For Luhmann, ethics is a theory reflecting on morality and, since for him morality is a type of communication, ethics becomes an analysis of communication—including its pathologies.

Luhmann's understanding of morality as a type of communication must be understood in the context of his general theory, which conceives of society as an encompassing system of communication—and not, for instance, as a sum of people. The economy, as one of the major social sub-systems, is thus not understood as constituted by people who operate economically by, for instance, selling, buying, and investing, but as constituted by sales, purchases, and investments, etc. as forms of economic communication. The theory, of course, does not deny the existence of people, but it assumes that people's bodies, and even their thoughts or intentions, do not play an operative role in communicative processes. Bodies and thoughts are necessary environmental preconditions for communication to take place, but, as environmental conditions of the existence of communication, they are still not communicative or social phenomena as such. This leads Luhmann to the following controversial, but, in my view, obviously correct insight:

> Within the communication system we call society, it is conventional to assume that humans can communicate. Even clever analysts have been fooled by this convention. It is relatively easy to see that this statement is false and that it only functions as a convention and only within communication. The convention is necessary because communication necessarily addresses its operations to those who are required to continue communication. Humans cannot communicate; not even their brains can communicate; not even their conscious minds can communicate. Only communication can communicate.
>
> *(Luhmann 1994a: 371)*

The radicality of this statement has to be acknowledged, but also the ultimately simple fact it expresses: Humans have bodies, including a brain, and they have thoughts, but in communication "we" do not exchange thoughts. This is only a metaphorical way of speaking, but in fact your thoughts never become mine, they remain yours. Most of what is considered to be essentially human, such as brain activity and thoughts, is not communication, but part of the environment within which communication takes place—and, of course, without which it could not take place.

As a sociologist, Luhmann is interested in social phenomena and does not attempt to reduce them to non-social events such as brain activity or thoughts. He wants to understand how society as a complex communication system functions and does not believe that it is determined by non-social structures. Society—and, within it, moral communication—has evolved into a self-reproducing and self-sustaining communication system whose functioning must be understood in terms of social theory. Luhmann therefore does not attempt to identify any extra-social (such as physical or rational "a priori") foundations that would determine moral communication. From the perspective of a Luhmannian ethics—i.e., a theory of moral communication—morality has little to do with the inherent goodness or badness of individual human beings, or with the correctness of the principles supposedly informing their actions, but is simply one quite prevalent way in which communication proceeds.

According to Luhmann, contemporary society consists of a number of social systems which have evolved into highly complex self-reproducing communication "organisms." (Luhmann does not use this metaphor, but his theory is strongly influenced by biological theories of evolution.) Among them are, for instance, the economy, politics, education, mass media, law, medicine, and sports, to name just a few. All of these systems have developed their own codes (such as legal/illegal in the sphere of law), media (such as money in the economy), organizations (such as parties in politics), etc., and all of them fulfill specific functions in society (the political system, for instance, allows society to generate "collectively binding decisions"). Luhmann therefore also calls them "function systems" and defines modern society as based on "functional differentiation," i.e., as basically divided along the lines of these various systems.

However, contemporary society has not developed a solid self-generating "morality system" with specific functions, programs, and organizations. There are, for instance, careers in politics, law, medicine, and the mass media, but there is no career in morality. There are political parties, religious congregations, sports clubs, or franchises, but no moral unions. There are banks, universities, and courts, but no moral institutions—and if so-called ethics commissions are created, they are in the service of other economic, political, or educational institutions. At the same time, all systems can and do use moral communication in various degrees and forms. Moral communication is, simultaneously, ubiquitous and "homeless," it is everywhere and nowhere at the same time. Political, legal, or mass media communication is at times moral and at times not. We can talk morally to our family members, but we do not have to. Some philosophers write books on just wars, while others write on military strategy.

In Luhmann's definition, morality is

> a special form of communication which carries with it indications of approval or disapproval. It is not a question of good or bad achievements in specific respects, e.g. as an astronaut, musician, researcher, or football player, but of the whole person insofar as s/he is esteemed as a participant in communication. Approval or disapproval is distributed typically according to particular conditions. Morality is the useable totality of such conditions at any time.
>
> *(Luhmann 1990: 84)*

As "the useable totality" of the conditions for distributing approval/disapproval of "people" as participants in communication, morality is a social, or communicative, construct, which, in multiple and always changing ways, configures and reconfigures "the conditions on the market of approval" (1990: 84). Moral communication introduces a dimension of overall social approval or disapproval of persons into communication—and this without necessity. Most communication does not need this dimension to function properly. In education, we can assign good or bad marks to students without, at the same time, signaling our general approval or disapproval of them as persons. Likewise, in other systems, such as the law, a fine can be issued without at the same time sending a message of overall personal disapproval to the person violating the speed limit.

The introduction of the dimension of personal approval or disapproval of participants in communication makes moral communication, in Luhmann's view, risky, because it can lead "to an over-engagement of the participants" (1990: 86). Once communication is morally charged, the stakes are raised. According to Luhmann, moral communication is "risky because it leads to a rapid fixation of positions, to intolerance, and to conflict" (Luhmann 1987: 92). More concretely, and menacing, Luhmann outlines the "problem of morality"—namely, the risk that moral communication will fuel social conflict:

> Whenever the catchword "morality" appears, the experiences Europe has had with morality since the Middle Ages should actually demonstrate this problem well: religiously adorned upheavals and suppressions, the horrors of inquisition, wars all about morally binding truths and revolt arising in indignation.
>
> *(Luhmann 1993: 359, my translation)*

Luhmann assesses moral communication as risky and socially pathological because of its tendency to generate conflict and its capacity to intensify it. It can cause severe harm, and thus one should "only touch it with the most sterile instruments and with gloves on"; it is a "highly contagious substance" (1993: 359, my translation). Ethics, as a theoretical endeavor reflecting on moral communication, must keep a safe distance from its object of investigation. Contrary to traditional approaches to ethics, its function is not to find out which moral characteristics, actions, or principles are correct, but to understand the problematic role of moral communication in society and thus to contribute to an immunization, as far as possible, from such communication. Luhmann's negative ethics treats morality as a potential sickness and, in stark opposition to current trends, suggests that "ethics has to be in the position to limit the sphere of application of morality" (1990: 90). Not so different from the Daoists, albeit in a very different historical and conceptual context, Luhmann paradoxically conceives of ethics as an activity that counters moral cultivation and that, in a way, promotes moral foolishness in the form of minimizing the application, and the appeal, of moral communication.

Luhmann's analysis of the functioning of moral communication in contemporary society also explicitly renounces another central element of traditional ethics: namely, the implicit or explicit demand that society as a whole may ascribe to one specific type of morality or set of moral principles (such as a specific list of foundational "human rights"). Simply put, contemporary society is too complex and too pluralistic to be reduced to one fundamental communicative system that would determine all others—as the failures of the ideology-centered (Soviet Union) or religion-centered (Iran) social experiments demonstrate. No single system, and much less all of society, can be "integrated" by one form of moral communication that everyone has to ascribe to—and, if so, it would be the end of modern functionally differentiated society. Society would collapse into a one-dimensional moral dictatorship, not a brave new world, but a "good new world" of one morality. Luhmann states:

> Above all it must be conceded that none of the functional systems can be integrated into the social system by means of morality. The function systems owe their autonomy to their individual functions, but also to their individual binary coding, e.g. the distinction between true and untrue in the scientific system or the distinction between government and opposition in the democratic political system. In neither case can the two values of these codes be made congruent with the two values of the code of morality.
> *(1990: 85–86)*

In order to fulfill their functions, contemporary social systems have developed their own non-moral codes, such as the distinction between true and false in science or the academic system, the distinction between healthy and sick in the medical system, or the distinction between gain and loss in the economy. None of these codes is moral as such, and none of them can be sensibly reduced to a moral distinction. To be unsuccessful in school, sick in medical terms, or a poor person in the economy is, normally, not equated with moral failure. In all these cases, there has been amoral progress in society. In the 19th century, for instance, bad students could still be deemed morally deficient, sick people could be blamed for their illness, and poor people could be perceived as lacking proper economic virtue.

When refuting another academic's claims as false, academics set out to prove their own claims as true—and vice versa. Once the discourse is overshadowed by moral communication, and truth is identified with moral goodness while falsity is identified with moral evil, the academic or scientific system is threatened. At this stage, academic communication ceases to aim at refuting opposing claims and may turn into a "witch hunt" which can aim at the social destruction of anyone who defends "evil" falsities. In any functioning academic dispute, one would not expect to identify academic judgments about truth and falsity with moral judgments about good and evil. Even more risky seems the over-moralization of political communication. Luhmann says: "We do not want the government to be declared structurally good and the opposition structurally bad. This would be the death sentence for democracy" (1990: 86).

That modern society, under present circumstances, is not and cannot be morally uniform leads to the conclusion that "a society differentiated into functional systems must accordingly renounce moral integration" (1990: 86). This means that "the functional codes must operate on a level of higher amorality because they must make their two values available for all operations of the system" (1990: 86). Again, the political system is a prime example. While appeals to morality—and pressures to communicate morally—are central to contemporary politics, a modern political system can function properly and effectively only if it is capable of maintaining its higher amorality (i.e., the amorality of its basic code which is not to be equated with a moral distinction) and, for instance, refrains from interpreting an election victory as a condemnation of the opposition as evil. While politicians may tend to rely heavily on moral communication—for instance, during election campaigns—and while morality usually does play a role in a functioning political system (as the deadly political effects of scandals or revealed cases of corruption show), the political system, like any other system, still has to be able to prevent its own code from being overtaken or equalized with moral coding. Thus, it seems, no current social system functions entirely amorally, but, at the same time, each has to maintain a form of higher amorality in order to be able to safeguard its own coding, and thus itself.

The higher amorality of all social systems in contemporary society does not extinguish moral communication, but keeps it in check and offers alternatives to it. Thus, according to Luhmann, contemporary society, despite the risk it imposes on itself by communicating morally, has so far managed to avoid moral "overkill." At the end of one of his essays on amorality, Luhmann provides some room for optimism and personal relief: "Now, individuals in particular can feel relieved as they come to realize that today nobody who takes a moral point of view can claim to speak for the whole of society" (Luhmann 1994b: 36).

While Luhmann shares the Daoist concern with the pathologies of morality, his theory is not geared towards the promotion of a lifestyle; in fact, he often stresses his intention to avoid any normative claims since the shift from a diagnostic to a normative discourse can easily lead towards the pitfalls of moral communication.

Not unlike the Daoists, Luhmann first and foremost offers us a disengaged analysis of moral communication and thus invites us to broaden our views beyond the confines of moral distinctions. Like Daoist philosophy, Luhmann's theory puts moral communication into perspective and opens up amoral horizons. Most importantly, it shows how higher amorality is neither a distant utopia dreamed up by amoralists, nor a dystopian nightmare that haunts moralists, but rather a decisive characteristic of the basic communicational codes which structure contemporary social life and make it effective.

4 The Carnivalization of Morality: Concluding Remarks on Moral Foolishness

For Daoist philosophers, the cultivation of moral foolishness is an exercise aimed at calming the heart-mind and preventing pathological afflictions. For Luhmann, moral foolishness takes on the shape of the "higher amorality" of social systems which thereby maintain their communicative integrity, self-reproduction, and efficacy. Both avoid a direct engagement in moral argumentation and rather try to show amoral alternatives to it.

But how do we practically manage to avoid a pathological affliction with moral communication and moral reasoning? In his influential essay "The Conscience of Huckleberry Finn" (1974), the philosopher Jonathan Bennett has discussed a quite exemplary case of suspending pathological morality through moral foolishness. Here, Bennett analyses Mark Twain's depiction of Huckleberry Finn's crisis of conscience when helping his friend Jim to escape from slavery. While on the run with Jim, Huck is plagued by a sincere moral guilt about his actions. As Bennett explains, virtually without exception all (pathological) moral principles available to Huck tell him that it is wrong to help a slave escape, and yet his human sympathy and "irrational" feelings make him do just that. Bennett stresses:

> The crucial point concerns *reasons*, which all occur on one side of the conflict. On the side of conscience we have principles, arguments, considerations, ways of looking at things . . . On the other side, the side of feeling, we get nothing like that.
>
> *(1974: 127)*

What Huck has to do in order to be able to act in accordance with his human sympathy and to save Jim is to become morally foolish—he is incapable of finding any moral reason or argument that would replace the morality of his time with a superior one. He has to suspend the framework of moral communication and, in Bennett's words, "give up morality altogether" (1974: 131). Huck gains some relief from his bad conscience about having found it impossibly "troublesome" to do the "right thing" and not let Jim escape, only by saying to himself:

> Well, then, says I, what's the use you learning to do right, when it's trou-blesome to do right and ain't no trouble to do wrong, and the wages is just the same? I was stuck. I could not answer that. So I reckoned I wouldn't bother no more about it, but after this always do whichever comes handi-est at the time.
>
> *(quoted in Bennett 1974: 131)*

Saving Jim, for Huck, is not a moral achievement that he adorns himself with, but something he does foolishly by ceasing to "bother about" moral judgments. The story thereby provides a very vivid example of the practical use of applied moral foolishness: Given the sometimes-overwhelming social power of moral communication, we may find ourselves unable or unwilling to engage with it on its own discursive terms. In such cases, the most effective way to avoid being pathologically afflicted by it is to cultivate a morally foolish attitude.

What the story also illustrates is, in Bennett's words, a "finely wrought irony" (1974: 127) for which Mark Twain is rightly famous. He is a literary jester par excellence, someone who not only often ignores but also mocks and ridicules the morals and the moral modes of communication of his time. While the character of Huckleberry Finn in this episode illustrates moral foolishness as applied moral restraint, the story by Mark Twain depicting Huck represents moral foolishness as an applied art providing ironic respite from moral communication and opening up alternative modes of communication and thought. In this way, the notion of moral foolishness refers to both the moral abstinence exemplified by Huckleberry Finn in the story and the ironical deconstruction of morality performed by Mark Twain as its writer.

Moral foolishness as a morally subversive art of ironic communication prac-ticed by jesters of all kinds is nothing new. It may well be traced back to the comedies of ancient Greece, with Aristophanes and his satirical portrayal of Socrates, the moralist, in *Clouds* as an early example.

In the past century, the Russian historian of literature Mikhail Bakhtin has introduced the term "carnivalistic" to describe the social practice of ironic amo-rality embraced by the art of moral foolishness. With this term, Bakhtin relates to the medieval carnival, which (according to him) served as a humoristic counter-culture that established a topsy-turvy world of behavior, values, and social roles. Through the mockery of the dominant morality, as represented at the time by the Catholic religion and its institutions, the carnival provided space for relief and relaxation within a world of strict hierarchies and suppression. Along with the carnival, as Bakhtin says, "clowns and fools . . . are characteristic of the medieval culture of humor" (in Morris 1994: 198). Bakhtin's carnivalistic moral foolishness represents the "laughing truth" (in Morris 1994: 210): mocking, unmasking, and annihilating that which is, under normal circumstances, sacrosanct, holy, and untouchable. Thus, the moral fool represents the (temporary) overcoming of the fear and awe imposed by moral communication and installed in the moral heart-mind. For Bakhtin, this fear—which includes, for example, the fear of social exclusion because of the violation of moral norms, the fear of punishment for immoral behavior, or the fear of one's bodily desires which may be considered immoral—is a "moral fear," and the carnival serves to suspend it:

> The medieval person experienced in laughter the triumph over fear. And this triumph was not only experienced as a victory over mystical fear (the "fear of God"), and over the fear of the forces of nature, but most of all as the victory over moral fear, which subdues human consciousness, and suppresses and numbs it.
>
> *(Bakhtin 1990: 35, my translation)*[14]

What Bakhtin describes here, "the victory over moral fear, which subdues human consciousness, and suppresses and numbs it," is also described in Mark Twain's story about how Huckleberry Finn helped his friend Jim escape slavery. And, as in the medieval carnival, Mark Twain, the artist, assumes the role of a jester to facilitate this victory. As applied amorality, a carnivalistic practice of moral foolishness can be more powerful and provide more immediate relief, and thereby sanity, than an argumentative engagement with morality and its "reasons."

The carnivalistic aspect of moral foolishness can perhaps be further illustrated with a simple joke. It is one of many (by now old-fashioned) German jokes about two local characters from the city of Cologne named Tünnes and Schäl. Walking across the big bridge over the Rhine, Tünnes encounters Schäl crying and deeply upset. Asked by Tünnes what the matter is, Schäl replies that someone just threw his sandwich into the Rhine. Showing concern, Tünnes asks: "Was it on purpose?" Still devastated, Schäl answers: "No, it was on rye."[15]

From the perspective of (a)moral philosophy, it can be said that the joke first builds up and then and ironically dissolves common moral communication patterns. Thereby, on a very simple level, it provides carnivalistic amoral relief. Since Tünnes sees Schäl in emotional distress and finds out that someone threw his sandwich away, the question of whether this had been done "on purpose" evokes a moral scenario and implies connotations of conflict and expectations of revenge or retribution. Schäl's foolish answer that "it was on rye," however, disappoints this expectation and destroys any moral anticipations. Rather than relating the question to the potentially sinister motives of the person who threw the sandwich into the Rhine, Schäl wrongly relates it to the sandwich he has been craving. Schäl's foolishness, however, which prevents any further moral discourse, is precisely what makes us laugh about the joke. Schäl thus turns out to be a moral fool like Huckleberry Finn, who, while being concerned with more pressing and powerful feelings, is incapable of coming up with moral reasoning. At the same time, the joke as such, like Mark Twain's story, becomes a carnivalistic tale that humorously dissolves moral communication.

A moral fool does not argue, but ridicules. Humor and deconstructive irony are among the most effective communicative tools countering an attitude of moral seriousness. Conversely, the taboos imposed on humor and irony usually indicate very accurately the most moralized types of communication in a society. That which cannot be joked about is that which is most intensely moralized: Those who draw a caricature of Mohammed are threatened with death; those who make "politically incorrect" jokes may lose their jobs and endanger their reputation. From a Luhmannian perspective, moral foolishness can play a vital part in minimizing such social risks of moral communication, while, from a Daoist perspective, it can contribute to cleansing the "heart-mind" of its moralist afflictions.

As an applied form of negative ethics, the "carnivalistic" variant of moral foolishness cannot engage head-on in academic debates on moral or amoral propositions, and it cannot be reduced to a specific "-ism" proposing a specific set of propositions. Instead, it is a communicative practice that parodies moral self-assuredness. Moral foolishness thus presents an invitation to cultivate not only a critical but also a light-hearted attitude toward morality and thus to minimize the restricting influence of moral communication on one's conceptions of the world, of others, and of oneself. It does not primarily oppose moral propositions because of their inaccuracy, but because of the potentially risky mode of communication they introduce into society and the reductionist kind of thinking they promote or express. Just as it is not very helpful to transform a fundamentalist religious believer through argumentation into an equally fundamentalist atheist, it is not very helpful to transform a fundamentalist moralist through argumentation into an equally fundamentalist amoralist. The point of moral foolishness when practiced in a humorous form is to loosen rigid good-bad distinctions and right-wrong dichotomies by exposing the vanity that is often attached to them.

Notes

1   "Negative ethics," according to Hans Saner, refers to a variety of philosophical positions that critically reflect on morality, including: (a) a total renunciation of ethics, (b) a conception of ethics as ineffable, (c) an ethics which holds that morality is always concrete and cannot be generalized, (d) an ethics promoting (moral) non-agency rather than moral agency (Saner 2005: 27–30).
2   See Garner 1994 for a contemporary amoral perspective.
3   A contemporary New Daoist treatise on negative ethics is Wohlfart 2005.
4   *Encarta World English Dictionary* (1998–2005).
5   Passages from the *Daodejing* are my own translations from Moeller 2007.
6   See Feng 1961: 80–81. See also Feng 1947: 78.
7   The numerical indication of passages of the *Zhuangzi* in this chapter follows the electronic edition of the text by the *Chinese Text Project* at http://ctext.org/zhuangzi/
8   For such approaches to the *Zhuangzi*, see Kjellberg & Ivanhoe 1996.

9 Moeller 2008: 117–123.
10 My translation.
11 This is a quotation from chapter 10 of the *Daodejing*.
12 This form of motion is called *you* 遊 in Daoism. It is central to the philosophy of the *Zhuangzi*. Graham has translated it (in the phrase *xiao yao you* 逍遙遊) as "going rambling without a destination."
13 The image of "dead ashes" is used several times in the *Zhuangzi* and refers to the "empty heart-mind."
14 Cf. Morris 1994: 209.
15 Richard Garner kindly helped translating the joke in a way that makes it work in English.

References

Bakhtin, M. 1990. *Literatur und Karneval: Zur Romantheorie und Lachkultur*. Frankfurt am Main: Fischer.

Bennett, J. 1974. "The conscience of Huckleberry Finn." *Philosophy* 49: 123–134.

Feng, Y. 馮友兰. 1947. *The Spirit of Chinese Philosophy* (trans. E. Hughes). London: Kegan Paul.

Feng, Y. 馮友兰. 1961. *Xin Yuan Dao* 新原道 (*A New Treatise on the Nature of Dao*). Hong Kong: Zhonguo zhexue yanjiu hui 中國哲學研究会.

Garner, R. 1994. *Beyond Morality*. Philadelphia: Temple University Press.

Graham, A. (trans. and ed.). 2001. *Chuang-Tzŭ. The Inner Chapters*. Indianapolis: Hackett.

Kjellberg, P. & Ivanhoe, P. (eds.). 1996. *Essays on Skepticism, Relativism, and Ethics in the Zhuangzi*. Albany: SUNY Press.

Luhmann, N. 1987. "The morality of risk and the risk of morality." *International Review of Sociology* 3: 87–101.

Luhmann, N. 1990. "Paradigm lost: On the ethical reflection of morality." *Thesis Eleven* 29: 82–94.

Luhmann, N. 1993. "Ethik als Reflexionstheorie der Moral." In N. Luhmann, *Gesellschaftsstruktur und Semantik. Studien zur Wissenssoziologie der modernen Gesellschaft*, Vol. 3. Frankfurt am Main: Suhrkamp. 358–447.

Luhmann, N. 1994a. "How can the mind participate in communication?" In H. Gumbrecht & K. Pfeiffer (eds.), *Materialities of Communication*. Stanford: Stanford University Press. 371–387.

Luhmann, N. 1994b. "Politicians, honesty and the higher amorality of politics." *Theory, Culture and Society* 11: 25–36.

Luhmann, N. 2000. *The Reality of the Mass Media*. Stanford: Stanford University Press.

Moeller, H.-G. 2007. *Daodejing (Laozi): A Complete Translation and Commentary*. Chicago: Open Court.

Moeller, H.-G. 2008. "Idiotic irony in the *Zhuangzi*." *CLEAR* (*Chinese Literature. Essays, Articles, Reviews*) 30: 117–123.

Morris, P. (ed.). 1994. *The Bakhtin Reader: Selected Writings of Bakhtin, Medvedev and Voloshinov*. London: Edward Arnold.

Saner, H. 2005. "Formen der negativen Ethik: Eine Replik." In O. Henning (ed.), *Negative Ethik*. Berlin: Parerga. 27–30.

Wohlfart, G. 2005. *Die Kunst des Lebens und andere Künste: Skurrile Skizzen zu einem euro-daoistischen Ethos ohne Moral*. Berlin: Parerga.

PART II

The Case for Abolitionism

4

AFTER SUCH KNOWLEDGE—WHAT?

Living and Speaking in a World Without Objective Morality

Russell Blackford

1 Introduction: Mores, Morality, and a Horrible Mismatch

Morality is not what it seems: there is a mismatch between its appearance of objective authority and its role—important, but not so grand—as a useful social technology. In what follows, I explain the mismatch, then turn to practical questions. How might we respond to a disconnection between our assumptions and the colder truth? How are we to live, speak, and seek to influence others in a world without objective morality?

This brings us quickly to the nature of morality itself. Human societies display complex systems of behavioral norms: systems of rules and expectations governing conduct, including expectations relating to dispositions of character. A society's most basic and strongly enforced norms are referred to by social scientists as its *mores* (see "mores" and "norms" in Calhoun 2002), and they are typically maintained by such methods as hostility, shaming, and ostracism, if not by more formal (perhaps harsher) punishments. In what follows, I refer to this observable social phenomenon when I write of "morality," "moral norms," and "moral systems."

The moral systems of the world's past and present societies vary greatly, but they also have features in common, since they are grounded in universal human needs, abilities, limitations, and evolved emotional tendencies. The latter (it seems) include inhibitions against aggression toward each other, a degree of natural kindness and reciprocal loyalty, positive attitudes to helpfulness, and a tendency to punish non-cooperators and seek vengeance when betrayed (see, for example, Greene 2013: 28–65). Moral systems and the psychological elements underlying them are studied empirically by scholars and scientists, and general conclusions can be drawn. One prominent scientific view is that the emotional tendencies underlying morality evolved for cooperation among otherwise selfish members of a group or society, and for competition with other groups (Greene 2013: 23–27, 185–186).

A similar understanding of morality is well represented within the Western tradition of moral and political philosophy from classical antiquity to the present day. In *Ethics: Inventing Right and Wrong*, J. L. Mackie takes up the theme with his suggestion that morality has a recognizable point or purpose, which he identifies as countering limitations that tend to make human life go badly. On Mackie's account, morality is a "device" that counters our limited resources, rationality, information, and intelligence, and, above all, our limited sympathies. It helps us live successfully in communities, reduce conflict with each other, and obtain a measure of peace, security, and cooperation (Mackie 1977: 107–115, 227).

In what follows, I'll assume an understanding of morality along such lines. That is, morality is a useful, somewhat limited social institution underpinned by our species' evolved emotional tendencies. But at the same time, morality is often regarded as something with more imperious claims. Its rules and expectations are seen as "part of the fabric of the world" (Mackie 1977: 15) or as possessing "ubiquitous and inescapable authority" (Joyce 2001: 104). As Richard Garner formulates the idea, "According to the moralist, some things are *really* wrong— forbidden, as it were, by Reality itself" (1994: 48). From the viewpoint of an ordinary person who has been socialized into the local moral system—someone who views the system from within, so to speak—there seem to be *objective require-ments* for our conduct. Certain evaluations of conduct appear to be necessitated, and certain actions demanded or prohibited (or perhaps encouraged, discour-aged, or merely permitted), by a mind-independent reality transcending anyone's ends, goals, purposes, desires, and so on, and any social institutions that prescribe behavior. Even if this illusion of objective moral authority is not universal to all human societies, it is plainly widespread within current Western populations.

Thus, many people in Western societies—and probably far beyond—are suf-fering from a horrible mismatch between their understanding of the world and the truth about morality. They believe in objective requirements and a form of authority that are entirely illusory. There is a disconnect between morality's appearance of a special authority and the reality that moral systems are all-too-human inventions.

2 Mackie: Morality as Technology

Mackie's *Ethics* clearly identifies this mismatch between the appearance and the reality of moral systems, but before going on I should pause to note that Richard Joyce and Simon Kirchin (2010: ix–x) interpret him as also putting forward a "stronger and more metaethically interesting view": a claim that objective moral authority is part of what our ordinary (affirmative first-order) moral judgments *mean*, systematically rendering them false, or at least untrue. Whether or not

Mackie is committed to such a strong claim, however, Joyce and Kirchin seem to accept that this is not his emphasis. It's another matter, of course, whether they are correct about what is or is not more "metaethically interesting"—that is in the eye of the beholder.

For reasons that will become apparent, I doubt that the "more metaethically interesting" thesis is strictly correct, and I'd be disappointed if debates about Mackie's work—or about what is now known as "moral error theory"—turned out to be merely a back-and-forth about such a doubtful thesis. The truth is more complex, I believe, and (though this is still in the eye of the beholder) more fascinating. As the subtitle (*Inventing Right and Wrong*) of his 1977 book suggests, Mackie's emphasis is actually on a claim that morality is a human invention, a kind of social technology, with a fairly clear function. He argues that moral norms and systems can be revised or extended (perhaps to cover new circumstances) or, in principle, even replaced.

Early in the book, Mackie makes two crucial points. First, there are no "objective values or requirements, which many people have believed to exist" (Mackie 1977: 17); and, second, this "is an ontological thesis, not a linguistic or conceptual one" (1977: 18). As he proceeds, however, and especially in chapter 5, he goes far beyond this starting point to develop his account of morality as a human invention or "device." In the upshot, *Ethics* is mainly devoted to an analysis of what content morality should henceforth include if it is to perform its function effectively, particularly in the light of changing circumstances. Mackie wants us to understand that existing systems of moral norms can be modified and to some extent even repurposed.

As he explains, the reasons why human beings and/or human societies need morality can change somewhat over time. Historical changes in social organization, technological capabilities, and the relationships among rival human societies may require an ongoing reinvention of moral systems (Mackie 1977: 121–124). Thus, moral norms that might once have been required for small communities to survive in competition with other species might not be what is required to maintain a stable nation state (1977: 121). Something different again might be needed for participation in a geopolitical order that involves far greater worldwide dependence of some human beings on others, together with the availability of much greater powers to do good or produce harm (1977: 121–122).

Mackie suggests that our entirely fictional "objectification of moral values and obligations" may be useful to human societies. To the extent that it is useful, "it might be thought dangerous, and in any case unnecessary, to expose it as a fiction." As we extend the scope of morality to the circumstances of modern political conflict, however, there are practical reasons to understand morality's real nature and to think more explicitly about how to develop its content (Mackie 1977: 239). Thus, Mackie wants at least *some* of us (including, we may suppose, anyone who is likely to read his books) to understand that objective moral authority is an illusion. At the same time, he hedges his bets as to whether this should be more widely known.

I can't deal fully with the issue here, but we might wonder whether Mackie was inclined to a form of elitism, similar to the "Government House utilitarianism" identified by Bernard Williams in the work of Henry Sidgwick and others (Williams 1985: 108). Williams accused them of envisaging societies with two classes of people: an elite group of moral theorists aware of the utilitarian justification of moral attitudes, and the rest of us who could be expected to adopt them unreflectively. Perhaps some remarks in Mackie's *Ethics* suggest, by analogy, a tendency toward Government House moral error theory.

In a later discussion of the issues in *Hume's Moral Theory*, however, Mackie displays more willingness to consider arguments for doing away with what he calls the "moral overlay" that reinforces a "basic practice" of behavioral norms and reciprocal sanctions (1980: 154–156). His discussion of the pros and cons is notably inconclusive, but he observes that unwanted side effects from moral practice might be reduced if we understood morality for what it is and could "see through its claim to absolute or objective authority" (1980: 156). Even here, however, his emphasis is not on the falsity of moral judgments so much as the usefulness of morality as a social technology, particularly if we (or whoever among us can influence opinions and attitudes) are able to modify it as needed to meet new problems.

3 Many (Tricky) Questions

Still, isn't there something unsatisfactory about this? However much Mackie finesses the issue throughout the careful chapters of *Ethics*, doesn't it remain the case that an affirmative moral judgment such as "Torturing babies to pass the time is morally wrong" comes out as false (or at least untrue) insofar as it seems to mean "Torturing babies to pass the time is objectively prohibited"? Even more disconcertingly (or so it may seem), the negative moral judgment "Torturing babies to pass the time is not morally wrong" appears to come out as true. On Mackie's approach, which I generally endorse, *nothing* is objectively prohibited.

After such knowledge—what?[1]

Before we sort this out, let's take stock. Most people in current Western societies (and perhaps far beyond) evidently believe in non-existent objective requirements. They grant morality (a limited human invention with an important social function) an entirely fictional kind of authority that transcends our ends and social institutions. Furthermore, it seems clear enough that much moral language is seriously flawed. In particular, the terms "moral rightness" and "moral wrongness," in their everyday meanings, do not seem to refer to anything that actually exists. In that respect, moral wrongness is much like sin . . . assuming this refers to something like disobedience toward God and that there is no such God.

I hope, however, that anyone who is sufficiently sophisticated to grasp these issues will not be too disconcerted. People who talk about various actions as being morally wrong do, indeed, appear to mean that these actions are not merely prohibited by the local mores. Rather, they are prohibited in some more objective sense. In that case, "objectively prohibited" may be a reasonably approximate translation of "morally wrong." Strictly speaking, then, nothing is morally wrong, but, still speaking strictly, nothing is morally right or morally permitted. For example, torturing babies (to pass the time or otherwise) is not required or permitted by standards that transcend human ends and social institutions. There simply are no such transcendent standards.

But for all that's been said so far, we still have compelling reasons to be opposed to torturing babies, to uphold social institutions that punish people for torturing babies, and for regarding the torture of babies as a cruel, bad, horrible thing. In section 5, I'll have more to say about moral language, but to foreshadow for the moment: I expect that much of our current moral language would survive even if we all became aware that objective moral authority is an illusion, and even if we gave up *some* of our moral language, such as talk of moral rightness and wrongness. (Note that secular-minded people have already pretty much given up the word "sin.")

Alas, new questions arise. Should we spread the (good? bad?) word about all this? Should we abandon our existing evaluative practices relating to human conduct and character, or can many of them continue? Should we ignore the moral norms of our respective societies, perhaps turning to new standards of our own choosing? More fundamentally, what is even meant, in a context like this, by such words as "should"?

At a personal level, we might worry about how to make our own decisions without belief in any objective requirements. We might also wonder how to evaluate and speak of such things as others' conduct and character. At another level, the question might be whether, or how, societies can hold together without the illusion of objective moral authority. In any event, what are the social implications of the horrible mismatch? Finally, recognition of the mismatch may have implications for science and philosophy. (I believe, as it happens, that they'll be positive ones, and I'll return to this in the concluding section.)

In the process of defending what he calls "Robust Realism," David Enoch raises a further problem: we do not know what the empirical consequences will be if we choose, henceforth, to speak in one way rather than another. He dismisses the debate about how to proceed if moral discourse is "systematically erroneous" not only because he rejects that assumption, but also because "pretty much all of [the debate] consists in empirical speculations about which consequences will follow if we speak in this way or that" (Enoch 2011: 116).

There are doubtless many more questions and complications, but (surely?) this is enough for one chapter. Let's turn to some possible answers.

4 Many (Dubious) Answers

I have a degree of sympathy for Enoch's concern about the empirical difficulties, but we can proceed cautiously. Even Richard Garner, one of the strongest critics of ordinary moral thinking and discourse, suggests, rather mildly, that "We can just cut back on our use of moral language and see how things go" (Garner 2010: 231). Mackie also offers some cautious advice: even if your society's existing moral system does not suit you, you probably should be glad that it exists. Rather than attempting to destroy it, or to transform it apocalyptically, you can try placing pressure on specific aspects of the system (Mackie 1977: 147–148, 190).

This immediately raises questions as to *how* we might place this kind of pressure on the details of our local moral systems, and I'll return to this (section 6). For the moment, however, note that Mackie's advice is less conservative than Jonas Olson's policy of "conservationism," proposed in his 2014 book *Moral Error Theory: History, Critique, Defence* (see also Eriksson & Olson, this volume; Isserow, this volume). Olson argues that we should go on speaking and thinking in the old way, allowing our knowledge that there is no objective moral authority to be silenced in everyday life (Olson 2014: 190–196). As he explains his position, we should continue thinking to ourselves that certain things are morally right and wrong, and continue saying as much, even though what we're saying is not literally true.[2]

According to Olson, this will not matter. At the same time as the speaker states a literal untruth, such as that stealing is morally wrong, she conversationally implicates a useful imperative, "Don't steal!" Thus, Olson predicts, things can go on much as before, either for an isolated individual who follows the conservationist policy or for an entire society of enlightened moral conservationists. Our current forms of moral reasoning will emerge unscathed. In arguing against any more radical approach, Olson claims that "it seems likely that if morality were miraculously abolished, it would subsequently be reinvented" (2014: 181). Taken in one sense, this last claim may be true, but it contains an equivocation that I'll bookmark for now and return to when we assess the options.

Joyce also offers a conservative (though not "conservationist") proposal: he sketches a form of moral fictionalism that could be adopted by individuals or ultimately spread across a society (Joyce 2001: 175–231). Once again, the idea is to carry on using our traditional moral language in thought and conversation. Unlike Olson, however, Joyce does not think we can continue entirely as we were. Rather, he recommends we entertain a fiction that we do not actually believe. He discusses problems for an isolated moral fictionalist who attempts to communicate with others who still believe in objective morality (2001: 203–205). Once enough people become moral fictionalists, however, those problems will recede, because familiar kinds of moral language will express only thoughts, not beliefs (2001: 204–205).

The content of the fiction will be mainly of a general kind: the idea that there are rights, obligations, prohibitions, and morally significant traits such as virtues; the idea that wrongdoers deserve punishment; and some minimal substantive content, such as the idea that torturing babies to pass the time is morally wrong, together with basic rules such as a reciprocal relationship between rights and obligations and the idea that painful consequences are morally relevant (Joyce 2001: 195). As will become clear, I am not convinced that *all* these things actually are fictional—but I can accept enough of them as fictions for current purposes. I'll return to this (along with other loose ends that are accumulating); meanwhile, the point remains that we could, according to Joyce, entertain the fiction that everything he lists is backed up by objective moral authority.

If we adopt Joyce's moral fictionalism, we will not believe that, for example, some actions have the strange property of being objectively prohibited. In settings where such questions arise for serious discussion, we'll deny that objective requirements and objective moral authority exist. However—so Joyce argues—we'll obtain benefits, as individuals, if we continue, in our quotidian self-talk and social discourse, to entertain thoughts of their existence. This will make us more trustworthy people (which will ultimately tend to our advantage) and act as a counterweight to self-destructive lapses. Thus, according to Joyce, moral fictionalism can be justified partly on the basis of enlightened self-interest (Joyce 2001: 214–228).

I'm inclined to reject moral conservationism and moral fictionalism. First, I am unimpressed by Olson's claim that if we abolished morality we'd have to reinvent it. As previously mentioned, I see an equivocation here. Olson's claim might be true if it meant abolishing the naturalistic phenomenon of moral systems. If these somehow disappeared or were forgotten, we might, indeed, need to invent new rules and expectations to constrain our conduct. Since these would be shaped by facts about human limitations, emotional tendencies, etc., I'd expect the newly minted behavioral norms to conform to what H. L. A. Hart calls "the minimum content of Natural Law," and to include such features as limits on acceptable forms of aggression, the provision of a system of property (though not necessarily individual property), and an institution of giving and honoring promises (Hart 1994: 186–212).

It does *not* follow that we'd have to regard the new rules and expectations as backed by objective moral authority. That is a separate point which Olson has not established, although it's the premise that his argument appears to need. For what it's worth, I am continually surprised at the strength of norms that are well known *not* to have any objective authority: norms of etiquette, for example, and norms of fashion.

Second, I am dissatisfied with ultra-conservative proposals such as those of Olson and Joyce, because they downplay what is arguably most important and interesting about Mackie's analysis: it offers the prospect of deliberately acting to *modify* the available social technology. We can take Mackie's advice and proceed cautiously, but we needn't be quietists about the defects of current moral systems.

Third, it would be intellectually dishonest and psychologically difficult to go on employing language whose semantic content we know to be straightforwardly false (or at least untrue). Of course, I don't claim that we are *objectively required* to avoid speaking falsely. All the same, many of us would find too much personal value in intellectual honesty to maintain exactly the old ways of thought and speech if we took to heart the conclusion that objective moral authority is an illusion. I predict that we'd find it easy enough to cut back (as Garner encourages us to do) on at least some kinds of moral language and judgments.

5 Minding Our Language and Making up Our Minds

By now, I owe some explanation of various words that we use every day, some of them even peppering this chapter: words such as "good," "well," "bad," "ought," "should," and "must." In this section, I'll argue that all these words would survive even a general loss of belief in objective moral authority. At a more personal level, I see no reason for us to avoid them as we go about our business, although we might find ourselves using them more self-consciously and perhaps more sparingly.

These words are not used solely in our moral judgments. In their more general meanings, we employ them to indicate various kinds of fit (or lack of it) between some action, choice, plan, event, person, situation, object, etc., and some end that might be desired (or perhaps feared, or even merely contemplated or tacitly assumed). For example, the word "good"—as in "a good hammer" or "a good quarterback"—means something like "with such features or properties as to be effective for our ends" (compare the similar analysis in Mackie 1977: 50–59). In his book *Confusion of Tongues*, Stephen Finlay attempts a more precise definition that relies on the probability of something's contributing to conversationally relevant ends (Finlay 2014: 19–47). Whether or not we should go all the way in adopting the details of Finlay's account, the general idea is attractive. The adverb "well" has a closely related meaning to that of "good," as do the comparative "better" and the superlative "best."[3]

Likewise, "bad" can be used to characterize the properties of a thing that make it unlikely to assist our purposes or other ends that might be relevant in a conversational context (compare Finlay 2014: 41). In many contexts, the word might signal that something's properties are such as to lead to outcomes that are definitely not desired by the speaker. In other cases, it can function slightly differently, relating to ends that we entertain in our imaginations but do not actually endorse. So, in an appropriate context, a *bad* thief is one who is incompetent at stealing property from other people. When we speak in this way, we don't endorse innocent citizens losing their money.

In its primary, most general, meaning, the word "ought" communicates that there is a certain relationship between a course of action and an end of some kind: if I say "You ought to X," it means, roughly, that X-ing is your most reliable or probable means to bring about some end that you desire or that is otherwise relevant in the context of our conversation. (Again, compare Finlay's more elaborate analysis [2014: 48–84].) The word "should" has a similar meaning, while the word "must" conveys something stronger, perhaps that a course of action is the only one that is at all likely to achieve the end (Finlay 2014: 72, 172).

None of this language would vanish from our vocabularies even if we all agreed that objective demands and prohibitions do not exist, and that no moral judgments bind us with an objective authority. Even if that were agreed, we would still need to talk about the relationships between various features, actions, and so on (on the one hand) and (on the other hand) various ends that we desire to achieve or that we are otherwise interested in discussing.

Similarly, I submit that we cannot dispense with so-called thick moral terms such as "kind," "cruel," "nice," "loyal," "courageous," "mean," and "lewd." Words such as these are necessary to draw attention to naturalistic features of actions, things, and people that we find especially important for our attitudes and choices. Many of these words—and cognates such as "cruelty" and "kindness"—can refer, in appropriate contexts, to dispositions of character that would remain socially important even in a world acknowledged to be without objective morality. For this reason, I accept the existence of traits such as virtues (kindness, loyalty, honesty, and so on) that are morally significant in the sense that they play an important role in existing moral systems. Likewise for vicious traits (such as cruelty and dishonesty). We do not need to regard these psychological characteristics as fictional.[4] If we miraculously abolished our existing moral systems (as Olson contemplates in the thought experiment discussed in section 4), whatever replaced them would continue to have a role for virtues and vices of character.

In that respect, Mackie correctly acknowledges that "kind" and "cruel" have naturalistic descriptive content (Mackie 1977: 16–17). What is false, following from all that's been said, is an assumption that might be made by a speaker and/or her audience that cruel actions have a further property of being objectively prohibited. I doubt, however, that this is part of the *meaning* of the word "cruel." The property of cruelty relates to deliberate infliction of gratuitous pain or harm (compare Väyrynen 2013: 4). If this is widely regarded as objectively prohibited, the further claim that X-ing is objectively prohibited might be conversationally implicated when I describe it as a cruel practice, but that will depend on the context. In some cases, I might convey no more than the word's literal descriptive content, or I might convey that *I* have a negative attitude to the action, or perhaps I might convey that the action is *bad* in the sense that it produces effects that I and/or my audience don't desire. It's worth reminding ourselves that communication is a very complex activity.

Note, though, that we might have reasons to avoid some thick moral terms because, in typical contexts, they convey a kind of badness, even if that is not part of their strict semantic content. For example, "lewd" arguably refers to something like overt, socially transgressive sexual display (Väyrynen 2013: 58). Its strict meaning possibly does *not* include "and therefore bad"—let alone "and therefore objectively prohibited"—but should I go on using the word if I have no objection to overt, socially transgressive sexual display? Perhaps I should not if social patterns relating to the word's usage result in a false impression (about myself and my own value system) whenever I use it. Likewise, I might avoid using the loaded words "chaste" and "unchaste" if I reject the attitudes to sexuality that lie behind them.

The point here is that some specific words may be worth giving up because of social baggage that they carry, even though their strict meaning does not necessarily include any false claims about objective moral authority. (Note that a refusal to employ these particular words is just one small way in which we can exert pressure to alter the local moral standards.)

My somewhat tentative conclusion is that disbelief in objective moral authority will not comprehensively change the everyday language that we use in our thoughts and conversations. But it can't leave everything in our moral language as it was, and it will lead to a greater degree of awareness of the language we are using. We are likely, without even making a deliberate effort, to cut down on such expressions as "X-ing is morally wrong" or "Y-ing is morally required": this sort of language—or even less formal variants such as "Z-ing is just wrong!"—will sound hollow and pretentious. Yet we may go on expressing, say, our disapproval of X-ing, our belief that Y-ing is *bad* (it leads to outcomes that we don't desire), or our conviction that only a *horrible* person would engage in anything as *cruel* as Z-ing.

Another element of our lives that might not change comprehensively (or much at all) if we came to disbelieve in objective prescriptive authority is how we make our serious decisions. Enoch's main argument for the existence of objective values, and with them objective moral requirements, is that their existence is somehow an "indispensable" assumption for serious deliberation. But that claim is not convincing.

He offers, as an example, deliberating on whether to practice law or undertake graduate work in philosophy. He describes a process in which somebody in that situation might ask many questions: "Will I be happy practicing law? Will I be happier doing philosophy? What are my chances of becoming a good lawyer? A good philosopher?" After a litany of further such questions, Enoch gets to what he considers crucial:

> Even with answers to most—even all—of these questions, there remains the ultimate question. "All things considered", you ask yourself, "what makes best sense for me to do? When all is said and done, what should I do? What *shall* I do?"
>
> *(Enoch 2011: 72)*

All these questions employ language that would still be available to someone who denies the existence of objective moral authority. Most of them involve the agent in either introspection about her own values and ends or trying, as well as she can, to ascertain elusive and complicated empirical facts. Even "What should I do?" can be seen merely as a question of which path is most likely to meet the agent's subjectively weighted ends, to the extent that she can identify them.

"What shall I do?" asks for the actual decision. Nothing in the example requires the agent to ask whether one choice or the other would be objectively demanded or prohibited.

Thus, the example can be reinterpreted to show how complex deliberation can take place without the assumption that there are objective requirements or that our various moral systems and norms are backed by objective authority. As it happens, I once faced almost exactly the situation Enoch describes: I needed to decide whether to return to legal practice after a break to recharge my batteries—perhaps taking my career to a new level by training as a barrister—or to embark on a doctoral program in philosophy. Although it was a difficult decision, none of my conscious thinking had anything to do with supposed objective values, objective requirements, or respect for the objective authority of any moral system that might have made claims on me.

Much more could be said about the processes by which we make up our minds. Although we often do ask ourselves the sorts of questions in Enoch's list—"Will I be happy practicing law?" and the rest—it's doubtful that we proceed by obtaining clear answers to these questions and then sorting through to find the most rationally justified answer to the final question of "What shall I do?" In reality, our decision-making is likely to be more intuitive, inchoate, and unconscious. If, after the fact, we explain it in prudential or moral terms, or a mixture of these, we are probably engaging in a degree of rationalization and self-deception. Still, nothing in my dispute with Enoch turns on this point.

Our life decisions can involve anxious deliberation that frequently delivers only approximate and ambiguous answers. The process takes place, however, and life goes on. It need involve no assumption that some actions are objectively demanded and others prohibited, or that some outcomes are good or bad in ways that transcend human ends and institutions.

6 Morality, Metaethics, and Meta-morality

This brings me back to what I see as Mackie's emphasis. Once we view morality as a form of social technology, the new perspective can liberate our thinking about many cultural and political issues. If morality's original function was to promote intragroup cooperation, perhaps we can reshape it to assist with our modern predicament, where particular societies consist of many tribal groups and no society can flourish in ruthless competition with others. Four decades after *Ethics* was first published, it seems clearer than ever that the scale of our problems has expanded. Human societies need to cooperate closely for mutual benefits and to handle global threats such as climate change, epidemic diseases, weapons of mass destruction, large-scale cultural and religious conflicts, and the emergence of extremist organizations such as Islamic State.

If we care about ends that morality has not served, or has not served well, such as ameliorating the suffering of non-human animals, we can attempt to repurpose morality to some extent. If, moreover, some moral norms are no longer socially functional, or perhaps never were, we have a reasonable basis to discard them. Some traditional moral rules and attitudes—such as many of those relating to sexual conduct and expression—seem to produce misery and oppression without significant countervailing benefits. Away with them, then! We can criticize them with suitable harshness and make vigorous efforts to consign them to history. It is possible, indeed, that much in our traditional moral norms does more harm than good. If so, perhaps we cannot overturn our local moral systems all at once— recall Mackie's words of caution about this—but it might be justifiable to ignore, or publicly defy, the most oppressive requirements.

To be clear and consistent, there is no *objective moral demand* that we act in any particular way. If, however, we understand morality as a form of social technology, we might find ourselves examining current moral systems and norms with a certain critical detachment. Once we do so, we are less likely to imagine that everybody, deep down, really accepts the same standards, or that the local ones are correct and immutable. With a more detached understanding, we may see obvious possibilities for change. There are then questions as to how we can help to produce it.

As I mentioned in section 5, even refusing to use certain words, such as "lewd" (or the pair of "chaste" and "unchaste"), exerts a small pressure. So can other forms of refusal: a refusal to laugh at certain kinds of jokes, for example, or to participate in certain kinds of mockery and exclusion. There are many courses of actions we can take, ranging from the quiet example of how we live our lives, and in whose company, to how we raise and educate children, to more public interventions. In some cases, it might be a matter of giving pointed support to people whom we regard as decent and good but who are being treated unfairly. On other occasions, we might wish to take part in high-profile organized actions that express our values, such as political demonstrations and boycotts. Much of this will depend on our individual priorities, opportunities, financial resources, talents, developed skills, assessments of likely consequences, and degrees of personal courage.

Some of us are especially privileged in our ability to exert pressure on the general culture through products that reach the public and (subtly or otherwise) influence perceptions of what counts as good, flawed, or bad behavior and character. We may, for example, have opportunities to write novels, stories, and plays, or scripts for movies or television. All of these can convey what certain kinds of experiences are like—perhaps expanding the sympathies of the audience—and can otherwise express attitudes and influence perceptions. Most of us don't have such opportunities, of course, but we may still have some ability to participate in cultural conversations (it might be something as simple as reviewing a new movie on a blog) and to exert a degree of influence.

None of the possibilities just sketched requires that any of us must take a public stance on metaethical debates about the existence of objective moral authority. I doubt that this would be effective, at least for the large majority of people who are not in the position of being able to publish academically respectable books, book chapters, and papers on metaethics; for most of us, most of the time, there is more prospect of achieving useful social outcomes in other ways.

I don't advocate Government House moral error theory, but I suspect that something like it may be almost inevitable for the foreseeable future. Existing moral systems tend to be intertwined with entire worldviews, often religious ones, that include commitments to belief in objective moral authority. It will not be a straightforward matter to persuade anyone to abandon those commitments, which will probably include her belief that the moral system she was taught as a child is the true one. In a very large class of cases, efforts to de-convert people from belief in objective moral authority will be futile unless we can first (or perhaps simultaneously) persuade them to change their entire worldviews. Although that can sometimes happen, popular worldviews, particularly religious ones, have shown impressive resources in evading straightforward falsification and maintaining their psychological hold over adherents (for more, see Blackford 2012: 11–12).

In these circumstances, it appears to me unrealistic to expect a majority of people—at any time in the foreseeable future—to accept that their various moral systems are human inventions. Therefore, if we're tempted to think that widespread acceptance of this difficult truth will solve any of our social and global problems, it's a temptation that I recommend we set aside. Some opinion leaders may well accept the truth, and like Mackie I expect this could be beneficial, but I don't expect acceptance of the cold truth about morality to extend widely under any current or foreseeable circumstances.

Nonetheless, as Joshua Greene emphasizes throughout *Moral Tribes* (2013), we do not live in culturally closed societies with unitary moral systems; rather, modern societies blend different groups with complex, diverse, yet intertwined, histories, and with many religious and moral traditions. Day by day, different moral systems confront each other within the same society, often struggling for political supremacy. How should we respond to this, keeping in mind that the rival groups make equally false claims to the objective authority of their preferred moral systems?

Greene argues that we need to devise higher-level "meta-moral" principles to cope with contemporary tribalism, but he acknowledges that we can't expect these to "feel right" or be intuitive in the same way as a group's traditional morality feels right for its members (Greene 2013: 26). He proposes that we adopt utilitarian principles for this purpose, employing them for the public policy and the law-making activities of the state. I doubt, however, that this is realistic: we cannot expect entire populations to agree on a comprehensive normative theory that many citizens will experience as implausible and even alienating. But, in any event, I doubt that anything so ambitious is necessary.

In this section, I've argued that we can exert pressure on our local moral systems in numerous ways, large and small. In my own lifetime, I have seen much change—such as the increasing social acceptance in Western liberal democracies of gay men, lesbians, and people who identify as bisexual or transgender. What we probably cannot do is convert most of our fellow citizens to disbelief in objective moral authority (even if that would produce benefits) or persuade them to adopt an academic normative theory, such as utilitarianism, as a "meta-morality" for use in public policy deliberation. In the next section, I propose an alternative that appears more realistic.

7 Morality, Public Policy, and the Law

I am pessimistic about any efforts to persuade whole societies to abandon belief in objective moral authority, or to persuade their citizens to view morality as a social technology. It may, however, be more realistic to expect some societies to move toward a secular and liberal understanding of the function of law and government: an understanding within which *these*, at least, are regarded as useful and modifiable social technologies. While moral systems can present themselves as timeless and immutable—often even as God-given—legal statutes are transparently the products of human activity. They are enacted, modified, and sometimes repealed as part of a ubiquitous (if often bewildering) political process.

Notwithstanding the continuing efforts of theorists working in various natural law traditions, the detail of formal law is obviously something that human beings create (and no reflective natural law theorist denies this much). In democratic countries, indeed, differences of opinion about matters of regulatory policy are inevitable and must inevitably be accorded a form of legitimacy, however vaguely this is understood by the citizens. Furthermore, the laws of liberal democracies must be generally acceptable to—and seen as pragmatically useful by—a wide range of people with varied worldviews. The success of political parties and the viability of political programs require coalitions of interested voters who may differ in many ways among themselves—both in their political and economic interests and also in their values and general understandings of the world. By contrast, moral systems tend to be integrated with specific worldviews. This tends to create a disanalogy between morality, on the one hand, and the workings of law, political deliberation, and state power, on the other.

Just as crucially, historical reflection may suggest to people with otherwise conflicting viewpoints that the officers of the state cannot be trusted to decide which might be the correct overall worldview, conception of the good, or detailed moral system. That task might take politicians and public servants into far-reaching issues concerning which religious revelations can be trusted and how they ought to be interpreted, what actions might conduce to spiritual salvation, and so forth. It might be better, perhaps from many viewpoints, if the legislature and other branches of government concentrate on more pragmatic concerns relating primarily to the welfare of citizens.

Welfare can be understood in a commonsensical, somewhat imprecise, way, but in any event it will be restricted to benefits and protections relating to life in this world. It will not extend to spiritual salvation or any otherworldly dimension in human flourishing. What is required to reach this position is not necessarily atheism or philosophical naturalism, but merely a certain wariness about the role of the state and the uses of organized political power.

In *Freedom of Religion and the Secular State* (2012), I argue for such familiar political principles as secular government, freedom of speech, the Millian harm principle, sexual privacy, and the rule of law. These may eventually achieve consensual acceptance, at least in societies where they are not directly opposed by hegemonic religious and moral traditions. I certainly do not claim that any of these principles can be made rationally compelling to all comers, irrespective of their philosophical, moral, cultural, or religious starting points. (In Blackford [2012: 41, 82], I acknowledge this with respect to a Lockean conception of secular government.) The arguments in support of these and related principles may, however, be acceptable from many points of view.

That remains to be seen, but I've addressed some aspects of the problem in other publications (again, prominently, in Blackford 2012), so I will not reargue the details here. Let it suffice to say that some political principles, even if defined rather roughly and understood by different individuals in somewhat different ways, may end up being accepted by a range of citizens with diverse worldviews and backgrounds. This is partly for pragmatic reasons: people with varied moral and religious positions need to find ways to get along in the same society. It is also partly because some political principles can be supported by premises that might be acceptable to people with many substantive worldviews or conceptions of the good. These premises include rather pragmatic ones about the desirability of civil peace and the incompetence of the state when it comes to deciding the deepest issues.

It might be most realistic to permit citizens to live in accordance with their varied moral systems and overall worldviews, to the extent that they can do so without harming or oppressing others. On this conception, the law can be relevantly minimalist in its impact on many private decisions, while developing more detail when it comes to matters of public safety, worker and consumer protection, environmental sustainability, and international cooperation. In particular, we should welcome the expanding role of formal legal norms to deal with many of the emergent social and global problems that our inherited moral systems handle poorly. I include here the development of public international law, even though many international norms that govern the responsibilities of the state and seek to restrain abuses of state power cannot be straightforwardly enforced.

Perhaps I am biased by my legal training, but at this stage of human development it seems to me that formal law is where the action is. Modern societies increasingly rely on its resources to solve problems that lie outside of traditional moral teachings. Legal norms and the institutions of the state have partly super-seded morality as guides to human action, though less formal kinds of moral evaluation and enforcement continue to interact with the law and to play an important background role.

8 Conclusion: Metaethics and a Science of Morality

If we free ourselves from the illusion of objective moral authority, we may nonetheless continue approving of (and abiding by) current moral norms that require mutual reliance, such as norms relating to debts and promises. These can be regarded as good for the widely shared goal of getting along together socially and enjoying mutual benefits from our interactions. Likewise, nothing discussed in this chapter prevents us from continuing to value such character-istics in others (and ourselves) as kindness, loyalty, non-violence, and various kinds of intellectual and general honesty. In sum, a more accurate understanding of the nature of morality will not lead to our acting entirely independently of valuable local norms.

We may go on using much of our old language, including such words as "good," "bad," and "should," along with many thick moral terms such as "cruel" and "kind." Given what I take to be the general meanings of these words, some of our statements that contain them will be true. At the same time, some elements of our moral practice may fall by the wayside as we view the local mores from a relatively detached and anthropological perspective. Likewise, some elements of our moral language may fall into disuse (much as the word "sin" and its cognates have for many secular people). Still, all this can be construed as proposing only a mild or partial form of moral abolitionism.

A final issue, foreshadowed in section 3, relates to the implications for science and philosophy. Some philosophers, especially those in the utilitarian tradition of normative ethics, have aspired to establish the study of morality on a scientific basis: they have hoped that moral questions could be answered by systematic, naturalistic, empirical investigation. By contrast with that vision, academic moral philosophy currently appears deadlocked, marked by seemingly intractable disa-greements over questions of metaethics and fundamental normative theory. Of course, the moral systems of various societies and cultures can be studied at a descriptive level by anthropologists and other social scientists. Unlike philoso-phers, however, they usually avoid reaching conclusions on which, if any, moral system might be best, true, or justified.

Once we accept that there is no objectively authorized moral system or nor-mative theory—and, with this, accept the thesis that morality is an invention, device, or social technology—much falls into place. With this adjustment to our assumptions, we are ready to investigate the phenomenon of morality in something more like a scientific way, but without constraining ourselves in the manner of social scientists. We can investigate not only the content of various moral systems and moral norms, but also how effectively they satisfy human needs and desires in various circumstances.

Such a reconstructed field of inquiry—a science of morality, perhaps, or simply a more scientific practice of moral philosophy—would not involve determining which actions are objectively demanded or prohibited. Instead, the field's theoretical foundations would include the proposition that no such objective demands and prohibitions exist. The systematic study of morality would continue, I am sure, to encounter many practical difficulties: consider those faced by existing social and behavioral sciences such as economics, anthropology, and psychology. Perhaps, therefore, the study of morality will never merit classification as a "science"—but that depends on exactly how we choose to distinguish between the sciences and the humanities (a question for another day!).

A reconstructed, systematic approach to the study of morality could draw on the methods and findings of other disciplines, and it could be carried out with an entirely naturalistic methodology. We could investigate what human beings seem to want in the vast range of circumstances that have confronted humankind so far. We could investigate, too, what social rules, character traits, and courses of action seem, on the evidence available, to be most effective for obtaining what we want. All of this could be studied in an integrated way, involving people with complementary training and skills. We would not assume that all human beings want the same thing, so we would not prescribe the same courses of action for everyone.

A framework is available, therefore, within which we can examine morality as a social technology that human societies have invented and can modify. This follows as a logical outcome from the philosophical tradition of Hobbes, Hume, Mackie, and others, and it is consistent with much current work in fields such as social and moral psychology. It is potentially, perhaps endlessly, fruitful—more so, I believe, than other approaches that have been more prominent in moral philosophy. I commend it to philosophers, social scientists, and others who seek an understanding of morality based on evidence and reason.

Notes

1 Astute readers will have picked up an allusion to T. S. Eliot's 1920 poem "Gerontion": "After such knowledge, what forgiveness?" (line 33).
2 My discussion of moral conservationism and moral fictionalism in this section elaborates slightly upon that in Blackford (2016: 98–100).
3 In this paragraph and the two that follow, I adhere closely to the analysis in Blackford (2016: 20–21), where I discuss the terms "good," "well," "bad," "ought," and "must" in slightly more detail.
4 If we did come to regard virtues and vices as fictional it would be the result of empirical investigation; it would not follow merely from a rejection of belief in objective moral authority. It would take us far afield to consider the empirical case against psychological characteristics that could qualify as virtues, but see Doris 2002. Joyce (2011: 171–178) questions whether such characteristics, even if they exist, could play the role required of them in standard presentations of virtue ethics.

References

Blackford, R. 2012. *Freedom of Religion and the Secular State*. Malden, MA.: Wiley-Blackwell.

Blackford, R. 2016. *The Mystery of Moral Authority*. Basingstoke, Hampshire: Palgrave.

Calhoun, C. (ed.). 2002. *Dictionary of Social Sciences*. Online version. New York: Oxford University Press.

Doris, J. 2002. *Lack of Character: Personality and Moral Behavior*. New York: Cambridge University Press.

Enoch, D. 2011. *Taking Morality Seriously: A Defense of Robust Realism*. Oxford: Oxford University Press.

Finlay, S. 2014. *Confusion of Tongues: A Theory of Normative Language*. Oxford: Oxford University Press.

Garner, R. 1994. *Beyond Morality*. Philadelphia: Temple University Press.

Garner, R. 2010 "Abolishing morality." In R. Joyce & S. Kirchin (eds.), *A World Without Values: Essays on John Mackie's Moral Error Theory*. Dordrecht: Springer. 217–234.

Greene, J. 2013. *Moral Tribes: Emotion, Reason, and the Gap Between Us and Them*. NewYork: Penguin.

Hart, H. L. A. 1994. *The Concept of Law*. Oxford: Clarendon Press.

Joyce, R. 2001. *The Myth of Morality*. Cambridge: Cambridge University Press.

Joyce, R. 2011. "The accidental error theorist." *Oxford Studies in Metaethics* 6: 153–180.

Joyce, R. & Kirchin, S. 2010. "Introduction." In R. Joyce & S. Kirchin (eds.), *A World Without Values: Essays on John Mackie's Moral Error Theory*. Dordrecht: Springer. ix–xxiv.

Mackie, J. 1977. *Ethics: Inventing Right and Wrong*. London: Penguin.

Mackie, J. 1980. *Hume's Moral Theory*. New York: Routledge.

Olson, J. 2014. *Moral Error Theory: History, Critique, Defence*. Oxford: Oxford University Press.

Väyrynen, P. 2013. *The Lewd, the Rude, and the Nasty: A Study of Thick Concepts in Ethics*. Oxford: Oxford University Press.

Williams, B. 1985. *Ethics and the Limits of Philosophy*. London: Fontana.

5

A PLEA FOR MORAL ABOLITIONISM

Richard Garner

1 The Moral Error Theory and Moral Abolitionism

Moralists and social critics have long lamented the popularity of moral skepticism, but while moral skeptics inevitably attract curiosity and criticism, they have always been relatively few in number and easily dismissed. Almost everyone else appears to think that we face a world of objective facts, some about what there is and others about what there ought to be. The belief in objective values is embraced without a second thought by ordinary users of moral language, and it appears to be no less popular among moral philosophers, who are often more interested in advancing their ideas of what is right or good than in asking whether anything is. But "often" does not mean "always," and I shall suggest that a growing minority of cautious moral philosophers are busy rethinking what almost everyone else believes about the objective reality and practical value of morality.

Proponents of what has come to be called "the moral error theory" do ask whether anything is right or good, answer "No," and add that those who accept or presuppose the reality of "objective values" are making a serious error. In 1977 John Mackie defended a version of this theory, and 10 years after that Ian Hinckfuss took the next step and advocated abandoning moral language and moral thinking—a view he called "moral nihilism," and that others have called "moral eliminativism," "moral abolitionism," "amoralism," or "amorality."

By the end of the last century, neither the moral error theorist nor the moral abolitionist had gained a seat at the metaethical table. The authors of a survey of ethics at the end of the 20th century (Darwall, Gibbard, & Railton 1992) observed that work by Mackie and by Gilbert Harman (who also rejected the belief in objective moral values) had made certain questions about the semantic, epistemic, metaphysical, and practical status of morality "hard to ignore."

Hard, perhaps, but not impossible, because the authors managed to give "scant or no attention" to "approaches to metaethics based on blanket irrealism or antirealism." They mentioned this only one more time, again to note that Mackie's error theory is to be one of those "passed over in what follows" (Darwall et al. 1997: fn. 24, fn. 35). In this century the neglect is fading, but the result is deeper and more interesting criticism.

Neither the neglect nor the criticism should surprise us. The moral error theorists, as well as the other irrealists and antirealists, are accusing almost all past and present moralists and moral philosophers of participating in a massive wild goose chase; and the moral abolitionist is suggesting that since morality is not only a myth, but a harmful one, we might do better if we stop talking and thinking in moral terms.

Mackie's book has become a classic, but since he did not favor abandoning our error-infested morality, he was content to continue using moral language as he had always done: to encourage or discourage certain behavior. But if there is no fact of the matter about what is morally right or wrong, then moral arguments only end when at least one of the parties tires of arguing. As we learn how easy it is to develop moral arguments to support whatever we want to do, we increase our praise for moral discourse, and our abuse of it. As this process accelerates, skepticism about moral objectivity begins to look like common sense.

When it dawned on people that moral abolitionists are really saying that morality is so flawed that it makes sense to consider abandoning it, some hasty moralists reacted by accusing moral abolitionists of claiming that it is morally wrong to moralize. But it would be most uncharitable to suppose that someone with enough skill to find a path to the moral error theory would fall so quickly into inconsistency. Here it is the critic who needs to be criticized for the indolent assumption that moral abolitionism can be so easily dispatched. What else can the defenders of morality say?

Counter-examples are a philosopher's weapons of choice. They come easily because our original equipment includes the ability to notice useful generalizations as well as exceptions to them. Harman argued that the position of the moral error theorist (or, in his terminology, the "extreme nihilist") implies that there are no moral constraints and "that everything is permitted." It also implies "that there is nothing wrong with murdering your father—that slavery is not unjust and that Hitler's extermination camps were not immoral." "These," he remarked, "are not easy conclusions to accept" (Harman 1977: 11).

But they are not easy counter-examples to accept, either, at least not when we understand what the moral error theorist is saying. Moral error theorists will not be willing to say these things are "not morally wrong" unless they can count on being understood to be emphasizing the rejection of moral objectivity, and not as supporting, or even urging the toleration of patricide, slavery, or genocide. They count on the fact that our world teems with actual laws, and with conventional rules, understandings, and obligations. As a result, much is forbidden and required—just not by the rules of an objective morality.

Yet it seems important to many that there be objectively true moral claims that depend on more than the whims or even the good sense of fallible humans. When we believe we have a genuine moral obligation, then we may take the matter to be decided—we "must" do the thing, period. Or so we say. But in real life we often disobey ourselves and choose the "morally worse" option. This deviation is evidence that we are influenced by a richer set of factors than just the moral beliefs we happen to have. Alongside those moral beliefs are habits, inhibitions, routines, policies, and our ever-shifting personal values. This motivational stew has taken us a lifetime to assemble, and a recognition of its awesome complexity can reassure us that a loss of our moral beliefs, which are at most one of the factors at play in the making of our decisions, is not going to send us into a life of crime or destroy our compassionate impulses.

2 Ethics and Morality

We say that words can mislead, but it is actually the users of words who do that. This chapter is about ethics and morality, and "ethics" and "morality" are two words whose users require particularly close supervision.

a) Ethics

Some use the words "ethics" and "morality" synonymously, some use one and avoid the other, and some distinguish between them. Bernard Williams once proposed a useful way to understand a distinction between ethics and morality. He identified the "ethical" as a vague area that includes, among other things, ideals, policies, practices, and obligations that arise from agreements, contracts, and from the roles we occupy or take on (Williams 1995: 7; see also Garner 2014: 16–19). I shall use "ethics" to refer to this collection of the non-moralized (but moralizable) components of what can be called our "motivational set." This assortment of conscious and unconscious factors is constantly changing, and the parts of it that are open to our awareness can be explained, criticized, or modified. Those who feel the need to defend their personal values or ethical practices often do so by appealing to something they consider to be more authoritative than feelings, habits, and policies, and more "worthy" of respect than self-interest. Our inherited, invented, or evolved ethics, it is said, must be brought into line with morality itself.[1]

b) Objective Morality

If ethics is seen as subjective, morality can be seen as objective. Ethics exists because of what people think and say; morality, that is, objective morality, doesn't exist at all, but those who think that it does imagine that it exists "on its own" and is independent of anything we think, say, desire, or decree. It is "real"—hence the label "moral realism"—and it is thought to "apply to" everyone without exception. As Kant once insisted ([1783] 1981: 48), a moral rule is not a mere "phantom of the brain," but an expression of an inescapable and binding requirement. The evidence that people think of morality in this way is found in what they say and in their eagerness to impose these requirements on others who subscribe to a different morality or none at all.

c) Subjective Morality

While most people never question the objectivity of their moral beliefs, there are those who think that Kant was wrong and that morality *is* a mere phantom of the brain, something we have constructed from our inherited tendencies, our life-experiences, and our desires. As reasonable as this subjectivism may seem, people often reject it because they fear that if morality were understood in this way there would be no need to take it more seriously than a demand from a group of strangers or a decree from a committee of philosophers. They may be right about that.

Mackie and Hinckfuss agreed about the subjectivity of morality, and Mackie called his version of morality "subjectivism" and opened his book *Ethics: Inventing Right and Wrong* with the words: "There are no objective values."[2] Hinckfuss agreed, but, as I have noted, Mackie proposed continuing to use "the moral overlay," while Hinckfuss argued in favor of eliminating it. The option I hope to clarify and defend here is the abolitionist option. I shall treat our "ethics" as our collection of non-moralized resources for making decisions, and I will argue that we are reasonably competent deciders, as long as ignorance, fear, and morality don't intrude.

3 Can We Abolish Morality?

There are those who claim that moral abolitionists are doomed to fail because moralist ways of thinking and talking are essential skills of any civilized human. Whatever the moral error theorists and abolitionists *claim* to believe, these critics insist that we are *all* moralists, even if we don't admit it, or even know it.[3] When a moral error theorist becomes annoyed at careless drivers or stubborn moralists, a moralist may claim that this proves that the would-be error theorist is a moralist after all, since anger is a symptom of an underlying moral judgment. But annoyances and dissatisfactions come upon us frequently and in many forms, and it is hard to believe that each and every minor irk involves anger and triggers its own negative moral judgment. In any case, anger made its appearance on the scene long before we developed the habit of moralizing and, its essential tool, language.[4]

Another way to argue that morality is inescapable is to say that when people, even moral error theorists, help others or tell the truth, this shows that they do have moral principles. Those who treat others well can be accused of believing in benevolence, and those who tell the truth can be charged with holding moral principles of truthfulness. But these charges can be dismissed on the grounds that some people help others just because they see a need and choose to fill it, and non-duplicitous error theorists may simply have a policy of telling the truth.[5] This can be filed under what I call their "ethics." Moralists might say that this policy is evidence of a moral principle, but error theorists will not think of it in the way moralists think of a duty to tell the truth. They will not see their policy as a response to an "objective demand or requirement," and they will be flexible enough to realize that sometimes it is foolish or even disastrous not to lie.

Even if it is psychologically possible to purge our moralist impulses and thoughts, or at least to reduce their number and strength, it is no simple chore. Daniel Nolan, Greg Restall, and Caroline West have argued that moral concepts "so pervade ordinary thinking and discourse" that we would find it "difficult and inconvenient" to do without them (Nolan et al. 2005: 311). But whether we find the practice of moral abolitionism *too* difficult and inconvenient to adopt will depend on how thoroughly we have been indoctrinated. Even if there is, as Richard Joyce observes, a genetic basis to "believe that moral obligations exist," we have managed to tame other once useful but now dangerous natural traits.[6] A moralist might say that we evolved to think and act morally, but an error theorist could explain the same behavior by saying that we evolved to have helpful impulses and to value and nourish relationships. Some speak of *moral* feelings and considerations, others just speak of feelings and considerations. What turns a feeling of dislike into a negative moral feeling or thought? It is the insertion into our active vocabulary of a few words by which our inchoate feeling is categorized and shaped into a moral feeling, which then can be presented as a moral thought. This requires knowing how and when to use words such as "evil," "immoral," "bad," "wrong," "despicable," and their ilk and opposites. If we can monitor our inner monologue, we can learn to identify and to treat these unwelcome concepts and feelings as intruders. We may occasionally have no control over when a moral feeling or some morally loaded thought jumps at us, but if we remember that these thoughts are expressions of what we feel, and not characterizations of objective features, then their power will wane, and eventually they may migrate to our inactive vocabulary—understood, but rarely if ever used.

So the answer to the question of whether we *can* abolish morality is a bit complicated. We become moral error theorists (just as a person becomes an atheist) by stepping or being shoved over the fuzzy line that separates believing from not believing.[7] There may be people who, for whatever reason, can't step over that line. But others can, even if it involves letting go of the belief in objective moral values. So the question that now looms is this: How does coming to accept the moral error theory influence what one does and says about morality? As Björn Eriksson and Jonas Olson ask (this volume): "What should you do about your moral practice if you come to believe that moral error theory is true?"

4 Should We Abolish Morality?

It is already clear, I hope, that the "should" here is meant as a practical rather than a moral "should." Do we have reasons based on our own (not always self-ish) concerns to mute our moralism? If we were asking about society, we might have been asking whether our own society would be better off, or happier, or less violent, without the moralistic beliefs we have been exploiting for all these years. But as everyone acknowledges, no such question is going to get a definitive answer, and people are bound to disagree. So let us ask whether adopting some version of moral abolitionism might serve *a person* well.

That will depend on the person and his or her circumstances, so the way to learn whether moral abolitionism has a payoff for *you* is to try it. Just observe how often unbidden moral thoughts show up in what you find yourself saying to yourself and to others. Next, combat some of these moralistic *thoughts* by raising questions about their etiology. Ask "Where did *that* come from?" Sometimes you will not like the answer. If you are eventually able to reduce the frequency of morally loaded words and the associated feelings, you will probably like the result. But an experience isn't an argument, so you should not expect moralists to be influenced by your report of your successful experiment.

So where does the argument go from here? The usual strategy of the moral objectivist is to attack the subjectivists and skeptics with well-worn counter-examples, disingenuously launched from the rhetorical perch of someone who can't even *imagine* that anyone would doubt, abandon, or urge anyone else to abandon, morality.

a) The McEnroe

A common reaction to moral error theorists and moral abolitionists can be called "the McEnroe." The moralist glares at one of these characters and says loudly and emphatically: "You *cannot* be serious!?!" A non-verbal version of this move has been called "the argument from the incredulous stare" (Lewis 2001: 86). In a "Full McEnroe," some such gut reaction is followed by a volley of moral judg-ments that "no reasonable person" could deny. How can there be nothing wrong with bear-baiting, slavery, torture, genocide, or hammering nails into a living baby, chopping it into a billion pieces, boiling the remains, and then forcing its mother to drink the concoction? (This last horror was provided by Russ Shafer-Landau [2004: 88], who claimed that it is an "eternally true" moral principle that this is something it would be wrong to do.) But avowals of certainty and litanies of atrocities are wasted effort because no description of some act or event, how-ever dramatic, is likely to cause a moral error theorist to return to believing in moral objectivity. However, a deeper than average grasp of the extent and depth of human suffering may lead anyone, even a moral error theorist, to lend a hand to someone in need, or to criticize those who do not.

Some may argue that moral error theorists have no standing to criticize the behavior of others, and that moral abolitionists have abolished the very language necessary to do so. The answer to this is that *not all criticism is moral criticism*. There are plenty of non-moral things to say to the bear-baiters and baby-punchers, or about anyone who hurts or oppresses others. Moral error theorists and abolitionists are reduced to silence or inaction only if they are unable to think of non-moral reasons for doing or refraining from doing things. But what are the chances of that?

b) At the Restaurant

In an earlier essay defending moral abolitionism, I mentioned some alternatives to moralizing:

> [I]nstead of telling others about their moral obligations, we can tell them what we want them to do, and then we can explain why. We can express annoyance, anger, and enthusiasm, each of which has an effect on what people do, and none of which requires language that presupposes objective values or obligations.
>
> *(Garner 2011: 19)*

Not everyone was convinced. Most responses were critical, but Jean Kazez, a professional philosopher with a blog called *In Living Color*, took the trouble to examine her own tendencies to moralize. She asked herself if there are times when moral language is "best thrown out altogether," times "when is it replaceable with something that 'does the job' equally well," and, finally, if it is "ever genuinely indispensable." She writes:

> Take this situation, which happened more than once when I was in graduate school back in the 20th century. You go out to dinner with a bunch of people and it's time to split the bill. Of course, you have to split the total bill, with tax and tip included. But some people don't do that. They put in less than their fraction of the total bill. Then, invariably, a couple of people say "oh well" and throw in a few more dollars. The low-payers, I think, anticipate the reaction of the high-payers, and the bill gets paid.
>
> The moral judgment I make in that situation is: NOT FAIR! I think the low-payer is taking advantage of others. Now, is that the sort of judgment I ought to abandon . . . period? I should think not—I'm not, after all, going to extremes and judging the person *evil*. I'm just thinking . . . what I said. So let's try the other possibility. Can we replace the moral thoughts here with non-moral thoughts? Instead of thinking "not fair" and "taking advantage" and "that was wrong," what might I think?
>
> Garner says I could think about what I want the person to do, and why. I'm allowed to be annoyed. But what is it that I want? I want

the low-payers to pay their fair share. But isn't fairness an irreducibly moral concept? What am I going to replace it with? Pondering my own moralizing, in this instance, doesn't take me in the direction of moral abolitionism—just the opposite.[8]

I understand Kazez's reluctance to retire the notion of fairness, but I think she may have overlooked a few effective non-moral ways to deal with her low-payer. Here is how I would reply to what she had to say about abolishing morality:

> Well, what you could have wanted is for the low-payers to pay more. There is no need to use the moralistic fiction of a "fair share" to make your point. That is usually an invitation to a moral argument, especially since low-payers who are aware of what they are doing will have preloaded rationalizations to defend their shortage. ("I didn't have any small bills" or "I paid more last time" or "I didn't have the lobster.") How much sense does the notion of a "fair share" make? Not everyone ate the same thing and some dishes, drinks, and desserts are more expensive than others. Are we supposed to put on our reading glasses, take out our calculators, and work out everyone's "fair share"? That sounds like a scene from a *Portlandia* episode. Even to bring up fairness here is to mar (if not spoil) a nice dinner, disturb your digestion, and maybe alienate a friend over a few dollars. If one member of your group does this consistently, then it should be enough to bring it up, in private, and in as non-moralistic and non-accusatory a way as possible. If that doesn't work, moralizing probably won't help, but there are other ways to deal with this kind of situation without going moralistic. You could just become a high-payer and forget about fairness. Call it a tranquility surcharge. Would you rather leave the restaurant with an aftertaste of resentment for the low-payer, or with the more palatable thought that you were able to resolve a potentially awkward situation by committing a (possibly) anonymous act of generosity?

c) Life Isn't Fair

I would say that the issue of fairness in *this* sort of situation is worth worrying about only if the low-payer is a serial offender; but there are other contexts where the stakes are more interesting. The controversies over fairness in taxation, representation, compensation, reparation, and incarceration are longstanding, momentous, and far more difficult to resolve than how to split the dinner check. But the questions we face at the restaurant have the same genesis as the ones that arise when we divide up expenses, responsibility, rewards, power, work, blame, or booty. It won't help to say that a division is fair when everyone gets what he or she deserves because it is no easier to compute what is deserved than it is to determine what is fair. Since we are endowed with various and unequal needs, skills, and advantages, we inevitably make different contributions to any joint project we undertake. Hence, there are few distributions of rewards and benefits that will not be contested by those who aren't willing to accept less than they wanted as "good enough." If John is required to divide 100 units three ways, no one is likely to complain if he gives each of the others 33 units and keeps 34 for himself. But if he assigns 50 to himself and 25 to each of the others, moralistically fueled complaints of unfairness can be expected.

In life, as in art and nature, the line between too little and too much is moving, blurred, and subject to interminable argument. We have no stable intuitive vision of such a line, nor any formula to allow us to construct one, but we do have a perfectly understandable concept of "way more," as in "John got way more than either of the other two." It isn't contrary to nature that this should have happened, and it isn't morally wrong for John to grab the "lion's share," but it will be noticed, and it will bother almost everyone but John and his friends and allies. When the inevitable criticism is raised, John is likely to bring out some well-worn rhetorical ploy, such as reflecting the accusation back on the accuser. ("It is you who are being unfair to me by denying me the share that I deserve.") That should be enough to guarantee that the argument will end in a stalemate, further arguments, or a fight.

d) Who Counts and How Much?

We have a natural inclination to take care of our own needs and the needs of those who matter to us, but questions of fairness and unfairness can put us at odds with our most intimate companions, our associates, and complete strangers. "How much shall I give to, share with, and demand from which others?" These are questions we all face every day, but the moralist asks different and supposedly prior questions: "How much *should* I give to, share with, and demand from which others?" Moral abolitionists and error theorists think these "prior" questions are unanswerable, but moralists, undeterred by centuries of inconclusive debates, still try to convince us that they can contribute to the happiness in the world by devising arguments to prove that we all have a moral obligation to promote it.

Peter Singer characterizes beings with "moral standing" as beings with interests it would be morally wrong to ignore. Humans are the prime example, but other "relevantly similar" beings also count (Singer 1975). As we learn more about non-humans, we discover ever more relevant similarities. Some supporters of "animal welfare" quote Jeremy Bentham, who set aside more complex criteria, and said "The question is not *Can they reason?* nor, *Can they talk?* but, *Can they suffer?*" ([1789] 1996: 283). This is generous, but less than helpful, because almost any living being can suffer. If *some* non-humans have moral standing, the question is "Which ones?" Opinions will inevitably and irreconcilably differ, as a great variety of non-humans are nominated by their human sponsors as worthy of protection and deserving of moral standing.

With the work of Singer in mind, Bernard Rollin observes that "the most powerful tool in the investigation of the moral status of animals" is the idea of a morally relevant difference: "If we can find no morally relevant differences between humans and animals, and if we accept the idea that moral notions apply to men, it follows that we must rationally extend the scope of moral concern to animals" (1981: 7). This argument may or may not be a powerful tool against speciesism, but it will fail to impress a moral error theorist, because it makes the assumption that "moral notions apply to men" (an obsolescent way of saying that humans have objective moral obligations). The moral error theorist is likely to suggest that when the argument cycles back to this point we need to change our strategy. Rather than starting all over by mounting an attack on, or a defense of, the very concept of moral objectivity, we might look for a less problematic way to resolve questions about how to deal with our fellow beings.

The idea of a circle that contains an expanding variety of beings with moral standing will generate endless disputes because there is no non-arbitrary way to draw the line between the ins and the outs. To most people, the line falls in the right place when it includes only the beings they wish to include. And yet the metaphor of an expanding circle is not useless. We can think of a *person's* circle of "consideration" as including those beings whose interests he or she actually considers when deciding what to do. Here the question is not who or what ought to be considered, but who or what has been, and is to be, considered. One person steps on a bug and another takes the trouble to brush it aside. This choice is not likely to be seen as a momentous or moral one, but the second person (at least on this occasion) included bugs (or that bug) within his or her circle of consideration. Lucky bug! Albert Schweitzer went a bit further than this when he insisted:

> A man is truly ethical only when he obeys the compulsion to help all life which he is able to assist, and shrinks from injuring anything that lives. He does not ask how far this or that life deserves one's sympathy as being valuable, nor, beyond that, whether and to what degree it is capable of feeling. Life as such is sacred to him.
>
> (Schweitzer [1923] 1987: 310)

e) Expanding Our Circle of Consideration

It is hard to deny that the animals we use for food live shortened lives, full of pain and terror. If we were able to witness, even for a day, the treatment of those animals at the end of their lives, many of us would modify our diets. It is not that we don't know how rare contented cows and happy chickens are, it is just that we have developed the habit of not thinking about that sort of thing. We can be aware of cold facts about chicken batteries, but still fail to *realize* what the system has in store for the chickens. Consequently, more people are attentive to the price of eggs than to the plight of the chickens.[9] To illustrate the difference between knowing something and realizing it, Rollin appeals to the idea of a gestalt shift: a radical event that sometimes transforms the way a person sees and feels about what is going on.

> We all know people who have stopped hunting when they suddenly real-ized that they are killing a living thing for amusement, rather than merely innocently participating in a sport. Or people who have stopped hunting when they first hear a wounded animal's exclamation as a cry. It is not that they have discovered some new fact, unavailable to them before. Rather, they have suddenly seen the same data in a new way.
>
> *(Rollin 1981: 44–45)*

Rollin is writing about extending consideration to non-humans, but the idea of extending it to more humans than we usually do is also something to think about. It is hard for most people to care about total strangers, but it is also hard not to be affected by realizing what it must have felt like to have been a slave, or what it does feel like to experience any moderate to intense human woe. An experience that leads us to realize what others are experiencing and how that feels is capable of unlocking a rich vein of compassion, and setting off the gestalt shift Rollin mentions.[10] Moral pronouncements, arguments, and demands, on the other hand, are more likely to harden our resistance and send us scurrying off in a search for counter-arguments and reasons not to care.

f) A Moral Compass

A magnetic compass points roughly north thanks to the influence of the unsta-ble but objectively measurable magnetic field that the Earth generates. A moral compass, by contrast, is not tethered to any objective feature of reality, and it is likely to point in a direction dictated by subjective factors such as its own-er's desires, biases, and dogmas. Moralists think of moral compasses as guides to proper behavior, and they seem to believe that someone without such a device would have no reason beyond self-interest to honor any promise, law, conven-tion, or moral principle. Luckily, we are capable of being moved by something other than "moral considerations" and self-interest. When we give in to some impulse to help a stranger (or even an insect), it is because we have resolved a storm of conscious and unconscious factors into an action, one that sometimes surprises even us.[11]

Moral error theorists will admit to lacking a moral compass, if that means lacking *moral* reasons for acting, but there are many other types of reasons—ones based on self-interest, self-respect, pride, affection, compassion, love, malice, and whimsy. Our general approach to life—what I have been calling our "ethics"—determines which moral considerations (if any) we will act on. Whether we choose to help or to harm, to give or to take, it is easy enough to make a moral case for our choice, which suggests that what we have done, or want to do, may have more influence on our moral compass than vice versa.[12]

Our moral compass may be as subjective, relative, and fictional as morality itself, but we each have a fully functioning collection of dispositions, habits, policies, and principles that make up our ethics (the non-moral factors in our motivation-set). For the moral abolitionist, "I will not" has replaced "I ought not," and a resolution has replaced a self-directed moral judgment.

5 Moral Fictions and Moral Fictionalism

The decision to be truthful is not a decision never to tell another lie, and sensible moral abolitionists will never resolve to refrain from moralizing "no matter what." It may be better to say that, mindful of the harm that can result from thoughtless and frequent moralizing, they prefer neither to use nor to encourage language that reinforces the errors of the moralists.

It is ultimately up to each person who has lost (all or some) faith in morality to determine whether, how thoroughly, and how quickly to abandon his or her moralist habits, and with what, if anything, to replace them. Hinckfuss looked forward to the day when the idea of "moral desert" would be abandoned and, as a result, "the perpetuation mechanism of morality would be lost and morality itself would rapidly become nonexistent" (1987: 40; excerpted in Hinckfuss, this volume). But that day may be far off, so here and now the task for moral error theorists is to find a way to operate in a society that many moralists would describe as moralistic rather than moral. We can watch out for intrusions of moral thinking, and stay alert when anyone uses language that presupposes objective moral values. There are times when even committed moral abolitionists will be tempted to rely on the power of the language of morality, but never as the first option. *Serious* moral abolitionists will take Kazez's question seriously: "Can we replace the moral thoughts here with non-moral thoughts?"

The answer to this question depends on the nature of the situation that may seem to call for a moralist response. In a typically implausible example, a moralist— say, George—is about to set out on some terrible course of action and the only way to stop him is to convince him that his plan would violate some moral principle that he accepts. If George "takes rights seriously," a moral abolitionist might remind him that going through with his plan would violate the moral rights of his potential victims; and that remark might save the day. This fictive use of moral language would be like telling a lie to save a life; and just as one lie does not a liar make, one moral utterance does not turn a moral error theorist into a moralist, or a moral abolitionist into a moral fictionalist.

Turning to a more ordinary kind of situation, Joyce introduces us to David, a moral error theorist who doesn't believe that baby-punching (or anything else) is morally wrong, but who is, like most of us, sickened by the very thought of it.

In the presence of a group of moralists, David is asked for an opinion on baby-punching, and he simply says: "Baby-punching?! Oh, that's just morally wrong" (Joyce 2011: 16). This keeps things simple, and perhaps prudently avoids a discussion of metaethics in a room full of moralists. Still, David could have answered the question put to him by just saying that the thought of baby-punching sickens him, and that should have been enough—unless the person who asked turns out to have been more interested in moral philosophy than in child abuse.

So far we have been looking at occasional uses of moral judgments by moral error theorists, but there are apparently moral error theorists for whom thinking and speaking in moral terms is a policy or a "life-strategy" rather than an occasional ploy. I noted above that Nolan et al. (2005) defend the practice of moralizing by arguing that it would be "difficult or inconvenient" to do without our moral concepts. Joyce also treats moral fictionalism as a useful practice. He agrees with Hume that rational self-interest can take us far into sociability, but he adds that, because we are not perfectly rational, moral beliefs can have an important role to play. When we deliberate about what to do, it is easy to cheat by adjusting our beliefs about what is likely to happen and about what we really want. But we can supplement and reinforce our practical deliberation if we can accept that the action dictated by it is "something that 'just must be done'." The important "instrumental value of moral beliefs," he says, is that "they are a bulwark against the temptation of short-term profit" (Joyce 2001: 212–214).

But if moral beliefs offer a bulwark against one temptation, moral doubts offer a bulwark against another, the temptation of easy and popular moralizing. We do cheat when we reason about what to do, but cheating is easier with moral reasoning than it is with practical reasoning. Experience limits what we can predict about and expect from the world we inhabit, but there is no such limit on what the moralist can claim about objective moral values and obligations.

Perhaps moral beliefs do influence moral believers, but what about the non-believers, the moral error theorists? Joyce rejects any form of fictionalism that encourages the belief in falsehoods, or the promotion of false beliefs in others, on the grounds that no such policy "will be practically stable in the long run" (2001: 214). But, because he values the usefulness of moral language, he has developed a form of "immersive fictionalism" or "fictive immersion" that aims to allow error theorists to use moral language without making or believing false assertions.

The jury is still out about this question, and immersive fictionalists can expect challenges from full-fledged moralists, from supporters of other types of fictionalism, and from moral abolitionists. Immersive fictionalism is a daring and interesting candidate but, as Joyce admits in *A World Without Values*, there remain questions about the "psychological viability" and the "pragmatic pay-offs" of the fictionalist program (Joyce & Kirchin 2010: xxiii).

The main question for the moral abolitionist is not whether *ever* to allow a moral claim to escape his or her lips. It is how to deal with the manifold opportunities the world offers for taking moralistic shortcuts, such as answering the "Why" question by saying, "Because it is the right thing to do."

6 Abolishing Morality and Applying Ethics

It's not easy being a moral fictionalist; pretend-moral arguments will be as endless, frustrating, and barren as "real" ones. Moral fictionalists can't be seeking moral truth, because they don't believe in moral truth. Instead, they use moral language to defend their actions, to influence others, and to stiffen their own resolve. Moral abolitionists look for other ways to do these things, since they realize that if a matter is widely considered important there will be plenty of enthusiastic moralists on every side.

A survey of the topics usually considered in applied ethics classes offers the moralist a rich field in which to work, and a moral abolitionist a chance to show how different things could be without morality. This is especially true when the intrusion of morality brings greater misery than did the problem it was designed to combat.

For example, we are a nation (even a world) of punishers. It has always been our tendency to lash out at those who displease, disobey, or disrespect us. Adam, Eve, and the serpent were the first to experience the effects of this cruel but effective policy. The inconsistent, racist, and misnamed criminal "justice" systems in the USA stand out as an ongoing example of how much harm the thoughtless and insensitive devotion to mere moralistic *slogans* can do.

Over 2 million citizens of the United States are "in the clink." But that jocular way of referring to incarceration hides the horror that awaits many who run afoul of the law. This is a larger proportion than in any other country on Earth.[13] Our practice of punishing "wrongdoers" is based on the controversial claim of deterrence (which I shall not discuss here) and on the moralistic idea of desert, according to which "justice requires" a punishment that "fits" the crime. This actually sounds reasonable and fair, but when we try to go beyond "an eye for an eye" or "a life for a life," the math gets difficult. Justice understood in this way sounds like a sadistic accountant's revenge fantasy. There is, of course, no objective measure of how much or what kind of pain a person deserves for annoying others, or damaging them or their interests, but we can be sure that few people ever think that the punishment they received was fair.

The call in Exodus (21:24) for "an eye for an eye" is an advance on death as the penalty for petty offenses, but it is based on the flawed moralistic idea that it is sometimes morally right, or even morally required, for us to cause suffering to someone because it is merited by his or her wrongdoing. When we have done something wrong, the scales of Justice, not anyone's anger or lust for revenge, determine how much we must suffer to pay for our wrongdoing.

There is much to argue about here, but fortunately the moral error theorist is not saddled with the need to calculate how much any person, even the most extreme offender, deserves to suffer. If it is *moral* desert we are talking about, nobody deserves to suffer. Of course, the word "desert" has plenty of uses that have nothing to do with morality. The winner of the race deserves the prize and one who fulfills a contract deserves the agreed-on payment. But this kind of desert does not need the extra embroidery of morality. If we could manage to keep morality and the emotions it amplifies out of the picture, then we might find ourselves in a position to discuss a wider range of responses to crimes and incivilities without having to pander to moral ire and posturing, and without pretending that the thirst for revenge is really a desire for justice.

One alternative to a moralist approach to crimes is restorative justice. John Braithwaite, a critic of systems of law that look first or exclusively to punishment, characterizes restorative justice as an attempt to restore the offender, the victim, and society to a state of harmony through understanding, remorse, restitution, and forgiveness (see Braithwaite 1989, 2002). The method is to bring involved parties together to work out some resolution of the disruption in the social order caused by the crime.

Braithwaite claims that such a system can be more effective in reducing offenses than our current punitive system, more satisfying to the victim, and better for the community. The research is promising. According to the webpage of the Centre for Restorative Justice, affiliated with Simon Fraser University, many studies do indicate that "offenders diverted to restorative justice programs tend to recidivate less, and that all who are involved in the process generally feel more satisfaction when compared to traditional methods."[14]

Successful restoration also depends on the willingness of the injured party or parties to forgive. Anyone can say "I forgive you," but it is harder for those who buy into the ideas of good, evil, duty, desert, and the other elements of morality to forgive deeply, because they need to deal with an entire layer of moral offense that requires additional forgiveness. The greatest barrier to a more humane and effective criminal justice system remains the belief that morality requires justice, that justice means people getting what they deserve, and that offenders deserve to suffer enough to make up for the evil that they have done. We may forgive them, but only after we have punished them for their misdeeds. Restorative justice may be impossible on any large scale until this unkind manifestation of moralism is purged from our criminal justice system, if it ever is.

Notes

1 I shall say that "moralists" believe in the objective and binding nature of moral judgments, whether they keep those judgments to themselves or express them publicly. Usually moralists subscribe to a traditional (or "nice") set of moral values (loyalty, non-duplicity, no killing or stealing, and so on). But occasionally a moralist will suggest that our true duty is to honor the opposite of the usual values, as Nietzsche urged—a move that brings to mind Milton's Satan's cry: "Evil be thou my good." Ayn Rand is famous for admiring those who prosper at the expense of others, and for inspiring the Gekko

dictum "Greed is good." A more traditional moralist might say that these characters have an immoral morality.

2 His main target was moral values, but he also included "non-moral values, notably aesthetic ones, beauty and various kinds of artistic merit" (1977: 15). The title of a 2002 book by Louis Pojman, *Ethics: Discovering Right and Wrong* (Belmont, CA: Wadsworth), expresses a rejection of the main thesis of Mackie's book.

3 Here one thinks of the infuriating claim that even atheists believe in God. Theosophists try to defend this claim by "defining" God as something that actually does exist: the laws of nature, love, or the universe. The same trick, which amounts to an effort to change the subject, is performed by those who define (or "reconstruct") morality in terms of what some imaginary people would, under certain conditions, desire.

4 Richard Joyce argues that animals cannot have moral thoughts, since language is a prerequisite for having moral concepts (Joyce 2006: 75–76).

5 Well, not so simply. Habits of helpfulness and policies of truthfulness do not arise out of the blue. They arise from conditions and causes most of which are quite beyond our ken.

6 In Chapter 6 of *The Myth of Morality*, Joyce explains how evolution has given us a "hardwired predilection to believe that moral obligations exist" (2001: 146). In a 2002 Princeton dissertation, Joshua Greene observed that "we may conclude that the wide-spread error embodied in moral realism is an error that makes sense—a mistake, one might say, that we were born to make" (Greene 2002: 188).

7 Someone who believes in moral objectivity can still, for some unusual reason or other, want to abolish morality—to give it up, to cause its general demise. Maybe he thinks it makes us weak. But the usual route to abolitionism leads through a rejection of objective values and moral obligations.

8 http://kazez.blogspot.com/2011/04/breaking-morality-habit.html

9 Today's hen houses are not like your grandfather's hen houses. www.humanesociety.org/issues/confinement_farm/facts/cage-free_vs_battery-cage.html. As for pigs, see the shocking scenes at www.youcouldsavetheworld.com/animal_cruelty3.html

10 Google offers a list of words that can be used to characterize this outcome: "pity," "sympathy," "empathy," "fellow feeling," "care," "concern," "solicitude," "sensitivity," "warmth," "love," "tenderness," "mercy," "leniency," "tolerance," and "kindness." The moral abolitionist would urge us to act from these rather than from a sense of moral obligation, and so would almost all those who receive our help.

11 Moral psychologists have discovered that the scent of fart spray or a sticky desk can influence the way subjects morally respond to questions they ask in their "thought experiments."

12 When we have thrown away our moral compass and given up the hope of finding the right thing to do or the correct amount to offer, one option is to adopt a vague policy of relatively painless generosity occasioned by a greater than usual awareness of the serious needs of some person or group who has come to our attention. This may be another tranquility surcharge, but, in the world as in the restaurant, there are reasons for paying it, not the least of which is that it makes life easier by eliminating an entire level of pointless calculation.

13 See www.prisonstudies.org/

14 See https://lawessay.net/restorative-justice/, www.anu.edu.au/fellows/jbraithwaite/lectures/index.php, and www.cehd.umn.edu/ssw/RJP/default.asp

References

Bentham, J. [1789] 1996. *An Introduction to the Principles of Morals and Legislation*. Oxford: Clarendon Press.

Braithwaite, J. 1989. *Crime, Shame and Reintegration*. Cambridge: Cambridge University Press.

Braithwaite, J. 2002. *Restorative Justice and Responsive Regulation.* New York: Oxford University Press.

Darwall, S., Gibbard, A. & Railton, P. 1992. "Toward *fin de siècle* ethics: Some trends." *Philosophical Review* 101: 115–189.

Garner, R. 2011. "Morality: The final delusion?" *Philosophy Now* 82: 18–20.

Garner, R. 2014. *Beyond Morality.* Battleborough, VT: Echo Point Press.

Greene, J. 2002. *The Terrible, Horrible, No Good, Very Bad Truth About Morality and What to Do About It* (PhD dissertation). Department of Philosophy, Princeton University, NJ.

Harman, G. 1977. *The Nature of Morality.* New York: Oxford University Press.

Hinckfuss, I. 1987. *The Moral Society: Its Structure and Effects.* Discussion Papers in Environmental Philosophy 16. Canberra: Philosophy Program (RSSS), Australian National University.

Joyce, R. 2001. *The Myth of Morality.* Cambridge: Cambridge University Press.

Joyce, R. 2006. *The Evolution of Morality.* Cambridge: MIT Press.

Joyce, R. 2011. "Moral fictionalism: When falsehoods are too useful to throw out." *Philosophy Now* 82: 14–17.

Joyce, R. & Kirchin, S. 2010. "Introduction." In R. Joyce & S. Kirchin (eds.), *A World Without Values.* Dordrecht: Springer Press. ix–xxiv.

Kant, I. [1783] 1981. *Grounding for the Metaphysics of Morals.* Indianapolis, IN: Hackett.

Lewis, D. 2001. *Counterfactuals.* Oxford: Blackwell.

Mackie, J. L. 1977. *Ethics: Inventing Right and Wrong.* New York: Penguin.

Nolan, D., Restall, G. & West, C. 2005. "Moral fictionalism versus the rest." *Australasian Journal of Philosophy* 83: 307–330.

Rollin, B. 1981. *Animal Rights & Human Morality.* Buffalo, NY: Prometheus Books.

Schweitzer, A. [1923] 1987. *The Philosophy of Civilization.* Buffalo, NY: Prometheus Books.

Shafer-Landau, R. 2004. *Whatever Happened to Good and Evil?* Oxford: Oxford University Press.

Singer, P. 1975. *Animal Liberation.* New York: HarperCollins.

Williams, B. 1995. *Ethics and the Limits of Philosophy.* Cambridge, MA: Harvard University Press.

6

BEYOND THE SURF AND SPRAY

Erring on the Side of Error Theory

Joel Marks

[T]he things to which we ourselves more naturally tend seem more contrary to the intermediate. . . Hence he who aims at the intermediate must first depart from what is the more contrary to it, as Calypso advises: Hold the ship out beyond that surf and spray.

(Aristotle)

1 Ethics Without Question Begging

It is a pleasure to embark on a discussion of ethics without having first to disabuse you of the belief in the existence of morality, which is a belief in the existence of right and wrong, good and evil, duty and desert, prohibitions and permissions, etc., as objective features of the universe. As J. L. Mackie, Ian Hinckfuss, Richard Garner, Richard Joyce, Hans-Georg Moeller, Russell Blackford, and yours truly have each argued at book length,[1] morality is a myth. Since there is so much else to discuss once morality has been taken to be mythical, it is, as I say, a pleasure to be able to get down to business.

Morality is to be distinguished from the *belief* in it, as well as the multitudinous practices, institutions, emotions, attitudes, etc., that accord with that belief, such as guilt feelings, conscience, outrage, condemnation, etc., for of course all of these do exist—alas. I have previously used the terminology "empirical morality" to refer to this real realm, and "metaphysical morality" to refer to the unreal realm it presumes.[2] So, for example, it is an instance of empirical morality for somebody to believe that lying is wrong as a matter of metaphysical fact. My position is that that belief, while surely existing, is nevertheless false because there is no metaphysical morality. In this chapter I use "morality" to refer to metaphysical morality.

Moralists are thus *ipso facto* in error, this being the gist of so-called moral error theory. What now? I assume that many, perhaps most, people at least implicitly hold a belief in objective, absolute, categorical, universal rules of conduct and/or standards of character and/or values[3]—in a word, morality. Laypersons and specialists alike would therefore seem to be left in confusion[4]: laypersons because we all seek a "guide to life," and ethical specialists because most assume that ethics is all about morality.

I still find it useful to recognize an area of inquiry that could be called "ethics," but I see it as asking questions that leave open the possibility that the answers will *not* involve absolute commandments, or inherent value or worth, or any of the other members of the metaphysical menagerie of morality. The more typical conception of ethics begs the very question I now see ethics as asking. For it is common to put ethics' central question as "How ought one to live?" or "What is the right way to live?" or "What is the good life?" Yet every one of these formulations incorporates a moralistic term: "ought" or "right" or "good." I reject all of them, because I don't believe morality exists in the first place; so to me they are like asking whether the king of France is bald.

I suggest, instead, that ethics be conceived as asking "How *shall* I live?" (or "What shall I *do*?" or "What shall *we* do?" etc.). Moralism offers one kind of answer: *Obey morality's dictates*. But a different kind of answer, one that is amoralist, is also possible—for example, *Act in accordance with your considered desires*. That is the answer I favor, which I call "desirism."[5] There can also be "in-between" answers, which allow certain accommodations to be made to morality—for example, *Live as if morality existed* (even though you know it doesn't). This is so-called moral fictionalism.

Thus, all of these answers suggest a source of ethical guidance, but only one of them—moralism—depends on the actual existence of morality; that is, of metaphysical morality. The two others differ about the status of empirical morality: Fictionalism favors retaining it, whereas desirism advocates eliminating it. Desirism, then, is a form of so-called moral abolitionism, or full-blown amorality, according to which not only is there no (metaphysical) morality, but we are advised to eliminate empirical morality as well. Moral abolitionism is therefore a negative thesis. Desirism seeks to offer a positive ethics to fill the void left by the total elimination of morality from both the noumenal and phenomenal realms. It offers reasoned desire as an adequate basis for living.

2 Desirist Ethics

The primary injunction of desirism is to *find out what you really want and then find out how to get it*. There is a typical first reaction to this, which I wish to dispel at once; namely, that desirism is egoistic.[6] The desire in desirism does indeed refer to what "you" or "one" wants. But what you or I or anyone wants need not be anything self-serving, not even in our enlightened self-interest (not to mention be outright selfish).[7] Your heart's desire could be to end human starvation in the world, at whatever cost to yourself; mine could be to liberate other animals from human exploitation, no matter what personal sacrifice this might entail. And yes, of course, somebody else's might be to grab whatever he can for himself and to hell with everybody else. So an individual desirist could be selfish, but she could also be altruistic, or anything in between.

Still, it might be thought that desirism, if not necessarily egoistic in theory, would be egoistic in practice. I cannot deny that as an empirical possibility, but I find it to be exactly as questionable as the claim that human beings are innately selfish. Both everyday observation and evolutionary argument seem to put the lie to that attribution. Yes, one can always concoct some selfish motive to account for seemingly selfless acts; for example, "You gave all your money to Oxfam only because you believe you will be rewarded in heaven." But there might also be leprechauns in the forest. The question is, "What is the evidence?" "What is the reasoning?" I see every indication and reason to believe in human generosity and self-sacrifice—in addition to selfishness, of course. Furthermore, there are countless other motives that are neither egoistic nor altruistic, but simply "for their own sake," such as wanting to build flying machines.

But suppose that human beings were, as a matter of fact, incorrigibly selfish. Would that be an argument for morality and against desirism? I don't see how. For even morality presumes that *ought* implies *can*, so if we were largely impervious to altruistic injunctions, morality itself would have to be egoistic. The moralist's objection to desirism on the ground that it would be egoistic in practice thereby loses its point.

The arguments for psychological egoism, it seems to me, tend to rest on cynicism and fallacy. The fallacy is to argue that human beings are perforce selfish because we always do what *we ourselves* desire. But the fact that a desire is always "one's own" does not mean that it is selfish—no more than the fact that a *belief* is always "one's own" means that you are always thinking about yourself. A desire becomes selfish (or at best egoistic) only when it is a desire "*for*" one's own welfare (in some way, to some degree). Many desires clearly are not so.

An attribution to desirism that is definitely on the mark, however, is rationality, for implicit in desirism's maxim is the idea that—to the degree that circumstances permit—one will bring to bear on any ethical question knowledge, experience, and logic. Of course, this is plausibly true of moralist practice as well. The difference is that the desirist will be reflecting on her own actual desires rather than on mythical obligations; hence the upshot will be not a mere conclusion or judgment but, in one's own case, the desired action itself. (Let me add "*ceteris paribus*" since, of course, the desired action would automatically result only absent an equally strong or stronger conflicting desire, or some other intervening contingency, such as a heart attack or intrusion by a prankster scientist who has surreptitiously planted electrodes in the desirer's brain.) So, for example, if you have the temptation to lie to someone on some particular occasion, and, after careful reflection, are actually motivated to do so and hence (other things being equal) tell the lie, your action will be neither right nor wrong. It will simply be the upshot of careful reflection and hence, by definition, what a desirist *would* (not "should") do.

Similarly, if I were to seek your counsel about whether to lie to someone on some particular occasion, or if you simply felt like butting in with your two cents, you might, after careful reflection, recommend (advise, urge, whatever) that I not do so. But again, what you would *not* be doing is asserting that it was *wrong* for me to lie or that I *should* not lie, etc.[8] Desirism is therefore both more and less than morality. On the one hand, desirism could appear to be but the pale shadow of morality, for, in lieu of objective requirements or "commandments," it offers to others only recommendations. On the other hand, desirism is inherently more efficacious than morality, since, in one's own case, it issues in actual behaviors (other things being equal) and not mere directives which could be ignored.

These facts have significant implications, for they enable desirism to detour around the chasm between *ought* and *is* that has perennially blocked ethical traffic in both directions. Going from *is* to *morally ought* is not a real problem to begin with, according to desirism, simply because, consistent with its error-theoretic roots, there is no such destination. You can't get there from here because there is no *there* there. One need not attempt to explain, for example, how "Lying involves treating somebody merely as a means" implies that "One morally ought not to lie," because it is not true that one morally ought not to lie (or ought or ought not anything else in the moral sense). Similarly, going from *ought* to *is* has no *point of departure*, so one need not be perplexed about how to motivate people to do what they morally ought, since there is *nothing* they morally ought, or ought not, to do.

But desirism has both departure point and destination. Thus, it is straightforward how one might go about explaining why Joel Marks's believing that lying involves treating somebody merely as a means might cause me (for whom Kantianism remains an ideal), after careful reflection, to refrain from lying. This would involve only the *is* of a belief resulting in the *is* of a behavior, presumably via the *is* of my desire to live in accordance with my Kantian ideal of myself or the world. Thus, filtering everything through one's own desires guarantees (*ceteris paribus*) one's own compliance. Furthermore, I submit, presenting the reasons by which one has oneself been moved is a more effective way of winning *another's* concurrence than to issue an edict. To those who doubt the persuasive power of speaking of one's own desires, I would recall to mind the "I have a dream" speech of Martin Luther King, Jr.

Can anything more be said about ethics? That is, would an amoralist of the desirist kind be able to offer any substantive recommendation(s) about how to live, etc., other than the procedural recommendation to examine one's own desires? I myself have certainly formed a number of general desires about conduct and character and so forth; for example, I want everyone to refrain from eating other animals (unless they need to in order to survive or to meet their nutritional requirements for health as standardly conceived). Furthermore, this is how I myself behave; and I go about *recommending* it to others on the basis of my belief that most people would desire the same thing if they were relevantly informed and experienced and reflecting rationally.

But I also recognize that my belief, despite its "rationality," could contain a large component of wishful thinking; there is enough wiggle room in the imaginable or even available evidence to allow for sincere disagreements on this score. Furthermore, I do not doubt that some people simply *would not* share my vegetarian ideal even if they were as well informed and rational as I am. Hence I could not honestly *recommend* vegetarianism to everyone willy-nilly, as much as I wish I could. Nevertheless the wiggle room might also be sufficient for me to say, "Try it, you *might* like it." If that were enough to count as a recommendation, then, yes, my brand of desirism would offer the universal and substantive recommendation to refrain from eating animals.[9]

But even lacking the basis for an honest recommendation, a desirist has resources for promoting her views. What resort she would take in the face of others' recalcitrance depends in part on how strongly she desires what others oppose. But this is how people have always behaved, is it not? Thus, some people who desire an end to human carnivorism are content to change their own dietary behavior; others seek to convert meat-eaters by means of rational and civil dialogue; others do an end run around meat-eaters by rallying the faithful to boycott uncooperative restaurants, lobby legislators, and the like; yet others go so far as to deceive, intimidate, vandalize, even . . .? All that is different about desirism from everyday moralism is that it refrains from putting on objectivist airs.[10] Instead of invoking morality, desirism calls a spade a spade.

Thus do I characterize the distinctiveness of desirist ethics from morality. But there is still a fundamental way in which a moralist could misunderstand the nature of desirism, by failing to appreciate the new conception of ethics that desirism presumes. The moralist's inveterate thought habits could thus cause her to construe desirism's recommendations to be stipulating the *ethical* thing to do, in supposed substitution for the moralist's *moral* or *right* thing to do, or what would be *unethical* in lieu of *immoral* or *wrong*.[11] But desirism does no such thing. For example, suppose you correctly surmise that, if fully informed, etc., I would tell the truth in a given situation, and so you recommend that I tell the truth; but I go right ahead and lie anyway. Have I done anything wrong or unethical? My desirist answer is "No" to *both*. I have simply ignored your recommendation and, assuming your recommendation was based on a correct surmise, done what I would *not* have done had I carefully reflected on the matter. I may subsequently regret my lying, but not, if I am a desirist, because I (believe that I) had done anything unethical or wrong—rather, because I came to realize that things would likely have turned out more to my liking if I had told the truth.

This is a subtle point, and it may not be crucial. I have mentioned it as part of my campaign to rid our thinking of any impulse to moralism. It does seem to me that the very notion of there being an ethical thing to do suggests that there is a truth of the matter analogous to there being a truth about what is right or wrong. But I recognize that, strictly speaking, only the latter is a will o' the wisp; while, presumably, there is in fact a specific thing an individual would do, other things equal, if he or she reflected on the matter—hence, there is in this way an ethical thing to do. But the difference from there being a moral thing to do is twofold: (1) the ethical thing does not presume any universal principle(s), such as *eating meat is unethical*, or *one must treat all sentient beings as ends-in-themselves*, and (2) *failing* to do the ethical thing is not *wrong*. So I am only warning that speaking of something's being "ethical" or "unethical" might shunt one's thinking back into a moralist groove.

A final point about the ethics underlying desirism, which moralists also commonly fail to grasp, is that I am recommending desirism itself to you, and not, as it were, commanding it. For a curious phenomenon to note is that *moralists* not only tell us about all of the things that we ought to do, but also tell us that we *ought to be moral*. In other words, a typical moralist would say not only that it is wrong to lie (at least, on most occasions), but *also* that it is wrong to ignore the dictates of morality. Thus, amoralists such as myself hear this all the time from critics: that, even though we might in all other respects be sterling citizens, always telling the truth and so forth, we are nevertheless morally wrong and possibly even evil for forswearing morality, which is to say, not acknowledging moral reasons for our truth-telling and so forth.[12] Alternatively, our critics often argue that our very amoralism is itself a kind of morality, since we are implicitly asserting that it is morally wrong to be moralistic.

But I deny these charges.[13] A desirist is desiristic about desirism itself, just as a moralist is moralistic about morality itself. I myself can't help but be desirist because, having reflected on the matter these several years, I am sufficiently motivated to be so. And I recommend desirism to you, whoever you are, because, having reflected on the matter these several years, I am convinced that, if you were to reflect on it as I have, you too would be desirist. (I offer additional considerations for you to reflect on in the next section.) But that is as far as the justification of desirism goes. It presumes no higher authority.

3 Why Be Amoral?

I cannot deny that under certain circumstances a desirist might decide that feigning moralism is the best strategy to achieve her ends. ("It is *wrong* to eat meat!") A moral fictionalist recommends this—in the manner of a shared pretense rather than an outright deception—as standard procedure. A moral abolitionist such as myself recommends against this under almost every circumstance. But, of course, there will be exceptions. At the end of this chapter I will explain just how far I would go in deracinating objectivism. But first let's consider the case for retaining a hefty dose of faux moralism in the world.

The most straightforward way to preserve a moral presence, in light of accepting moral error theory, would be to perpetrate a deception; thus, despite myself disbelieving in the metaphysical reality of absolute obligations and so forth, I might encourage others to believe in them. . . or at least I might not discourage others from believing so. This could manifest a cynical attitude. (What atheist wag said, "I want everyone else to believe in hellfire, especially my wife and my business partner"?) But it could also spring from totally benign motives. Dostoevsky's Grand Inquisitor and Plato's Guardians stand for the hypothesis that too much truth about ethics could be detrimental to society. Thus the "noble lie."[14]

But who is to say whether the widespread disbelief in morality in particular would result in social chaos or some other state of affairs that most of us would clearly not prefer to the present arrangement? We are left with our educated guesses or hunches or "intuitions," which is the time-honored method of philosophers, for better or worse.[15] I have previously laid out my own reasons for believing that an overtly amoral society would be more to my and most people's liking.[16] I find a belief in morality to correlate with tendencies to be angry, captious, hypocritical, arrogant, arbitrary, imprudent, and intransigent, whereas a disbelief in morality correlates with tendencies to be tolerant, explanatory, compassionate, as well as, *ex hypothesi*, grounded in reality. Since I strongly prefer the latter set to the former, and imagine my readers do too, I embrace and promote moral abolitionism; that is, the elimination of all moralist beliefs and practices.

Perhaps my most general complaint against (the belief in) morality is that it exacerbates existing differences of desire between people, thereby making the resolution of disagreements more difficult. The "right thing to do" is, more often than not, just what the person so labeling it happens to desire, thereby providing her subjective desire with a (seemingly) objective imprimatur. This obviously makes compromise or negotiation with an equally ensconced opponent less likely.[17] But my view of the actual use of morality, as a means of trying to get one's way, runs counter to the view of morality as primarily a check on one's own impulses, as well as a spur to one's own virtuous behavior.[18] Who, as I say, is in a position to judge definitively which of these conceptions, or whether some other, rules the world?

Meanwhile, another of my empirical hunches or surmises is that, in the absence of a decisive argument or evidence, each theorist is unlikely to retain a studied neutrality but will instead favor one case over another because of personal factors.[19] And notice that this *ad-hominist* view of ethical methodology applies not only to matters of taste but even to matters of fact. Thus, I myself wish to discourage the belief in morality not only because I prefer the traits of tolerance, etc. to arrogance, etc., but also because I allow the ambiguous evidence for the respective empirical correlations between amorality/tolerance and morality/arrogance to sway me in my desired direction. I do not believe I am unusual in employing this procedure, but I admire the few who are aware of doing so and admit to it.[20] If I am correct about this, then ethics is a kind of idealism[21] in the sense of creating a guide to life out of the fabric of one's own desires, or in one's image, as it were.

With this same broad brush, I paint over other arguments and evidence that favor retaining morality in everyday affairs. A less extreme position than the noble lie is moral fictionalism, which seeks, not to publicly (and deceivingly) disavow a disbelief in morality, but only to relegate that disbelief to the background. An analogy might be the way we normally have our own death in the back of our mind, but live in the foreground. Just so, a moral fictionalist would know (i.e., believe) that amorality is reality, but act and even think and feel as if it weren't.

The reason given is, as with the noble lie, that the belief in morality does serve useful purposes;[22] furthermore, the belief and its attendant attitudes come naturally to us.[23] The evidence for the latter claim can be found in one's own experience. I myself can attest to the enduring power of my moralist reactions to various actions and traits and states of affairs, even though I have striven to suppress them for several years now. Is it not likely that they are trying to "tell me" something? Would evolution, biological or cultural, have instilled them in us with such force and staying power if they did not serve a valuable, even essential function? But I am no longer cowed by the undoubted utility and salience of belief in morality. For me, as indicated above, the disutility looms larger.[24]

Furthermore, the force of our moralist responsiveness can ultimately be ignored, analogous to sensory illusion, however compelling. I often cite the example of the straight stick that "looks bent" when partially immersed. In the normal case we will realize that the stick is *straight* even though we may never be able to shake the impression of a bend at the water's surface. Just so, I might never eradicate the moral outrage I feel whenever I see my friends eating meat; but over time I observe my responses to partake more of sadness (for the animals), empathy (for the carnivores), determination (to change the world's eating habits), and calculation (of how to do that) than of anger and condemnation.

Note that I do *not* mean to suggest that my moral feelings have sublimated into non-moral ones, as if a substratum of psychic energy were liable to redirection, analogous to the drawing which can be seen as either a duck or a rabbit. Or, to use a different well-worn image: morality does not have to climb a ladder to the unlocked second-story window of one's psyche in order to unlock the front door for amorality's entry. Having moral responses is not, I believe, a necessary developmental preliminary to having compassionate responses.

I also see the latter as likely to be more effective at furthering my (or one's) ends in the long run; for example, would not my meat-eating friends be more likely to hear me out if I approached them with caring (for both the animals and them) rather than accusation?[25] In sum, then, the fictionalist sees error theory as posing a problem—how to maintain society in the face of morality's demise—that fictionalism then purports to solve; whereas the abolitionist sees error theory

as presenting an opportunity—to make the world more to our liking—that abolitionism then seizes. Desirism presumes abolitionism and offers a positive program
to replace the "abolished" morality. The non-existence of morality is, thus, not
an inconvenient truth but the cornerstone of a new ethics.

4 Beyond Amorality

Despite my sanguine take on the possibility of amoralist transformation, I fully
acknowledge that the process can be difficult. That is why I prefer, to the bent
stick, the analogy of feeling yourself to be in motion when peering down from
a bridge at the water rushing under you (in the opposite direction). It is not so
easy to ignore the latter illusion, even though you are cognizant of its falsity. One
needs a clean break—to look away. Just so, I therefore embrace not the mere disbelief in morality (moral error theory), which is compatible with public and even
private moralism of the fictionalist type, but the full-blown public and private
avoidance of all things moralist (moral abolitionism). Indeed, my particular claim
to fame is to go to the opposite extreme from fictionalism and, so to speak, err
on the side of abolitionism. What I mean is that I recommend against using the
vocabulary and assuming the attitudes of not only morality but also of other value
realms to the greatest degree practicable.

The implicit strategy here is Aristotle's, or Odysseus's.[26] In the epigraph to this
chapter, Aristotle alludes to the episode in the *Odyssey* when the cunning captain
orders his helmsman to steer away from the whirlpool of Charybdis and toward
the cliff of Scylla. Both are dangerous, but the whirlpool more so. Once you are
sucked into its surf and spray, your ship is a goner; but cleaving to the cliff holds
out some hope of saving the ship, even though you may still suffer some losses (as
Odysseus lost six members of his crew to the hungry mouths of the mythologi-
cal Scylla). Analogously, Aristotle advises us to seek the virtuous mean that his
ethics recommends by erring on the side of the lesser extreme or vice. I would
say that the same applies to the project of achieving a genuinely amoral world:
since many or most or all of us(?) have a strong bias in favor of morality, we are
well advised to err on the side of amorality in our thinking, feeling, and action,
including speech behavior.

But this is not quite what I have in mind. The specific image I wish to convey,
like the present volume and the present study, already presumes that there is no
morality. Thus, the whirlpool (Charybdis) stands for fictionalism and the like—
that is, error theories that still pay some degree of obeisance to morality. They are
therefore the stronger "vice," because we are naturally moralist in our thinking
and feeling. Indeed, that is the fictionalist's argument for retaining some connection to morality. This "extreme" is therefore "more contrary to the intermediate."

What is the intermediate in my image? None other than moral abolitionism.
This is error theory in the raw, not moderated by any sort of moralist concessions or trappings. It is the regime I seek to promulgate. It is equivalent to sailing

straight through the Strait of Messina. But since doing so risks drawing us into the strong whirlpool, ultimately to drown in moralism, I propose instead that we cleave to the cliff, which is also dangerous, but less so.

What, then, does the cliff (Scylla) stand for in my conceit? It would have to be amorality in the sense of John Mackie's opening line: "There are no objective values" (1977: 15). Morality strictly so called concerns the (objective) value of rightness/wrongness only. But there are many other values commonly taken to be objective, and what I am proposing is that we attempt to treat *all* of them as subjective instead.[27] This is less "contrary to the intermediate"— moral abolitionism—because, like it, this "extreme" involves the project of subjectifying value in our thinking, speaking, and acting, whereas the extreme of fictionalism involves none of that.

In fact, I balk even at giving the *appearance* of objectifying moral value itself, for there are ways in addition to fictionalizing by which an error theorist might do this. One way is to assert hypothetical obligations, such as "If you want to spare other animals unnecessary distress and death, then you ought not to eat any," or employ hypothetical imperatives, such as "If you want to spare other animals unnecessary distress and death, then don't eat any." It might be thought harmless enough to use "ought" and related language so long as it were not intended categorically or absolutely. And, indeed, desirism does conceive ethics to be purely hypothetical, since desirist recommendations are contingent on someone's desire. Nevertheless, I want to avoid *any hint* of allusion to categoricity; therefore, I avoid even the mere locutions of the old morality[28] and, what is more, I see *no reason* to retain them.

What, after all, does "ought" add to the purely *predictive* "If you wanted to spare other animals unnecessary distress and death, then, other things equal, you *wouldn't* eat any"? I think the "ought" serves only to sustain the illusion of objective authority on matters of value. This is especially so, since we commonly omit the hypothetical clause in our assertions. Our excuse is that it is harmless and efficient to omit what everybody agrees about, such as wanting to avoid inflicting unnecessary distress and death on other creatures. But I have come to see this instead as an effort—however unwitting—to impose a regularity of preference where there may not in fact be one.

Another faux objectivity I now try to avoid, or at least not rely on, is to speak in what I call "moral mode." This would occur in the context of discussion with a moralist. Perhaps we are debating whether to support animal experimentation. An advocate of vivisection would typically argue that animal experimentation is justified because of its utility; namely, in speeding up progress in medical science and testing and treatments and the like. My natural response, having been well trained in moral argumentation, would be that the utility of animal research for the advancement of medicine has been abundantly questioned, and then to point out that it is arguable that *human* experimentation might be even more urgent on account of its utility for the same purpose, but we don't consider *that* justified.

Since this is a sufficiently stunning reply to the vivisectionist, I am tempted to use it.[29] However, a career in moral argumentation has convinced me that a dedicated opponent will always be able to reply with arguments that satisfy *her*. And my diagnosis of the whole situation is that this is only to be expected, since our primary use of morality is to advance our own agendas. So moral argumentation is indeed a temptation to me, but one which I feel is better avoided even in this "modal" usage; for the reality of indulging in it is to get stuck in a quagmire of endless dialectic. While that may be just fine for someone who enjoys debate for its own sake, it no longer appeals to me, since unending debate serves mainly to entrench the status quo,[30] whereas I have my sights on bringing about change in the world.[31]

5 The Full Mackie

Notice, then, that I have already steered away from "the intermediate" of strictly *moral* abolitionism and gone "beyond the surf and spray" in the direction of eliminating, in addition to the literal use of moralist language, the use of some of the same vocabulary in non-moralist contexts, such as the hypothetical and the modal. But I would tack farther still in this direction by avoiding talk of non-moral *values*. After all, Mackie wrote, "The claim that values are not objective, are not part of the fabric of the world . . . also includes non-moral values, notably aesthetic ones" (1977: 15). I seek to implement this claim in an abolitionist way by eliminating speech and attitudes that mistakenly uphold the objectivity of these values too.

Thus, I now strive to avoid declarations of the value of artworks or musical compositions or films, etc., that I happen to love or hate, and instead say things like, "This is my favorite song" (in lieu of "This is the best song ever written") or "I love so-and-so's paintings" or "This is what I especially like about so-and-so's writing." I also sidestep assertions about jokes or other (supposedly) *funny* things, opting for purely subjective "valuations" such as "This movie made me laugh more than any other I've seen" (in lieu of "This is the funniest movie ever made") or "This movie really tickled my funny bone; I think you might enjoy it too."

Am I thereby being too serious about humor, or about taking humor seriously? Possibly. We are not so used to viewing different senses of humor or different artistic tastes as pretexts for wars and such as we are used to viewing different convictions about right and wrong.[32] But keep in mind that my goal is to pass through the Strait of Messina—that is, rid myself and the world of moralist attitudes, for which, I am suggesting, it may be necessary not only to eliminate moralist trappings (which fictionalism fails to do), but also cognate attitudes and behaviors in far-flung realms, such as aesthetics and humor. I for one commonly experience a tenacity in the funniness of a joke or a cartoon or a film that reinforces my general belief in the existence of objective value; therefore I am now willing to risk "erring" by observing a perhaps too scrupulous literalness in my dealings with humor and other non-moral values, all the better to undermine moralism.[33]

Another, and perhaps the ultimate, value "beyond morality" that I would, ideally, banish from our external and internal discourse is good/bad. This is not to be confused with *moral* goodness or badness. Satan is morally bad, whereas a toothache is non-morally bad. Desirism asks (rhetorically), "What fact of the world does the attribution of goodness or badness to something assert other than that we do or don't like it (either for itself or for what it can get us)?" Admittedly there is also a functional use of "good"[34] that—analogous to the use of the hypothetical in the moral realm—does not have the same objectivist pretensions as good *tout court*. For example, one could speak of a good car even though one considered cars themselves to be baneful (since they pollute the environment and cause carnage on the highways to both humans and other animals and contribute to obesity and urban sprawl, etc.). However, as with hypotheticals, I discourage the use even here, and for the same sort of reason: what may seem harmless, and even useful, in itself nonetheless facilitates objectivist attitudes, whose overall effect is contrary to what I desire for myself and the world.

There is a special problem about the use of goodness in the defense of amorality as such, for it is tempting for both moral fictionalists and moral abolitionists to argue that retaining or eliminating moralism, respectively, would be a *good* thing—would lead to a *better* world than would the other. It is easy and natural to speak in this way. But it would only be to jump from the frying pan into the fire, according to an abolitionist such as myself who wants to go the "full Mackie." For "a good thing" could only be a way of speaking (since there is no objective goodness) and, in accordance with the standard abolitionist rationale, possibly a misleading and even dangerous way of speaking at that. To embrace the elimination of moralism on such grounds would be tantamount to a consequentialism, which is itself a form of moralism.[35] Hence, an error theorist who argues that either a fictionalist or an abolitionist regime would be a *good* thing is just as misguided as one who argues that either retaining or eliminating moralism would be the *right* thing to do.

6 Cleaving Still Closer to the Cliff

Avoiding the language of morals and other values, and substituting the language of desires and "liking," is the method I have been advocating for eliminating moralism from our thinking and behavior. But even that is not enough, for our psyches, and hence our lives, are saturated with moralism.[36] Hence, if we wish to uproot moralism, we must make a greater effort still. For example, if I encounter a meat-eater who defends the practice by asserting that other animals are not capable of experiencing pain or distress or suffering—which is false—or that the Bible condones meat-eating—which, true or false, is surely not logically relevant or at least not logically decisive—I discover in myself a kind of contempt for that person's intellect. And when I examine this contempt, I am impressed by its phenomenological affinity to the *moral* contempt or outrage I spontaneously feel for the meat-eater's meat-eating. Am I not, then, also feeling moral contempt for the meat-eater's ignorance and illogic? Similarly, am I not myself morally prideful in making my own assertions and inferences? But this will never do for a moral abolitionist.

What I have come up with as a *modus operandi*, therefore, is to try to refrain from assertions like "This is true" or "You are being irrational" and replace them with "This is what I believe and here's why" or "I don't see how that follows; could you explain?" This retreat to belief is of course analogous to my switching from moralist and other normative talk to talk about my desires. The difference is that the psychologizing and subjectifying I am doing now is epistemic rather than metaphysical, since the humility it manifests is purely instrumental and not indicative of a disbelief in truth and rationality. Hence, also, I am more tempered in my beliefism than in my desirism. I don't feel it incumbent on me or us in strict truthfulness to refrain from baldly asserting that $2 + 2 = 4$, whereas I do feel so constrained about asserting that kicking the dog is wrong. Even so, we need not pound somebody on the head with the former, while I would forcefully express my displeasure and intervene to prevent the latter.

But moralism is more pervasive still. Consider so-called thick concepts, which piggy-back descriptive notions with an evaluative connotation.[37] Thus, to call someone a liar is implicitly to condemn them. However, "lying" is first and foremost only a description; namely, of the act of saying something that you believe to be false for the purpose of convincing someone else that it is true. My advice for the aspiring moral abolitionist, therefore, is to put all of our thick concepts on a reducing diet and get rid of that unsightly moral fat. But this is more a matter of mind than of vocabulary. We cannot "abolish" the use of all such words and concepts, since we would be left practically speechless. But a "thin" vocabulary would be quite adequate for expressing our preferences. And isn't this a delightful prospect, especially for a society: to be able to speak forthrightly, yet without accusatory judgment? "You are lying, and I wish you would stop it" (with explanation and evidence if needed) rather than (in effect) "You dirty liar."

This ends my brief survey of what I consider to be the true scope of moral abolitionism if it is to be effective. I have argued that moralism is so widespread and entrenched (perhaps even "wired in") that we must go to extremes to expunge it. I have also tried to convince you that moralism is so baneful on balance (to what I and, I suspect, you most care about) that you, like me, will be motivated to go to these extremes. Eliminating explicitly moralist language is only the most obvious first step, for moralism can be found in the way we use almost any vocabulary. The ultimate goal, however, is not the reform of speech but the removal of an attitude from our psyche, and hence of its influence on our behavior and the world. Thus do I commend desirism to your consideration and experimentation: Try it—you might like it.

Notes

1 Mackie 1977; Hinckfuss 1987; Garner [1994] 2014; Joyce 2001; Moeller 2009; Marks 2013c; Blackford 2016.

2 See Marks 2013c.

3 This assumption has been challenged. For example, Stich (2008) has suggested that the belief in morality is peculiar to Western culture; Finlay (2008), that the assumption of the belief's prevalence is peculiar to antipodean philosophers; and Sarkissian, Park, Tien, Wright, and Knobe (2011), that the assumption of the belief's prevalence is peculiar to the folks like me who declaim against... the belief's presumed prevalence! The present volume presumes that these challenges have been met or at least not been proven. And in any case some people clearly do believe in morality as I have characterized it, so my remarks are addressed to them.

4 I certainly was, and in both capacities, when I first had my "anti-epiphany" of the unreality of morality. I relate the story in Marks (2013b).

5 See Marks 2013d, 2016.

6 I thank Bill Irwin for vigorous debate on this issue.

7 I take egoism to be the "enlightened" form of self-interest, whereas selfishness—when not just the generic term for caring about oneself—would be the "unenlightened" form. So, under normal circumstances, taking the biggest piece of the pie for oneself would be selfish because short- and narrow-sighted, while an egoist would share equally with everyone since this would likely serve her best interests in the long run (by helping her cultivate circumspection and self-control, keeping her weight down, not alienating others, etc.).

8 Making a recommendation to someone else is also a behavior of one's own, of course, so complications can arise. For example, you might conclude, after careful reflection, that, if you were me, you would, after careful reflection, want to lie. This suggests that you recommend that I lie. But you might also conclude, after careful reflection, that you wanted me to tell the truth. This suggests that you recommend that I tell the truth. What to do? The desirist answer depends on (the relative strength of) another desire; namely, how much, after careful reflection, you want to be completely honest with me. If this desire were stronger than your desire that I tell the truth, then, other things equal, you might make no recommendation yay or nay but simply explain to me why you felt stymied. If you were more desirous of *my* telling the truth than of *your* telling the truth, then, ironically, you might lie to me or mislead me by recommending that I tell the truth.

9 I need not even say "*other* animals," since I don't think most of us would, under most contemporary conditions, care to be cannibals, either!

10 Although it could do so *deceptively* under exceptional conditions.

11 Lederman (2014) appears to be doing this, but in fact his main point is a different one (personal communication), about the rationality of desirism, with which I agree.

12 Cf. Dworkin 1996.

13 I sought to circumvent them at the very outset by reformulating the central question of ethics as "How *shall* we live?" rather than "How *ought* we live?"

14 Garner (1993) offers a critique of this tendency.

15 Cf. Pigliucci's definition (2013) of philosophical analysis as "a matter of critical reflection on empirically underdetermined issues."

16 Marks 2013c: chs. 3 and 4.

17 The exacerbation of disagreement is not the only problem, however, since there can also be a stifling of healthy conflict and change from the hardening of attitudes in the absence of disagreement—conative (as well as cognitive) sclerosis, if you will.

18 I thank Mitchell Silver (personal communication) for reminding me of this.

19 Cf. Nietzsche: "Gradually it has become clear to me what every great philosophy so far has been—namely, the personal confession of its author and a kind of involuntary and unconscious memoir" (*Beyond Good and Evil*, trans. W. Kaufman [New York: Vintage, 1966], sec. 6). Whether or not my own philosophy of desirism is a "great" one, I have attempted to discern the purely personal causes of my predilection for it in the "Ad Hominem Addendum" to Marks 2013d.

20 Cf. Joyce (2001: 222): "I do not pretend to have established the truth of this claim with any assurance, but rather to have proposed considerations in its favor."

21 "Or narcissism?" asks Richard Garner (personal communication).

22 Thus Joyce (2001: 223): "The whole point of [morality, although Joyce at this point in his monograph is describing the function of "the moral *fictive* stance" since he, like me, denies the existence of morality as such] is that it is a strategy for staving off inevitable human fallibilities in instrumental deliberation. Without the stance, the knave [Joyce's stand-in for 'the average person'] will be vulnerable—he will make mistakes; he will rationalize to himself poor decisions; he might get what he immediately desires, but not what he values; he will defect on deals and he will pay the price."

23 "[M]oral thinking . . . suits our psychological configuration [and so] can be fast and frugal" (Joyce 2011).

24 Perhaps this is a change from humanity's previous circumstances. (Hans-Georg Moeller alludes to Dylan in this context: "The times they are a-changin'" [2009: 108].) Thus, if we do not take control of our own destiny by eliminating or at least moderating our moralism, evolution/nature might do it for us by wiping us out.

25 A scientist would see my question as substantive rather than rhetorical. But I am skeptical about science's capacity to answer the *general* question of morality's versus amorality's relative efficacy. And one reason for my skepticism is the perennially contested nature of the concepts involved; thus, some ethicists would label the *caring* attitude as the truly *moral* one, either intrinsically or because of its instrumental efficacy.

26 Or Circe's? Aristotle appears to have erred in attributing this advice to Calypso, for in Homer's *Odyssey* it is Circe who warns Odysseus about Scylla and Charybdis, and Odysseus does not meet Calypso until after traversing the Strait of Messina.

27 Call this "axiology"?

28 Hinckfuss drew explicit attention to the fact that "certain words of constraint that are commonly used in making moral statements can also be used within contexts that are logically unrelated to morality" (1987: section 1.3.1). However, he also observed that "'ought' and 'should' do not change meaning as we move from moral to non-moral discourse." I (unlike Hinckfuss) am urging on that basis that we might want to avoid using them altogether.

29 And have done so; see, e.g., Marks 2012.

30 I expand on this in Marks 2013a.

31 What I have called the "moral mode" might be viewed as an occasional variant of moral fictionalism, as it is used only on particular occasions for strategic purposes. But I think that is not quite right, since the moral fictionalist is indulging in a pretense even as regards his own awareness, whereas the user of moral mode is well aware of speaking only hypothetically.

32 And yet one may wonder what would be the correct analysis of, for example, the violent protests around the world against the publication by a Danish newspaper in 2005 of cartoons depicting the prophet Mohammed.

33 Of course, I do not want to be so "scrupulous" as to impose on others an offputting hence counterproductive political correctness.

34 See Blackford 2016; cf. Mackie 1977: 53–58.

35 Consequentialism holds that one *ought* to do whatever will have the best consequences.

36 Cf. Pettit and Knobe 2009.

37 See Kirchin 2013.

References

Blackford, R. 2016. *The Mystery of Moral Authority*. London: Palgrave Macmillan.

Dworkin, R. 1996. "Objectivity and truth: You'd better believe it." *Philosophy and Public Affairs* 25: 87–139.

Finlay, S. 2008. "The error in the error theory." *Australasian Journal of Philosophy* 86: 347–369.

Garner, R. 1993. "Are convenient fictions harmful to your health?" *Philosophy East and West* 43: 87–106.

Garner, R. [1994] 2014. *Beyond Morality*. Brattleboro, VT: Echo Point Books & Media.

Hinckfuss, I. 1987. *The Moral Society: Its Structure and Effects*. Discussion Papers in Environmental Philosophy 16. Canberra: Philosophy Program (RSSS), Australian National University.

Joyce, R. 2001. *The Myth of Morality*. Cambridge: Cambridge University Press.

Joyce, R. 2011. "Moral fictionalism: When falsehoods are too useful to throw out." *Philosophy Now* 82: 14–17.

Kirchin, S. (ed.). 2013. *Thick Concepts*. Oxford: Oxford University Press.

Lederman, Z. 2014. "Amoralist rationalism? A response to Joel Marks." *Journal of Bioethical Inquiry* 2: 115–116.

Mackie, J. L. 1977. *Ethics: Inventing Right and Wrong*. London: Penguin

Marks, J. 2012. "Accept no substitutes: The ethics of alternatives." *Hastings Center Report* 42 (S16–S18).

Marks, J. 2013a. "Animal abolitionism meets moral abolitionism." *Journal of Bioethical Inquiry* 10: 445–455.

Marks, J. 2013b. *Bad Faith: A Philosophical Memoir*. North Charleston, SC: CreateSpace.

Marks, J. 2013c. *Ethics Without Morals: In Defense of Amorality*. New York: Routledge.

Marks, J. 2013d. *It's Just a Feeling: The Philosophy of Desirism*. North Charleston, SC: CreateSpace.

Marks, J. 2016. *Hard Atheism and the Ethics of Desire: An Alternative to Morality*. New York: Palgrave Macmillan.

Moeller, Hans-Georg. 2009. *The Moral Fool: A Case for Amorality*. New York: Columbia University Press.

Pettit, D. & Knobe, J. 2009. "The pervasive impact of moral judgment." *Mind & Language* 24: 586–604.

Pigliucci, M. 2013. "Experimental philosophy is not an elephant." *Rationally Speaking* [Blog], March 15. http://rationallyspeaking.blogspot.com/2013/03/experimental-philosophy-is-not-elephant.html.

Sarkissian, H., Park, J., Tien, D., Wright, J. & Knobe, J. 2011. "Folk moral relativism." *Mind & Language* 26: 482–505.

Stich, S. 2008. "Some questions about Richard Joyce's *The Evolution of Morality*." *Philosophy and Phenomenological Research* 77: 228–236.

PART III
Alternatives to Abolitionism

7

MORAL PRACTICE AFTER ERROR THEORY

Negotiationism

Björn Eriksson and Jonas Olson

1 Introduction

What should you do about your moral practice if you come to believe that moral error theory is true? That is our leading question in this chapter. Several philosophers have approached this question in different ways during the last few decades, and they have all come up with different and mostly conflicting answers.[1] The aim of this chapter is to reconsider the issue, and to improve on extant answers to the question.

We first deal with a few preliminary matters and discuss what—if any—*distinct* impact belief in moral error theory should have on our moral practice. Second, we describe what is involved in giving an answer to our leading question and take notice of some factors that are relevant to what an adequate answer might look like. We also argue that the specific details of adequate answers to our leading question will depend largely on context. Third, we consider three extant answers to our leading question: fictionalism, conservationism, and abolitionism. Of these three, conservationism seems most promising. However, conservationism leaves pertinent questions unanswered. In order to provide answers to these questions, and ultimately to provide an answer to our leading question, conservationism needs to be supplemented, yielding an account we call "negotiationism." This final proposal is not neat and tidy, but it might work reasonably well in the moral environment in which error theorists are likely to find themselves.

2 Preliminaries

2.1 Moral Practice and Moral Error Theory

First, by "moral practice" we mean our ordinary moral thought and discourse in a broad sense, including our practice of morally blaming and praising and of judging certain actions morally wrong and others morally permissible, as well as our moral theorizing and principled moral reasoning. Second, by "moral error theory" we mean the view that moral judgments purport to refer to moral facts and state moral truths, but since there are no moral facts and no moral truths, no moral judgment is true.[2] (Henceforth we simply use the term "error theory" for this view.)

While we are sympathetic to error theory, we shall for the purposes of this chapter remain largely non-committal regarding what considerations might motivate the view. But we chiefly have in mind considerations according to which moral facts are for one reason or other metaphysically problematic.[3] Our leading question is relevant to anyone who inclines towards error theory, but in this chapter we do not defend or presuppose any particular motivation for error theory: it is belief in error theory and the upshots of such belief for moral practice that are in focus, not the truth of error theory.

We address our leading question to each and every one of us. Our question is thus not the collective and idealized question of what would be best if adopted as a moral practice by some group, perhaps everyone.[4]

2.2 Can Error Theorists Answer the Question Without Undermining Error Theory?

Critics, as well as sympathizers, of error theory have recently pointed out that many standard arguments against moral facts and in favor of moral error theory apply not only to moral normativity, but also to normativity more broadly.[5] If there is nothing we ought morally to do, it seems that there is nothing we ought to do, or should do, in the more general normative sense. This invites the objection that when error theorists ask what they should do about moral practice, they undermine their own position in that the question presupposes that there is something that they should do, which according to error theory there is not. What the objection achieves is to highlight the point that "should" in our leading question signifies a mere means–end relation. When the error theorist poses the leading question, she presupposes that she has certain ends, and the question concerns how to employ moral practice in order to realize those ends. This is not an idiosyncratic sense of "should." Sometimes when we say that a person should go and see a certain film, for example, we mean merely to say that she would enjoy it (we presuppose that enjoyment is an end that all or most people have), not that she *should* see it in the moral or more general normative sense of "should" (although in some contexts that is what we mean to say, of course).[6]

The error theorist can thus pose the leading question of this chapter without undermining her own position. It is important to see also that the question is an open and complex one, with no obviously correct answer. It is sometimes thought that if one believes that there are no moral facts and that ordinary moral thought and discourse is systematically mistaken, the only sensible option is to jettison moral thought and discourse, or at least the parts of it that embody the error. Simon Blackburn says that the moral error theorist J. L. Mackie "did not draw quite the consequences one might have expected from [his error theorist] position. If a vocabulary embodies an error, then it would be better if it were replaced by one that avoids the error" (Blackburn 1993: 149). But that is not obviously so. We have already seen that error theorists can understand questions about what should be done as means-end questions about how to realize desired ends. Similarly, the question whether some course of behavior is *better* than another can be understood as asking whether that course of behavior promotes realization of the relevant ends to a greater extent than the other. An error theorist may well think that her ends would be less likely to be realized were she to jettison her moral practice than they would be if she were to preserve it, in part or in whole.[7]

3 The Impact of Error Theory (and of Realism) on Moral Practice

Our discussion so far may suggest that the leading question arises only for error theorists. But things are not so simple. It may be reasonably doubted that belief in error theory has any *distinct* impact on what our moral practice should look like. And, perhaps surprisingly, this doubt may also arise, *mutatis mutandis*, for moral realism.

Let us suppose for a moment that moral realism is true and that facts about how one should or ought to moralize are within its scope. Presumably, if moral realism is true, there is a fact of the matter regarding how we ought to moralize. Though this may seem very different from an error theorist-cum-pragmatist position vis-à-vis moral practice, it need not be all that different. It all depends on what the facts are (assuming there are such) regarding how we should or ought to moralize. It is not far-fetched to think that the general truth about how we should moralize (if there is such a truth) is that we should moralize so that the goals, values, and principles of the true morality are fulfilled, promoted, and adhered to in the right way by our moralizing. Even believers in morality may need the services of pragmatic thinking and deliberation in its execution. It is a familiar idea within the utilitarian tradition that we ought to engage in moral discussion, deliberation, and argument only to the extent that it is conducive to the best overall consequences. Equally familiar is the idea that it might be morally desirable for an enlightened elite to keep the true morality a secret, and promulgate to the public false moral beliefs that would better promote the best overall consequences than would true moral beliefs.[8]

Moreover, to abolish moralizing altogether is consistent with belief in moral realism. We may imagine a person whose greatest concern is to promote the general happiness and who is also a moral realist. Suppose now that this person comes to believe, regrettably from her point of view, that there are side constraints on what it is morally permissible to do in order to promote the general happiness. It is not unimaginable that this person decides to jettison moral thought and discourse altogether, because she believes that some moral truths conflict with her greatest concern.[9]

Does this boil down to saying that error theory, by and large, is neither here nor there when it comes to settling on one or another set of guidelines for moral practice? Almost. One difference between the respective impact of realism and error theory concerns the status of the constraints on possible ways to mold moral practice. Given error theory, there are only pragmatic, attitude-dependent constraints. This contrasts with the inescapable and attitude-independent normative constraints that realists of various stripes endorse. But, as we have seen, even for the moral realist there will probably be some room and some reason to engage in focused practical deliberation about how to moralize, and hopefully the following discussion can be instructive for realists who take up that task. A second difference, to which we turn next, is that there may be aspects of moral practice available to the realist but not to the error theorist, such as moral belief.

4 The Error Theorist's Moral Toolbox and Its Content

If moral practice is worth preserving, from the perspective of error theorists, that is because the contents of what we might call the "moral toolbox" are useful. Let us consider some of this content.

When engaging in moral discussion and deliberation, we advance *moral propositions*, some of which are contents of *beliefs* that we hold, while others are put forward as ammunition for *reductios* and thus neither believed nor asserted. Sometimes we signal that we have certain *moral commitments* that are especially dear to us, so that we can be trusted not to compromise them. And we tie moral propositions together in arguments and draw moral conclusions. In sum, the standard toolbox of "normal" moral practice notably contains at least moral beliefs, the logical resources needed for argument, and certain psychological resources that underpin moral commitment and adherence to moral principles. Are any of these resources rendered unavailable by belief in error theory, or can error theorists retain legitimate access to them?

Belief seems problematic, but not fatally so. If the error theorist believes some (positive) moral proposition, she thereby has contradictory beliefs: a belief that, say, it is wrong to φ, and a belief that (implies that) it is not wrong to φ. These concerns can perhaps be handled, but there will be costs. We discuss these below, in connection with the idea that is most welcoming to moral belief even given error theory, viz. *conservationism*, which is roughly the view that error theorists should stick to their (pre-error-theoretic) moral practice. By contrast, abolitionism and fictionalism, although mutually incompatible, both reject moral belief and moral assertion.

When it comes to the logical resources for moral argument, the situation seems to be similar to that of moral belief. Moral arguments are available to any error theorist, but how useful they are in deliberation depends on how our leading question is answered. Error theorists who shun, or recommend against, moral belief will see little or no practical use in moral arguments, since they shun, or recommend against, believing the moral premises. Error theorists who take a fictional stance to moral practice can make practical use of moral arguments in the moral fiction. Finally, error theorists who recommend sticking to ordinary moral practice, and who succeed in so doing, may make the same practical use of moral arguments as any realist does.

What about moral commitment and adherence to moral principles? The important point here is whether the error theorist can be practically committed to such things as keeping her promises, helping friends in need, refraining from eating factory-farmed meat, and so on. And why couldn't she? The error theorist may not be committed to these things *because she thinks they are morally required*, but rather because she is concerned about being a reliable person and because she cares about the wellbeing of her friends and of non-human animals. Does that reduce the strength of the commitment? We think not.

There are, however, commitments that seem to be in a special way persistent and not under the voluntary control of those committed. A moral realist may see herself as committed, from the nature of things, to the belief that, for example, industrial meat production morally ought to be abolished; she may experience this commitment as not up for revision. An error theorist who holds a deep concern to minimize the suffering of non-human animals may be equally committed to the elimination of industrial meat production. The error theorist and the moral realist seem both to have access to practical commitments that they both experience as outside their direct and voluntary control, and as not being matters open to deliberation or decision.

But it is an all-too-familiar fact that human beings sometimes fall prey to weakness of will. As an illustration, think of an error theorist who holds general practical commitments to keeping her promises to friends. Imagine, however, that she finds herself in a situation in which she is strongly tempted to break a promise to a friend because doing so would lead to an immediate gain for herself. It is clearly not unrealistic to suppose that in such a scenario the temptation overrides the motivational force of the error theorist's general practical commitments. Several writers have noted that moral thinking is in such scenarios a useful tool to prevent deviation from general practical commitments.[10] The idea is, of course, that the principled thought "But it would be wrong!" silences or reduces the motivational force of immediate temptations and short-sighted and egoistic inclinations. Error theorists who reject moral thinking have no access to that kind of device, and that seems to be a cost of the abolitionist position. It is also worth noting that, in interpersonal contexts, signaling moral commitment may be a powerful pragmatic device. The abolitionists will have to explain how they manage without it, and that is indeed a weakness of that position. Conservationists have no problem with signaling commitment, and neither have fictionalists. We shall return to this important point in sections 8 and 9.

5 When, Where, and How Should an Error Theorist Moralize?

Thus far our discussion suggests that it is advisable for error theorists to foster pragmatic attitudes about when, where, and how to moralize. Obviously, the answer to the question of the proper time, place, and mode of moralizing will be determined largely by factors that vary considerably with context. Before we consider in greater detail some extant answers to our leading question, we will take notice of some such factors.

First, moral beliefs may be more or less malleable, in the sense that they are more or less sensitive to criticism in the form of counter-examples or counter-arguments. Moral beliefs based on no apparently good reason may be held with greater conviction and be less sensitive to criticism than moral beliefs based on purportedly good reasons. The absence of grounds or justification for a person's cherished moral beliefs may prompt fortification of those beliefs by in effect isolating them from criticism, however rationally compelling the criticism may be to observers. We should expect quite a lot of variation regarding the malleability of people's moral beliefs. And that variation will normally affect what may be reasonably expected from engaging in moral discussion and argument.

Second, and relatedly, moral beliefs are held with more or less hostility or disdain toward people who do not share them, which may also influence the costs and returns of entering into moral discussion and argument.

Third, some moral discussions may be "demoralized" in the sense that they admit reconstruction as non-moralized discussions concerning, for example, people's preferences or interests and how best to satisfy them. Moralized conflicts over the justice of some political issue, for example, may be disarmed in this way by widening the scope of the discussion (see Olsson Yaouzis, this volume). This is common in political bargaining, where an initially unacceptable, because deemed unjust, proposal is offset by another, often completely unrelated, offer that is in the interest of the party who felt that the initial proposal was unjust. She may then instead see the situation as one of "Some you win, some you lose" (rather than as a case of double injustice being done). Other discussions are not so easily demoralized. For example, it tends to be difficult to demoralize conflicts where large sacrifices have already been made in the name of morality. No matter how desirable it would be if concern for the wellbeing of people replaced the focus on conflicting moral rights and wrongs, large moral investments from all sides make demoralization all but impossible. The current situation in Syria (April 2017) comes to mind here.

When encountering a situation where an issue under discussion seems easily demoralized, the error theorist can consider trying to have a demoralized version of the issue accepted for discussion and thus avoid entering into moral discussion and argument. There may be distinctive returns from demoralizing differences of moral opinion: Disagreement over matters of non-moral fact are sometimes easier to settle than disagreement over moral facts, so conflicts may be made more tractable if demoralized. This is partly because of epistemic difficulties peculiar to moral investigations, but also partly because a demoralized conception of a conflict is more likely to describe it in terms that encourage cooperation and a sense of a shared problem to be solved rather than a conflict to be resolved. However, demoralizing conflicts may also incur costs, as we will discuss in sections 8 and 9.

In order to provide a useful answer to our leading question, complexities concerning malleability of moral beliefs, hostility and disdain towards dissenters, possibilities of demoralizing discussions, and probably others, should be taken into account. This means that the answer, in the form of a proposed best way of practicing morality (if at all) given belief in error theory, will be a description of a rather complex set of conditions for deploying moral arguments and assertions. The account we call "negotiationism" promises to be just that. Before describing this account, we will briefly highlight some suggestive shortcomings and virtues of the other strategies mentioned, with special focus on how well they succeed in accommodating the complexities mentioned above. Negotiationism will then emerge as the result of purging the shortcomings and compiling the virtues of the other proposals. We begin with fictionalism.

6 Moral Fictionalism

The most attractive version of fictionalism we find to be Richard Joyce's. Joyce is an error theorist, but like some fellow error theorists he emphasizes the usefulness of moral thought and talk as devices that bolster self-control and combat weakness of will.[11]

However, Joyce recommends that we give up on the systematically erroneous moral beliefs and assertions involved in ordinary moral thought and discourse. His brand of fictionalism recommends instead that we think moral thoughts without believing them, and that we utter moral sentences without assertoric force. Instead of believing that stealing is wrong, we *entertain the thought* that stealing is wrong, and instead of asserting that property is theft (and hence wrong), we *express that entertained thought* while withholding assertoric intent. Sherlock Holmes tends to loom large in discussions of fictionalism. The paradigmatic fictionalist is a Holmes fan who entertains thoughts, and freely expresses them, about Holmes, Watson, and Moriarty, and their doings and whereabouts. But the Holmes fan isn't deluded: she knows that Holmes is just a fiction. The moral fictionalist idea, then, is that we become "morality fans" in an analogous way. This seems to be in principle a psychologically possible move to make, but fictionalism faces several problems.

As one of us has argued in previous work (Olson 2011, 2014), it is not obviously that false moral beliefs and assertions are pragmatically costly, so it is not clear that Joyce has sufficiently motivated the move to fictionalism.[12] Here we shall let that objection pass, however. Instead we shall focus on what we call the "stability problem."[13] The problem arises from fictionalism's double ambitions to use moral thought and discourse as devices to bolster self-control and combat weakness of will *and* to avoid holding false moral beliefs and making false moral assertions.

The fictionalist is charged with the mission of inducing (in herself) not moral belief, but moral thoughts and talk—the fiction of morality, in other words. How is she to go about accomplishing this? She could try to moralize away in the hope that any day now her moral thoughts and the expressions of them will stop being disrupted by pangs of error theoretic insight, so that she becomes comfortable in her moral fiction. Accomplishing this seems a tricky task. The fictionalist must not, as it were, put the pedal to the metal and go for full-blown moral belief; in accordance with her own recommendation, she must proceed with caution lest she slip into real moral belief and assertion. Real moral belief is to be shunned because of the alleged pragmatic costs of having false beliefs. This is a prominent *raison d'être* for Joyce's fictionalism. This leaves the fictionalist precariously balancing between the alleged intellectual havoc of endorsing false beliefs and making false assertions, and the alleged pragmatic havoc of having no access to moralized thought and talk—of becoming a *de facto* abolitionist. One might wonder if this feat is at all possible even for short periods of time. Even if it is possible, fictionalism seems to us to lead to a severe practical tension. On the one hand, the fictionalist must practice cognitive self-surveillance and occasionally remind herself about the truth of error theory in order to prevent slipping into holding real moral beliefs and making genuine moral assertions. But, on the other hand, such cognitive self-surveillance and occasional reminders would seem to make moral thought and discourse much less effective in bolstering self-control and combating weakness of will. This should motivate the error theorist to search for alternative answers to our leading question.

7 Moral Conservationism

One such alternative is moral conservationism. The point of departure of conservationism is the same as that of fictionalism: the usefulness of moral thought and discourse. However, conservationism does not see real (as opposed to pretense) moral belief and genuine moral assertion as something to be shunned, but rather as something to be endorsed, insofar as they do indeed help bolster self-control and combat weakness of will. One might wonder whether it is at all possible for avowed error theorists to hold real moral beliefs, but it is not unlikely that peer pressure, emotional engagement, and the like, may give rise to beliefs that one rejects "in the cool hour."[14] Moreover, some philosophical beliefs—e.g., skepticism about free will or induction—are such that we are disposed to hold them only in the seminar room, while in less reflective everyday commerce we tend to believe that there is free will and that inductive reasoning is justified.

Such considerations may suffice as a possibility proof that conservationism is a position that is psychologically available to error theorists. One might doubt, however, that conservationism completely avoids the stability problem that fictionalism faces. The familiar problem is that in situations in which one is tempted to, say, shoplift or break a promise, one's belief in error theory may resurface and prevent one's belief that shoplifting or breaking promises is wrong from functioning as an antidote to weakness of will. We sometimes look for ways to escape our moral beliefs or opinions when the costs of acting on them are mounting. For an error theorist, there seems to be one ever-present escape route from the perceived requirement to act on one's moral opinions: dismissal of the moral belief or opinion.

There is, then, a threat of instability in the conservationist stance, especially in the face of temptation. Compartmentalization of moral and metaethical beliefs can probably be upheld at times, most easily in more impersonal contexts that don't put the moralizer's own interests on the line. But this instability in the face of temptation is a reason to be skeptical about the possibility and advisability of following the conservationist's recommendation as a general practice. So what does conservationism recommend for error theorists who are psychologically unable to hold real moral beliefs, either in general or on some isolated occasion, due, for example, to the force of temptation?[15]

We need first to distinguish interpersonal from intrapersonal cases. In interpersonal cases, a plausible recommendation is to keep making moral assertions, although one knows them to be false, since their pragmatic implicatures make them useful. Plausibly, one pragmatic aspect of moral judgment is *imperatival*. Noncognitivists at least since C. L. Stevenson (1937) have argued that the imperatival aspect constitutes the primary meaning of moral judgments. While cognitivist error theorists reject this, they need not reject the thesis that moral claims implicate imperatives.[16] Even among error theorists, the claim that breaking promises is wrong could be generally recognized as literally false but as conversationally implicating the imperative "Do not break promises!" Note that this conservationist recommendation does not amount to a concession to moral fictionalism. The idea is not that moral utterances are made with non-assertoric force. Neither does it amount to a recommendation to adopt noncognitivism as a replacement theory. The idea is still that moral claims express false propositions but that they conversationally implicate imperatives.

In intrapersonal cases, a plausible recommendation is to go on thinking moralized thoughts and say to oneself, for example, that breaking promises is wrong (although one believes that this claim is false). For it is plausible that there is a correlation between our motivationally efficacious attitudes of likes and dislikes and our moral judgments (people tend to judge morally wrong what they on reflection dislike and to judge morally right what they on reflection like), even if the correlation is not of the strong kind posited by some internalists about motivation. Thinking the thought—or saying to oneself—that breaking promises is morally wrong might resonate with one's dislike of promise-breaking and in this way function as a reminder that one normally (i.e., on reflection) dislikes breaking promises. In situations in which one finds oneself tempted to break a promise, such a reminder might bolster self-control partly because we normally want to avoid acting so as to become the objects of our own dislike and partly because we simply want to adhere to the attitudes presently under temporary threat from temptation, and the moral thought is a reminder of this.

It is fair to ask at this point why disliking breaking promises, or believing that one normally dislikes breaking promises, is not effective enough when it comes to bolstering self-control. In what way would self-control be bolstered further by moralized thoughts, such as the thought that breaking promises is wrong? A plausible answer is that in situations in which one finds oneself tempted to break a promise, one's dislike of promise-breaking and one's belief that one normally dislikes promise-breaking are typically not cognitively and motivationally salient, and perhaps even silenced. Thinking, or saying to oneself, that breaking promises is morally wrong (although one believes that this is false) might serve to evoke and make cognitively and motivationally salient one's dislike of promise-breaking.[17] How effective would such a stance to moral thought and discourse be in bolstering self-control? Probably not as effective as it would be if belief in objective prescriptivity or irreducibly normative reasons were in place, but it might still be effective enough to render a moral conservationist policy worthwhile.[18]

But we would now like to return to an issue that has hitherto gone largely unnoticed by both fictionalists and conservationists: namely, the issue concerning the when, where, and how dimension of moral practice, broached in section 5 above.[19] Let us say that "preservationist conservationism" is the view that recommends merely that moral practice be preserved for occasional use, but remains silent on the extent to which it should be used, and with what degree of intensity. Let us also say that "conservative conservationism" is the view that, not only should moral practice be preserved, but the extent to which we engage in it, and with what degree of intensity, should be unaffected by our belief in error theory. Conservative conservationism, then, may well recommend frequent and heavy moralizing.

For our purposes, preservationist conservationism has the obvious drawback that it does not provide a complete answer to our leading question, precisely because it remains silent on the extent to which moral practice should be used, and with what degree of intensity. Conservative conservationism has a different kind of drawback: namely, that heavy and frequent moralizing seems difficult to defend pragmatically, as we are about to argue next, with aid from the abolitionist camp.

8 Moral Abolitionism Redux?

We saw in section 4 above that abolitionism involves rejection of the seemingly useful employment of moral thought and discourse as intrapersonal and interpersonal commitment devices. That seemed a significant cost of abolitionism. We also saw that the putative usefulness of moral thought and discourse are among the main motivations of both fictionalism and conservationism. But perhaps fictionalists' and conservationists' concern to preserve moral practice is premised on excessive optimism about the usefulness of moral practice.

In fact, there is a case to be made for the claim that we should at least ease up a bit on moralizing regardless of whether we incline towards realism or error theory. As Richard Garner put it in defense of the abolitionist position, "the death of moralizing might be good for the individual and for society" (2007: 500; see also Garner, this volume). Much of our present moralizing may be part of the problem rather than part of the solution, partly due to the "arrogance and interference that a belief in the objectivity of morality often occasions" (2007: 500).

The error theorist *locus classicus* for reflections on the downsides of morality is Ian Hinckfuss's *The Moral Society: Its Structure and Effects* (1987; excerpted in this volume). Hinckfuss argues that "the moral society"—i.e., a kind of society where people try to act and get others to act morally to a high degree—is plagued by several problems that would dissolve if people stopped doing this. Chief among the features of the moral society are unnecessary feelings of guilt, perpetuation of unsound power relations grounded on perceived moral desert, and moral obstacles to the fruitful resolution of conflicts of interest.

A glance at some present-day conflicts seems at least partly to vindicate Hinckfuss's worries about conflict resolution. The convictions of both parties that they have morality on their side do not seem to help in the Israel-Palestinian conflict. The same can be said for the disagreements between militant Islamists and Western liberals. The fact that they see themselves as having got morality right (and the other side as having got it wrong) makes discussion and fruitful compromise much harder to attain. The polarization in present-day U.S. politics is another example of how paralyzing a conflict can become if it is seen as a moral conflict. The point about perpetuation of social power relations seems at least partly correct, too. Even in the light of some rather strong evidence that a more egalitarian society would be better for all, even for those who are at the top now, political proposals to the effect that resources and power be distributed more equally among people meet with objections that those presently in power and well off deserve their power and are the rightful owners of their material and monetary goods.[20] The moralization of success also weighs on the younger generations, who may feel that they must achieve whatever they think morality demands of them, irrespective of how those demands fit with their considered views of a worthwhile life.

Much of this seems correct: moralistic dogmatism, self-righteousness, and the pressure from conceptions of moral desert probably contribute to considerable social problems. But these coins have a flip side too. Even though one may agree with Hinckfuss that the practice of morality plays an infelicitous role in many social contexts, there are some considerations that speak in its favor. The idea of moral desert could, for example, work as a reinforcement of a judiciary system in a society. If (at least some) punishments are regarded as morally deserved, it may have a stabilizing effect on the system. And this could be a good thing if the system is a good one. And while the costs of experiencing the pressure of moral demands to be "worthy" and "deserving" may indeed provoke stress, they may also provide motivation and thus promote considerable achievements.

Regarding morality as an obstacle to fruitful conflict resolution—which arguably is the weightiest item on Hinckfuss's list of morality-driven problems—there are conflicts where it is important that one does *not* compromise, but sticks to one's proverbial or literal guns. Moralizing the issue or keeping it moralized may help do just that. This may be the wise thing to do, particularly in conflicts where the other side already is irrevocably committed to a moralized understanding of the conflict. In such cases the other side may not really take one seriously if one refuses to regard the matter in a moralized light.

These speculations, which seem correct from the perspective of our armchairs, have received some empirical support. A study by Ginges, Atran, Medin, and Shikaki (2007) seems, in fact, to show that having the resources of a moralized discourse may be necessary for finding acceptable compromises in some kinds of conflicts. Ginges et al. studied attitudes to the Israel-Palestine conflict. They asked three groups of people with stakes in the conflict—Israeli settlers in the West Bank, Palestinian students in Jerusalem, and Palestinians living in refugee camps—to consider and respond to different peace deals. The conflict between Israel and Palestine is regarded by people on both sides as involving "sacred" values, as Ginges et al. put it. Such values are crucially regarded by their champions as not tradable for non-sacred values. One result from the study is that in moralized conflicts over such "sacred" values, compromise may be seriously considered only if both sides make concessions regarding "sacred" values. And not only that: offering what the other side regards as concessions regarding non-moral, instrumental values (such as money or help restoring destroyed infrastructure) actually raises the resistance to compromise regarding the "sacred" values. Ginges et al. found that the proposal to give up one sacred value (the settlements on the West Bank for Israeli settlers; Jerusalem as the Palestinian capital for Palestinian students; and the sacred right to return for Palestinian refugees) for the sake of peace is met with *less* (albeit still strong) resistance than the proposal to make the same concession and be compensated in non-sacred currency such as money. The upshot of these studies seems to be that, if one has no "morality card" to play, then one may be left without any workable moves at all in conflicts of the kind most likely to prove difficult and serious. This is of course consistent with its being better if all sides to a conflict would drop all of their "sacred" moral values and focus on the problem as a future-directed matter of gains and losses in currencies directly connected to people's non-sacred interests. That far, Hinckfuss may be correct. But for many of the ongoing real conflicts haunting our societies, that is an irrelevant consideration: people will not leave their moral values behind when they approach the negotiating table, and suggesting that they should may only lower their motivation to reach an agreement. Indeed, they may not approach it at all if they don't believe that the other side has such values to concede.

Another relevant finding that has emerged in this area of research is discussed by Scott Atran and Robert Axelrod (2008). It concerns the importance of sincere apology and acceptance of responsibility. In many conflicts, the acceptance of responsibility for past "sins" is a prerequisite for moving on to negotiation over non-sacred instrumental values such as peace and monetary compensation. Not surprisingly, apologies and acceptance of responsibility only work if experienced as sincere. So, for example, Donald Rumsfeld's hedged "apology" for the events in the Abu Ghraib prison in Iraq, referring to "un-American" behavior on the part of a few wayward soldiers, met with angry dismissal and did not silence those who held the U.S. government responsible. To be able to deliver sincere-sounding apologies and acceptance of responsibility one must have recourse to a moralized discourse: one must accept that a moral transgression has been made (under that description).

These two seeming facts about conflict resolution and negotiation—the importance of having moral "sacred" values of one's own to concede, and being able to accept moral responsibility and apologize—speak heavily against abolitionism, at least as a unilateral undertaking of those convinced of error theory and morality's dysfunctional tendencies. As long as others continue to moralize their discourse, we may have to play along. So, morality may be a necessary tool for resolution of some conflicts, and this goes for many of those conflicts that are hardest to resolve and have the highest running costs. The lesson from this is that the problem regarding the effects of moralizing calls for case-by-case analysis and close attention to the details of the situation at hand, rather than a clear-cut purist choice of abolishing moral practice or conserving it.

This spells trouble for abolitionism, but it also suggests that conservationism is incomplete. It seems that abolishing moral discourse altogether would be unwise. But, in view of Hinckfuss's reasonable objections to a highly moralized society, it seems plausible that a pragmatically justifiable moral practice should be guarded and self-reflective. We should normally be on the lookout for adverse effects of potential moralizing, and be prepared to retract and go for demoralization if possible.

9 Negotiationism

The twofold lesson to draw is, first, that conservationism is a plausible account of the kind of moral thought and discourse error theorists should employ when they *should* pursue moral thought and employ moral discourse; in these cases, error theorists should endorse moral belief and assert moral propositions even if they believe them to be false; and, second, that conservationism needs to be supplemented with answers to the questions of *when* and *to what extent* to moralize. We will end this chapter by providing some brief thoughts on the limits of conservationist moralizing as well as on the different ways it can be pursued. The discussion will result in a kind of supplemented conservationism we call "negotiationism." Its aim is to open all doors for fine-tuning the occasions for, and manner of, conservationist moralizing to the needs of the moment.

What is needed along with the tools available to conservationism, in view of the complexity and variability of actual moral practice, is some regulation regarding both when to engage in moral discourse and the manner in which to do it. A conservationist should not moralize freely and regard moral discourse as the default practical discourse in important matters. The guarded attitude towards moralizing inspired by the abolitionists should be accommodated by negotiationism. And this component is a natural addition to a preservationist conservationist framework. The whole idea of conservationism is that use of moral discourse is justified to the extent that it produces desired effects. It is a natural corollary to this attitude that starting up the moral machinery in the first place should be subject to caution. So, our first explicit addition to preservationist conservationism to turn it into negotiationism is the imposition of strictures regulating when to moralize at all. It goes without saying that it is hard to know in general when a moralized discourse will be pragmatically justified, but some thoughts on the matter are worth considering.

If one enters into discussion with people who have already moralized an issue, and it seems that they will not consider a demoralized approach to the issue as worthy of serious response (a kind of situation that is not uncommon, we believe), a moralized approach may indeed be the best. The same goes *a fortiori* for a situation where the people engaged are aggressively moralistic. But if there is room for shifting the focus from explicitly moral categorizations to other practical ones, such as welfare and people's interests (or whatever runs the error theorist's pragmatic machinery), it may be advisable to abstain from moralizing in the hope that the issue at hand may be discussed and resolved with a view to these practical considerations. And where demoralization seems unattainable, a reframing of the moral values at stake may be feasible. This kind of move is discussed by Atran and Axelrod (2008), and the general idea is that, while "sacred" values are normally not negotiable (except in trade for likewise "sacred" values from the opposing side), they sometimes are sufficiently elastic or vague to admit reframing. The value of *equality*—"sacred" in the US, for example—has shown an impressive elasticity (from being seen as consistent with voting rights only for white men with property to today's ideal of equal opportunity). Likewise, the ideal of *Jihad* as a sacred duty may range from being conceived as the inner struggle to preserve one's own belief in God to an all-but-paramount injunction to actual violent war against those who in any way threaten Islam.

Such elasticity opens up the possibility for reframing values to make them more negotiable, a move that is often made possible by the sacred values being tied to things that may actually be accessible from the negotiating table, and thus fruitfully reframable. For example, Atran and Axelrod offer the following speculation about the possibility of reframing the "sacred" value of Jerusalem as the Palestinian capital, by reframing the area considered holy:

> If Palestinians, who simply refer to Jerusalem as "The Holy" (Al Quds), can reframe their idea of the city to include only its Arab suburbs and part of the Temple Mount (Haram Al-Sharif), then Israel might be willing to accept the Palestinian capital there. Constructively reframing the issue of Jerusalem in this way need not call into question "the strength of attachment" to the sacred value of Jerusalem.
>
> *(2008: 236)*

So, where a wise negotiationist does not see any possibility for demoralizing, she should consider the possibilities for fruitful reframing of "sacred" values. Our second and third additions to conservationism, to yield negotiationism, are thus recommendations to look for possibilities and possible benefits of demoralizing the relevant issue, and of reframing "sacred" values under dispute.

From an error theoretic perspective, moral disagreement or conflict will often seem suited for *negotiations* rather than collective inquiry aiming to converge on the true or correct answer. Conflicts suited for negotiations rather than inquiry are just those where no true answer is forthcoming. This does not mean that issues suited for negotiation are less urgent or important; it means only that other means of pursuing the discussion are more likely to be appropriate. For one thing, even though unanimity may often be a good thing, in situations suited for negotiation there is no requirement of unanimity. The best solution to a negotiated issue may have aspects that are unfortunate according to all the involved parties. There is, however, no need to worry that the *correct* solution is being overlooked. There is a legitimate worry that the *best* (as judged separately by the parties involved) may not be found, but that is another matter. The parties have to find a solution that all sides can go along with, given the circumstances.

Negotiationism sits well with error theory and provides the flexibility that different kinds of interaction demand. When entering discussion, there is, for the negotiationist, always the question of *how* to pursue the discussion. In particular, there is the question whether it should be conducted in a moralized fashion or not, and the further question of how any moral considerations that cannot be eliminated should be framed. And the negotiationist may naturally regard proactive moralization as a move in the negotiation; for example, saying that a certain course of action is "morally wrong" is to make a move indicating that one will not budge from that position (lest there are very tempting counter-offers in the other side's moral currency). A negotiationist may thus opt even for heavily moralized discourse in situations where it is effective to signal unfaltering commitment. Unfaltering commitment is admittedly one of the finest accomplishments (and dangers) of morality. The moralization of an issue may thus function as an ersatz moral commitment in ongoing negotiations. Of course, it will not be an *actual* unfaltering moral commitment, but the signal is sent and it may play a role in the discussion. This view of moralized discourse as containing ersatz moral commitments also carries the benefit that taking such a standpoint is not tantamount to locking down further nudging and compromise, as *real* unfaltering commitment does. As a move in a negotiation, the moral standpoint functions as a signal that this is final and not a matter for compromise, but as a negotiationist one need not take *that* as final.

Let us sum up. The negotiationist endorses conservationism in its preservationist version and supplements it with systematic consideration of proper occasions for conservationist moralization, paying close attention to such things as the degree of moralization of the issue, the depth of its moralization, and degree of open-mindedness of those involved, as well as the possibilities of reframing moral values that cannot be eliminated. The rule of thumb is to moralize just as much as is needed and to try and work towards demoralization when feasible. Furthermore, the "morality card" should be played as a move in a negotiation, as an ersatz moral commitment sending the signal that one has this "sacred" value to protect and that any serious counter-offer must be in kind.

Negotiationism is not neat or simple, just as we promised at the outset, but it just might work. And this should be good enough for serious consideration.

Notes

1 Notable contributions include Mackie 1977, 1980; Hinckfuss 1987 (excerpted in this volume); Joyce 2001; Garner 2007; Cuneo & Christy 2011; Olson 2011, 2014; Lutz 2014.
2 For a discussion of some details concerning the formulation of moral error theory, which we do not need to worry about here, see Olson (2014: 11–15).
3 For variations of such considerations, see, e.g., Mackie 1977; Lewis 1989; Joyce 2006; Olson 2014; Streumer 2017; Kalf 2018.
4 This is the kind of question Mackie (1977) sets out to answer after having established error theory.
5 See, e.g., Cuneo 2007; Olson 2014; Streumer 2017.
6 Olson 2011, 2014.
7 The converse is certainly possible too: among the ends that an error theorist cares most strongly about might be holding true and consistent beliefs and avoiding false and inconsistent ones, as well as being honest in conversation with others. In order to realize these ends, the error theorist will have to jettison moral thought and discourse and adopt abolitionism. However, our discussion proceeds on the assumption that the error theorist does not give overriding priority to ends concerning truth and consistency in belief and honesty in conversation. We thank Frans Svensson and Krister Bykvist for discussion here.
8 For a classical discussion, see Sidgwick ([1907] 1981: 489).
9 Abolitionism has recently been defended by Stephen Ingram (2015), who argues in particular that abolitionism and moral realism make for an interesting package.

10 For example, Joyce 2001; Nolan et al. 2005; Olson 2011, 2014.

11 Joyce 2001: ch. 8.

12 See Joyce (2001: 187ff.). It should be noted that Joyce's fictionalism is of the *revolutionary* kind. According to *hermeneutic* fictionalism, by contrast, ordinary moral thought and discourse is already fictionalist, i.e., akin to thought and discourse about Sherlock Holmes. In this chapter, we disregard hermeneutic fictionalism, since, if it is true, our leading question does not arise.

13 This problem is also discussed in Olson (2011, 2014) and in Cuneo & Christy (2011).

14 This is argued, by way of examples, in Olson (2011, 2014: ch. 9).

15 The following three paragraphs recapitulate material from Olson (2011, 2014).

16 Joyce seems at one point to hold that it is part of the meaning of moral claims that they express conative attitudes. See Joyce (2006: 54–57, 70); see also Joyce (2010). In our view it is more plausible that moral claims conversationally implicate imperatives. For a classical study of conversational implicature, see Grice (1989).

17 Thinking certain non-moralized thoughts might have the same kind of effects. For example, the thought that stealing would make one a thief might evoke the belief that one normally dislikes thieves, which, in conjunction with the desire not to become the object of one's own dislike, might bolster self-control. Thinking moralized thoughts, however, is likely to be especially effective in this regard, due to the strong correlation between moral judgments and motivationally efficacious attitudes of likes and dislikes.

18 Moral conservationism is rather similar to what Terence Cuneo and Sean Christy (2011) call "moral propagandism" (cf. Joyce 2001: 214). Propagandism, just as conservationism, recommends that we keep a moralized discourse, but just for illocutionary effect, as it were. Propagandism adds the recommendation that the truth of moral error theory be kept a secret among an enlightened elite (Joyce likens the view to "Government House Utilitarianism," 2001: 214). The Joycean fictionalist withholds assertoric force from moral judgments, whereas both the conservationist and the propagandist allow and indeed cherish full assertoric force for the greater good of effective persuasion and motivational fortification (in the intrapersonal case).

19 The "how" question concerns, e.g., the suitable degree of intensity with which to employ moral arguments, and the suitable degree of willingness to compromise.

20 For evidence that inequality actually has such widespread adverse effects, see Pickett & Wilkinson (2009).

References

Atran, S. & Axelrod, R. 2008. "Reframing sacred values." *Negotiation Journal* 24: 221–246.

Blackburn, S. 1993. "Errors and the phenomenology of value." In S. Blackburn, *Essays in Quasi-Realism*. Cambridge: Cambridge University Press. 149–165.

Cuneo, T. 2007. *The Normative Web*. Oxford: Oxford University Press.

Cuneo, T. & Christy, S. 2011. "The myth of moral fictionalism." In M. Brady (ed.), *New Waves in Metaethics*. Basingstoke: Palgrave Macmillan. 85–102.

Garner, R. 2007. "Abolishing morality." *Ethical Theory and Moral Practice* 10: 499–513.

Ginges, J., Atran, S., Medin, D., & Shikaki, K. 2007. "Sacred bounds on rational resolution of violent political conflict." *Proceedings of the National Academy of Sciences* 104: 7357–7360.

Grice, P. 1989. *Studies in the Way of Words*. Cambridge, MA: Harvard University Press.

Hinckfuss, I. 1987. *The Moral Society: Its Structure and Effects*. Discussion Papers in Environmental Philosophy 16. Canberra: Philosophy Program (RSSS), Australian National University.

Ingram, S. 2015. "After moral error theory, after moral realism." *Southern Journal of Philosophy* 53: 227–248.

Joyce, R. 2001. *The Myth of Morality*. Cambridge: Cambridge University Press.

Joyce, R. 2006. *The Evolution of Morality*. Cambridge, MA: MIT Press.

Joyce, R. 2010. "Expressivism, motivation internalism, and Hume." In C. Pigden (ed.), *Hume on Motivation and Virtue*. Basingstoke: Palgrave Macmillan. 30–56.

Kalf, W. F. 2018. *Moral Error Theory*. Basingstoke: Palgrave Macmillan.

Lewis, D. 1989. "Dispositional theories of value." *Proceedings of the Aristotelian Society* (supp. vol.) 63: 113–137.

Lutz, M. 2014. "The 'now what' problem for error theory." *Philosophical Studies* 171: 351–371.

Mackie, J. L. 1977. *Ethics: Inventing Right and Wrong*. London: Penguin.

Mackie, J. L. 1980. *Hume's Moral Theory*. New York: Routledge

Nolan, D., Restall, G., & West, C. 2005. "Moral fictionalism versus the rest." *Australasian Journal of Philosophy* 83: 307–330.

Olson, J. 2011. "Getting real about moral fictionalism." In R. Shafer-Landau (ed.), *Oxford Studies in Metaethics, Vol. 6*. Oxford: Oxford University Press. 181–204.

Olson, J. 2014. *Moral Error Theory: History, Critique, Defence*. Oxford: Oxford University Press.

Pickett, K. & Wilkinson, R. 2009. *The Spirit Level: Why Greater Equality Makes Societies Stronger*. London: Allen Lane.

Sidgwick, H. [1907] 1981. *The Methods of Ethics*. Indianapolis: Hackett.

Stevenson, C. L. 1937. "The emotive meaning of ethical terms." *Mind* 46: 14–31.

Streumer, B. 2017. *Unbelievable Errors: An Error Theory About All Normative Judgements*. Oxford: Oxford University Press.

8

MINIMIZING THE MISUSE OF MORALITY

Jessica Isserow

Introduction

According to moral error theorists, moral discourse is guilty of a systematic error, and so no positive first-order moral claims can be true. The striking consequence of a moral error theory is that nothing is morally right or wrong. Needless to say, this position doesn't exactly make for a good first impression; claims to the effect that there is nothing wrong with torturing kittens to pass the time are bound to strike us as counter-intuitive. Yet moral error theory has gained traction in recent years, and continues to rack up plausibility points.[1] Accordingly, many have thought it prudent to develop a contingency plan: if the moral error theory turns out to be true, then what ought we to do with our moral practices?

An increasingly popular response is to recommend that we do away with our moral practices altogether—that we cease using moral language, thinking moral thoughts, and invoking moral considerations when deliberating about what we ought to do. This is the route recommended by moral abolitionists, who take our moral practices to be harmful on balance (Hinckfuss 1987; Garner 1994, 2007; Greene 2002; Burgess 2007; Marks 2013; Ingram 2015). Since moral discourse can boast neither truth nor usefulness, abolitionists think that we have doubly good reason to get rid of it.[2] In their view, we ought to consign talk of moral rights and duties to the same scrap heap as talk of witches, phlogiston, and dragons.

Why think that our moral practices are on balance harmful, though? In defense of this claim, a common abolitionist strategy is to put forward an Argument from History (AFH). Though this style of argument is rarely laid out in a careful manner (more on which below), it comprises two key steps: a reminder of morality's supposedly grim past, and a warning of an equally grim future if appropriate action (i.e., abolition) is not taken. The first step is often anchored in concrete examples, which are taken to show that our moral practices exacerbate interpersonal conflict, too often lend a helping hand to war and violence, and render our societies authoritarian and elitist—to name just a few complaints (see Hinckfuss 1987, §§2.3–2.4, §4.2, excerpted in this volume; Greene 2002: 238; Garner 2007: 502–503; Ingram 2015: 240–241). In what follows, I will suggest that neither the first step nor the transition to the second is as straightforward as it may initially appear.

Before proceeding, however, let me note two important qualifications regarding abolitionists' ambitions. First, and *qua* moral error theorists, abolitionists are obviously not complaining that morality has been used for *immoral* purposes. Their real contention is that war, oppression, and the like, are contrary to our practical interests, and that these are precisely the sorts of things that morality tends to help along. Second, abolitionists do not aim to show that morality can be used *only* in service of malicious ends. What they wish to bring to our attention is the remarkable *pliability* of moral considerations. History suggests that we can offer a moral justification for just about any agenda, whether harmful or beneficial. Since morality can easily be put to harmful use, it would appear to be an especially dangerous tool—and one that perhaps we'd be better off without. Though it will be admitted that morality can be used for (non-morally) good purposes, we have ample evidence that it can be used for (non-morally) bad purposes as well.[3] And, though the good here may be very good, the bad seems especially horrid.

In this chapter, I evaluate the abolitionist's case and find it wanting. My first order of business will be to draw out the finer lineaments of the AFH (section 1). Doing so is needed, for abolitionists are seldom clear on the details here. The task for section 2 will be to assess what I take to be the most promising variety of the AFH, according to which moral considerations have often made things worse than they otherwise would have been. As we shall see, the abolitionist has a slight penchant for exaggeration. Though moral factors plausibly had a role to play, their role is not nearly as central as she would have us believe. This is not to suggest that the abolitionist's concerns are entirely baseless; she is correct in thinking that morality has the potential to exacerbate social hierarchies and oppression. However, she is wrong in thinking that this supports her abolitionism, for there are means by which we can minimize these abuses of the moral overlay. In section 3, I propose that we can do so by attending to the non-moral factors that typically underlie morality's misuse. I conclude that the AFH supports better standards of education and critical thinking going forward, rather than an abolitionist response to moral error theory.

1. The Argument From History

Abolitionists are particularly fond of drawing attention to morality's bad track record. Ian Hinckfuss points towards the massacre of the moral Catholic highlanders by the moral Protestants at Culloden and its aftermath, the genocide of the peaceful and hospitable stone-age Tasmanians by people from moral Britain, the mutual slaughter of all those dutiful men on the Somme and on the Russian front in World War I, the morally sanctioned slaughter in World War II . . . and the subsequent slaughter in Korea, Vietnam, Northern Ireland and the Middle East—all this among people the great majority of whom wanted above all to be good and who did not want to be bad.

(1987: §2.2)

Stephen Ingram pays special attention to the role that moral considerations have played in helping along social oppression:

If your group is in the business of subjugating some other group, one effective way to help sustain that subjugation is to convince everyone that your group is more competent at moral judgement . . . Plausibly, such methods have been used throughout history to help sustain oppressive social hierarchies. Take, for example, the subjugation of women. Opponents of women's suffrage commonly argued that married women did not need the vote because they would be best represented by their husbands.

(2015: 238–239)

These are the sorts of claims that characterize what I have dubbed the "AFH." The purpose of drawing our attention to these historical samplings is to motivate the idea that our moral practices are on balance harmful. Moral considerations are pliable; they can be used to further harmful agendas as well as desirable ones. Social conflict and oppression are bad enough on their own. Any mechanism that helps them along is surely (the thought goes) something we can do without.

Unfortunately, abolitionists are seldom explicit about the finer details here. It isn't clear, for example, who is included in the scope of this "we"—just whose interests are frustrated by these moralized agendas? Oppression and war are certainly not contrary to *everyone's* interests; profiteers and warmongers, for instance, often stand to gain. I will assume in what follows that by "we" abolitionists mean to refer to *most* of us, who presumably want to avoid an untimely demise, see to it that others are well, and live in a stable and cooperative society. Not everyone has these ends, of course. (Sensible knaves remain.) But we need not require that abolitionism be sound advice for everyone. It need only be sound advice for most of us, who share a broad variety of interests and concerns.

There is further ground-clearing work to be done. It's not obvious what sort of role abolitionists take morality to have played in these samples from our history: does morality make bad things happen, or does it simply make things far worse? It's also not entirely clear why abolitionists take moral considerations to have been especially helpful in promoting these unfortunate agendas. Addressing these questions will be useful for the purposes of distinguishing more plausible varieties of the AFH from those that can be dispensed with rather quickly.

1.1 The Role of Morality

Abolitionists argue that moral considerations have played an important role in their depressing catalog of historical events. But there are different roles that moral considerations may be thought to have played. One possibility is the following:

> **Strong role**
> Moral considerations were counterfactually responsible for these unfortunate events.

On this reading of the AFH, the unfortunate events in question would not have come to pass had it not been for the moral justifications that were offered in support of them. Certain remarks from abolitionists suggest that they intend to put forward this strong claim. Joshua Greene (2002) seems to think that nations could not garner requisite support for aggressive foreign policies without moral language:

> One might go so far as to say that nations require the language of moral realism to marshal popular support for aggressive actions. Has a military aggressor ever not claimed a moral right to carry out its plans? Has a nation ever been moved to war by leaders who said, "It would be good for us economically, and we can get away with it, so why not?"
>
> *(2002: 238)*

I think that we can safely dispense with this strong variant of the AFH, for our answer to Greene's question ought to be a resounding *yes*. I take it that Genghis Khan did not have to tread carefully around his marauders' moral sensibilities, ensuring that they felt morally justified in riding off to rape and pillage.[4] Desires for glory and conquest appear to have been sufficiently strong motivators. Of course, identifying the full range of causal factors involved in any particular historical episode is difficult. But identifying unwelcome social agendas that succeed without morality is not. Wall Street profiteers do not seem to require any moral justification to advance their own financial interests at others' expense. *Pace* Greene, "We can get away with it, so why not?" can sometimes suffice.

Let us therefore set to the side the proposal that moral considerations were needed for war efforts (etc.) to gain a foothold. Perhaps their contribution is better characterized as follows:

> **Moderate role**
> Moral considerations were causally sufficient for these unfortunate events.

One finds this suggestion in Hinckfuss (1987, excerpted in this volume). In maintaining that moral societies (i.e., those that participate in the institution of morality) are "elitist, authoritarian," and "inefficient in the resolution of conflicts," he does not intend to suggest that they would not be this way were they not *moral* societies. His claim is that that "the way morality perpetuates itself within a society is *causally sufficient* for the perpetuation and aggravation of these aspects of society" (1987: §2.2, emphasis added).

As I understand Hinckfuss's suggestion, it is perfectly possible that an *amoral* society could be elitist and authoritarian; morality is certainly not necessary for things to go awry. This is plausible. But the flip side of the sufficiency claim is not. Hinckfuss seems to think that introducing moral practice into a peaceful and well-functioning society would be enough to send it on the path to rack and ruin. And that seems false. Just how morality manifests itself within a society will presumably depend upon the nature of that society: its members, its social organization, and the like. I defer further development of this idea to section 2. If what I have to say there is right, then the moral edifice is certainly not enough to render a society conflict-ridden, authoritarian, and elitist (though a healthy dose of ignorance and insensitivity may sometimes suffice).

But all is not lost for the AFH. Even if morality was neither necessary nor sufficient for these atrocities, it is still possible that things would not have been nearly *as bad* were it not for moral considerations. The abolitionist may accord the following weaker role to moral considerations:

Weak role
Moral considerations made things worse than they otherwise would have been.

Quite a few abolitionists seem to have this weaker role in mind. Ingram (2015: 238) concedes that moral considerations do not themselves generate social hierarchies, but argues that they help to perpetuate them. Richard Garner does not think that moral conviction is what leads people to war, but he does think that moral considerations have often made things worse, since they can be used to "justify inflicting any cruelty deemed necessary for victory" (2007: 507). I take this weak variant of the AFH to be the most promising, and so I will assume in what follows that it is this argument that must be reckoned with.

There is one final matter in need of address. It is the abolitionist's contention that morality exacerbates war, oppression, and other social ills. But it's not obvious why portraying these agendas in a moral light would serve to make them even worse. Our final ground-clearing task will be to ascertain why abolitionists take morality to have such far-reaching consequences.

1.2 Why Morality?

A common theme underlying the AFH is that morality exacerbates interpersonal conflict, something which abolitionists put down to two factors.

First, as we have seen, moral considerations are *pliable*—they can be recruited to support almost any agenda. When someone breaks a promise to me, I may be quick to tout the values of honesty and commitment. But should I find myself guilty of any promise-breaking, I can instead elect to emphasize the greater good that was served by my actions. Perhaps the problem isn't too concerning for such trifling cases. But a substantial worry suggests itself once we consider more sinister agendas. Greene notes that terrorists "can justify their actions in terms that sound eerily similar to those used by their victims in other contexts" (2002: 237). Given this pliability, moralized conflicts seem especially difficult to resolve; it is difficult to convince the terrorist to come around if each of us can take morality to be on our side. One might suspect that inter-societal conflict is an inevitability in any case, but the problem is closer to home. Garner notes that morality can help along intra-social conflicts as well: "If the issue is not moralized, Roe v. Wade looks like a sensible compromise between two extreme positions, but when the right to life is set against the right to choose, neither side can yield without violating morality" (2007: 502).

Second, there is a distinct kind of *obstinance* that moral conviction seems to legitimize. This isn't to say that we don't butt heads over non-moral matters as well; we might disagree, for instance, over how to best divide an inheritance, or how to budget for an upcoming wedding. But at least, in cases of conflicting preferences and interests, there seems to be a light at the end of the tunnel; compromise isn't typically off the table. Yet matters seem different in moral disagreement. If I think that we morally ought to refrain from genocide, and you think that we ought to go for it, then ought I to meet you halfway by agreeing to wipe out just half of the relevant population? I don't think so. It seems that we often feel entitled to stand our ground when we butt heads over moral issues (Enoch 2011: ch. 2).

Some abolitionists have proposed to explain this obstinance by appealing to the idea that we invest moral requirements with *categorical authority* (Ingram 2015: 239–241). The demands of morality present themselves as inescapable; we take ourselves to have reason to comply with them independently of our ends (see Joyce 2001). This goes some way towards explaining why we tend to remain obstinate in the face of moral conflict. We may very well have ends that would be well served by reaching an amicable compromise. But insofar as one party takes the termination of fetuses to be wrong, they take themselves to have categorical reasons to oppose it—and such reasons do not cease to apply when they frustrate an agent's other ends.

These two aspects of morality make for a precarious marriage. The problem is not only that we can recruit a moral justification in service of almost any agenda.

Once these agendas have garnered moral support, they are apt to be seen as giving rise to inescapable obligations. I will not take issue with these claims in what follows. There are more important places to push. I think that we need to question the extent to which morality plausibly contributes to the harms that abolitionists have in mind. Later, I will suggest that we should also be deeply suspicious of the inference from morality's harmful potential to the recommendation that we do away with it.

2 Other Culprits

According to abolitionists, moral considerations have played an important role in the massacres and oppressive social structures of history, making matters worse than they otherwise would have been. I should acknowledge from the outset that this claim is not easy to assess. We can speculate, of course. But it is incredibly difficult to state with any great confidence how history would look without talk of moral rights, duties, and obligations. In any event, it is certainly not something that we ought to be confident of coming to know merely as a result of armchair speculation.

Let me be clear: I am no historian. My strategy will not be to tirelessly tease apart the many potentially relevant causal factors at play, finally arriving at a principled conjecture as to whether things would have been just as grim without morality. Instead, I shall simply grant to the abolitionist that moral considerations exacerbated the atrocities that she invites us to consider. Even granting this, I think there is something to be gained from turning our attention to the many non-moral factors at play. As we shall see (in section 3), doing so puts us in a position to challenge the assumption that the relevant harms are unavoidable.

2.1 Religion and Intolerance

I want to devote some space now to examining the non-moral factors that have plausibly helped along war and oppressive social structures. Needless to say, religion has often been an important contributing factor. The Crusades in Jerusalem were driven by a Christian objective to reclaim the Holy Land from Muslims; the Thirty Years' War was spurred by Protestants' refusal to comply with Ferdinand II's attempt to impose Catholicism upon them; and the French Wars of Religion were, at least in great part, the result of Catholics' intolerance towards Huguenots.

As far as social subordination is concerned, the role of religion in facilitating oppression can hardly be overstated. The inferiority of women is enshrined in religious scripture—as is the validity of slavery. Religious teachings can also legitimize the status quo in the minds of both oppressor and oppressed. Kevin Bales notes that for many slaves in Mauritania (which uses Sharia as its legal system), freedom is a dismal prospect. Deeply believing that God wants and expects them to be loyal to their masters, they reject freedom as wrong, even traitorous. To struggle for liberty, in their view, is to upset God's natural order and puts one's very soul at risk.

(1999: 108)

I do not want to pretend here that morality is easily dissociable from religion. Religious teachings do, after all, prescribe and prohibit certain kinds of behavior, and these directives are seldom free of moral language. Indeed, it is sometimes customary to interpret people of faith as (tacit) champions of a distinct kind of metaethical position, according to which God's will is the source of moral obligations. Religious wars and oppression may very well have been fueled by a sense of moral duty.

That said, we shouldn't swiftly infer that a sense of moral duty is what's doing the heavy lifting in these cases. Religious belief-systems tend to come prepackaged with threats to the non-compliant: a smite from above, an eternity of damnation, and the like. And a fear of divine reprisal has motivational force; whatever one's considered moral judgment on the matter of war and oppression, the threat of fire and brimstone can surely suffice to motivate supporting a religious agenda. The promise of avoiding divine reprisal was especially salient to those participating in the Crusades, who were promised absolution from their sins.

Religious conviction also has the potential to breed intolerance. The religiously affiliated have been found to be more intolerant of ethnic minorities than the unaffiliated (Allport & Kramer 1946; Hall, Matz & Wood 2010). Religious fundamentalism in particular seems highly correlated with prejudicial attitudes (Altemeyer & Hunsberger 1992; Kirkpatrick 1993; Hunsberger 1996).[5] And intolerance can certainly help along social oppression. The intolerant feel no need to refrain from exercising their power to interfere with others.[6] Even if religion is not easily dissociable from morality, then, it is far from obvious that a sense of moral duty is the dominant force at play in the cases to which the abolitionist appeals. Many of these atrocities were likely helped along by prejudicial attitudes as well.

2.2 Ideological Factors

The above considerations notwithstanding, we do need to be wary of using religion for target practice. The two world wars were not carried out in the name of faith. Nor has oppression always been rooted in religious belief-systems. Other sorts of ideologies have also proven effective in sustaining social hierarchies.

The Sambia of Papua New Guinea are an interesting case. The general attitude towards women in Sambia society is one of contempt; "abusive language, squabbling, and wife-beating, as well as suicides resulting from some such incidents, are pervasive in Sambia life" (Herdt 1982: 194). Hostility towards women is rooted in Sambia ideology, which prizes masculinity and takes women to be its greatest threat. In order for boys to transition to manhood, they must be removed from the contaminating influence of women (especially their mothers) at age 10, ingest the semen of older males during coming-of-age ceremonies, and undergo induced nose-bleeding to purge them of female contaminants that inhibit male growth (the latter continues throughout life). None of these aspects of Sambia ideology seems distinctively moral; masculinity very much seems to be a non-moral ideal—one that men are prepared to go to great lengths to achieve.[7]

That ideologies can breed contempt comes as no surprise—Nazism is a commonly cited example. Nazi ideology combined an especially toxic nationalism with an emphasis on racial purity. Added into the mix was a deep-seated anti-Semitism: many of the country's social and economic woes were put down to the scheming interference of German Jewry (mistakenly, I hasten to add). Once again, the boundaries can be murky; it is not unlikely that certain aspects of Nazi ideology may have been moralized. Nonetheless, many facets of Nazism can plausibly be taken to have represented people's non-moral values and preferences: values attached to racial purity and ambitions for territorial expansion, for example.

2.3 Epistemic Complacency

The list above should not be surprising; religion, intolerance, and ideological factors are the usual suspects. But there is a further suggestion that I want to develop here. It seems to me that there is one explanatory factor in particular that we find in almost all of these cases: many historical atrocities seem to have been marked by a staggering sort of *epistemic complacency*—an utter failure to carefully reason through the relevant issues or to challenge the dominant beliefs of the day. Many of the beliefs that these people held—beliefs regarding the legitimacy of slavery, the inferiority of women, or the contribution of the Jewish people to Germany's loss in World War I—were, by all appearances, simply taken for granted.[8]

It is my contention that epistemic complacency has played a substantial role in these samples from our past. This is, of course, an empirical hypothesis—one that would require further research and reflection before it could be pronounced with any greater confidence. But the hypothesis seems to have a high degree of *prima facie* plausibility; it is difficult to maintain that these undesirable social agendas would have been just as successful had the parties involved been epistemically *vigilant*. Showing that Nazism would have gained the traction that it did even if theories of racial purity and the stab-in-the-back-myth had been subjected to further scrutiny seems like a tall order (though I shall qualify my confidence somewhat in section 2.4).

The epistemic complacency hypothesis certainly seems to have something going for it, but let me say a little more to motivate it. It's important to appreciate that a culture's (dominant) moral belief-systems are seldom—if ever—divorced from its stock of non-moral beliefs. So-called *caste societies* attach moral significance to hierarchy and social order, but their moral systems have long been intertwined with mystical beliefs concerning purity and pollution (Haidt 2012). For much of history, moral justifications were offered for the enslavement of people of color—but, again, we cannot ignore the influence of the non-moral beliefs held by the subordinators. They regarded the inferiority of their slaves as scientific fact; studies from phrenology, for instance, suggested to them that certain races were more "advanced" than others (Hanlon 2003). Though abolitionists tend to emphasize the role of people's moral convictions in helping along social subordination, it's difficult to shake the impression that people's inaccurate *non-moral* beliefs were the primary source of harm.[9] If they hadn't held these false beliefs, then it is far less likely that they would have been in a position to offer a moral justification for their oppressive practices.

None of this is to suppose that there was anything *epistemically special* about those involved. As Gideon Rosen points out when discussing the sexism of the 1950s, a failure to "see through a pervasive and well-protected ideology need not be a sign of culpable negligence or recklessness . . . It might just be a sign of ordinariness" (2003: 67–68). Epistemic complacency isn't restricted to the epistemically challenged; few wander through life reflecting upon or questioning the presuppositions of everyday thought.

Ordinary or not, however, epistemic complacency seems very much to have played a key role in the cases under consideration. Members of oppressive groups don't tend to be very open to the possibility that they might be mistaken about the legitimacy of their status. That women might have had equal intellectual potential to men is a consideration that seems to have given pause to few who lived before the 20th century. But if that's right, then the real root of the problem would appear to be bad reasoning, or false empirical beliefs. If the abolitionist is really concerned to prevent war and oppression, then, it seems to me that she needs to be casting a much wider net; she ought to be taking issue with human stupidity as well.

2.4 A Lack of Human Feeling

I have suggested that epistemic complacency played an important role in some regrettable moments of our history. However, it would be naive to think that cognitive shortcomings were the only culprit. It is unlikely that things would have been any better had Genghis Khan's marauding followers been paragons of epistemic rationality (indeed, they may have been far *worse*). It is not merely epistemic complacency, but also a lack of human feeling that can help along undesirable agendas. I intend to refer to something quite broad here: everything from unbridled selfishness to acute hatred. It is remarkable just how little thought Genghis Khan and his posse seem to have given to the suffering of their victims. But, of course, it is not only them who exhibited such insensitivity. A strong willingness to be self-serving appears to have been a significant contributory factor in many of the abolitionist's examples. It is not in the least bit surprising that the institution of slavery was favored by those who stood to gain economically, nor that the elite had a penchant for social stratification (see Enoch 2011: 192–193).

My tentative hypothesis, then, is that epistemic complacency and a lack of human feeling (especially when working in concert) were important and under-appreciated contributory factors in the cases that the abolitionist brings to our attention. This is not to suggest that all warmongering and oppression can be put down to human stupidity and selfishness. But we should be careful not to under-estimate the damage that ignorance and insensitivity can do.

2.5 Taking Stock

The non-moral factors singled out for mention above are not exhaustive. But they will suffice for my purposes. When put together, these factors seem to form a large part of the explanation for the atrocities to which the abolitionist appeals. It is not implausible that they sometimes would have sufficed. If anything, our dark past would seem to be over-determined. The case isn't dispositive by any means; it's difficult to tease apart the many causal factors at play here. Nonetheless, we do seem to have good grounds for doubting that moral considerations were the only—or the even most important—culprits.

But just what is to be inferred from all of this? At this stage, not much. I have suggested only that many non-moral factors operate in tandem with morality in the cases that abolitionists invite us to consider; I have not denied that our moral practices play some role in generating harm. That said, empha-sizing the contribution of non-moral factors is important in our argumentative context. Doing so helps us to identify some promising avenues for minimizing the misuse of morality.

3 Minimizing the Misuse of Morality

I have suggested that abolitionists tend to ignore (or, at least, significantly down-play) the role that non-moral factors have played in the atrocities that they bring to our attention.[10] But I have not denied that moral considerations have played a role in helping along wars and oppressive social structures. I am certainly willing to grant that morality has something to answer for here. Perhaps moral considera-tions weren't necessary for women's subordination, but it seems difficult to deny that they helped.

My arguments would therefore appear to leave the abolitionist in a comfort-able position. It may very well be true that war and systematic oppression have resulted largely from a lack of human feeling, bad reasoning, and false empirical beliefs, but those who engage in faulty reasoning and disseminate false informa-tion do walk among us. And, so long as they do, it seems imprudent to hand them any tools that would serve to make their actions even worse. What is important to appreciate at this stage, however, is that the abolitionist doesn't think that morality can be used only in service of malicious or self-serving agendas. She concedes that morality can be and has been used for good purposes as well. What the AFH really shows, then, is that morality can be of great benefit or great harm, depending upon the manner in which it is used. However, the right response to this problem isn't necessarily to do away with morality. A better response is surely to seek a means by which we can reap the relevant benefits while avoiding the associated costs.

Suppose that we could *not* reap the benefits of moral practice while avoiding the costs. In that case, the AFH may very well support abolitionism.[11] Morality might be said to carry far too much baggage; we could not hope to enjoy the relevant benefits without opening the door to (or worsening) oppression and war. But suppose that we *could* reap the benefits of moral practice while avoiding (or, at least, substantially minimizing) the costs. If this were so, then abolitionists wouldn't so much have motivated abolitionism as they would have motivated the need for reform.[12]

In what follows, I will argue not only that that there are tangible benefits of moral practice, but that we can conceivably reap these benefits while controlling for the costs. Simply put, there are means by which we can *minimize* the misuse of morality. I won't, however, rely upon the abolitionist's concession that morality can do some good to make my case. Instead, I shall introduce a new player into our dialectic—*the moralist*. The moralist thinks that our error-ridden moral practices are useful to us on balance. And she has an AFH of her own.

3.1 The Moralist's Argument From History

The moralist takes our moral practices to be incredibly useful (on balance), and so she holds that the appropriate response to moral error theory is one that preserves moral discourse in some form. This may amount to holding onto moral discourse in its current error-ridden form (Olson 2014; see also Eriksson & Olson, this volume). Or it might involve preserving moral language in the spirit of a useful fiction (Joyce 2001, 2005; Nolan, Restall, & West 2005). The moralist might even make use of a revised moral discourse—one that has been liberated from error (Lutz 2014). For our purposes here, there is no need to choose.

Why think that our moral practices are on balance useful, though? In defense of this claim, the moralist advances her own argument from history. She argues that our moral systems have often been instrumental in overthrowing oppressive regimes, and putting an end to war and violence. Here, she draws our attention to morality's *good* track record: the role of moral values in the eradication of slavery, and the importance of women's rights discourse in their liberation from domestic servitude, and so forth. The moralist does not pretend that morality can be used only in service of desirable ends; she acknowledges that it can be put to harmful use as well. Nonetheless, she insists that there is ample evidence that moral considerations can be put to very good use indeed. And though the bad here may be rather bad, the good is especially helpful.

Moreover, and as the moralist is keen to emphasize, moral considerations offer us a particularly effective means of *countering* harmful uses of morality. Moral conviction might reinforce oppressive social structures, but it is also of great help in overturning them. As Caroline West notes:

> Ideas such as that women have a moral *right* to be treated with equal concern and respect, that current unequal social arrangements are *unjust*, that sexual discrimination is *wrong*, that men *ought* not be differentially advantaged, and so on, function as a check on the behavior of the powerful, protecting the comparatively powerless from suffering further at their hands.
>
> *(2010: 192)*

Thus, morality doesn't just get us into these unhappy situations, it's also often what gets us out. Slavery in the US might have been reinforced by twisted moral values, but the abolitionist movement was driven by moral conviction as well. On first appearances, this might not seem like much of a defense, for we presumably could have done without the years of systematic oppression in between. But recall the lessons of section 2. If we are right in thinking that much of our depressing past was over-determined—that religious differences, selfishness, or intolerance would, in many cases, have sufficed—then we should count ourselves lucky that there were folk around whose moral convictions moved them to challenge the status quo.

Of course, the moralist must say something more about the role that she takes moral considerations to have played. It is not completely implausible that moral conviction may have been necessary for the eradication of slavery and the enfranchisement of women. But a weaker claim will serve her purposes: she need maintain only that moral considerations played a key supporting role—that they amplified prosocial tendencies and added momentum to campaigns for positive social change. Perhaps morality is not necessary for social progress, but it can often make progress easier to achieve.

Yet why is morality in particular useful for such purposes? The moralist's answer parallels that of the abolitionist: moral demands have a distinct kind of practical import. When people judge that women have a *moral right* to be treated with equal concern, or consider their society *unjust*, they take themselves to have reasons to work against these oppressive social structures. And they take themselves to have such reasons independently of whether these arrangements happen to be to their benefit. Moral requirements are invested with *categorical authority*; they present themselves as inescapable demands. One cannot evade their force by citing an interest in non-compliance.

Of course, the moralist is an error theorist, and so regards the authority of morality as mere illusion. What is important is the instrumental value of a conceptual framework that presupposes such authority. When people conceive of oppressive social structures as the sorts of things that must be opposed independently of their ends, their motivation to work against them is likely to be stronger.[13]

Admittedly, there is no guarantee that morality will continue to play these roles once it is seen for the farce that it is. That will depend upon whether a fictional, revised, or conserved moral discourse proves an adequate stand-in for its error-ridden predecessor. But absent any reason for thinking that none of these proposals can deliver the goods, the moralist thinks that we have good reason to favor them over abolitionism.

3.2 How to Minimize the Misuse of Morality

Having made her case, the moralist concludes that it's not all doom and gloom when it comes to our moral past. She concedes that the abolitionist has identified a significant problem. However, she takes that problem to be surmountable.

To address the abolitionist's challenge, the moralist begins by revisiting the argument advanced in section 2. There it was claimed that epistemic complacency and a lack of human feeling have played a substantial role in many unfortunate incidents of history. Selfishness, and false empirical beliefs, though not the only culprits, have certainly helped along harmful social policies, allowing them to go about unchallenged.

The moralist takes these considerations to point toward a promising means by which we might minimize the misuse of morality. To begin with, we might cultivate people's dispositions to seek further evidence for their beliefs, to challenge existing dogmas, to question the ideologies to which they are exposed, and to carefully reason through the arguments in favor of competing social policies. In short, we might furnish ordinary folk with a philosophical toolkit of sorts—one that nurtures and encourages epistemic vigilance.

It's worth clarifying what this epistemic vigilance entails. It is certainly not the moralist's contention that oppression and violence can be curtailed by way of providing ordinary folk with the resources to acquire true *moral* beliefs. (She is, recall, a moral error theorist.) Her foremost ambition is to ensure that morality is not put to harmful use. And she thinks that we can partly circumvent this by preventing false *empirical* beliefs from gaining a foothold—beliefs in the inherent inferiority of other groups, say. By encouraging people to challenge or to further reflect upon the information that comes their way, we can hope to stop at least many harmful agendas in their tracks.

It should be noted that the case for epistemic vigilance doesn't rest *only* upon our interest in securing these particular benefits. We have good independent reasons to challenge what we take to be uncontroversial. Most of us care about acting in a way that furthers our ends, and we're generally better positioned to further those ends—whatever they may be—if we track truth effectively (see Kornblith 2001). However—and importantly—we are not epistemically infallible. Even that which strikes us as obvious may yet turn out to be false. This suggests a further reason to subject our beliefs to scrutiny (at least on a more regular basis) if we want to discover the truth.[14]

According to the moralist, then, it is reasonable to suppose that we can enjoy the benefits of the moral edifice while controlling for the costs. More specifically, we can work to prevent moral considerations from becoming attached to harmful agendas by encouraging epistemic vigilance—such agendas are less likely to gain a foothold if they have been subjected to scrutiny. When our empirical beliefs fall in line with the facts—facts regarding the equal intellectual potential of other groups, say—we are less likely to be in a position to offer a moral justification for warmongering and oppression.

But we are not done just yet. Though epistemic vigilance will be of considerable help, the moralist acknowledges that it is unlikely to put an end to all of our troubles. This becomes especially evident once we distinguish the participants from the promoters of conflict (e.g., the poor folk dying in the mud from those giving the orders). It may be in the interests of those in charge to encourage going to war (say), and they may be effective at manipulating others to do so (via skillful rhetoric or misinformation, perhaps) even with such epistemic safeguards in place. The problem is that we have restricted our attention to people's *beliefs* (or belief-forming methods). We have neglected to consider their *desires*; in particular, the degree to which they care for others. To the extent that people remain cruel and inconsiderate, the potential for morality's misuse is disquieting. When combined with a willingness to be self-serving, moral considerations will often make matters worse.

This suggests that better standards of evidence and critical thinking will need to be supplemented with particular emotional dispositions. We might, for instance, work to cultivate our capacities for empathy.[15] In coming to empathize more with others, we would be in a better position to understand and identify with their needs. This would by no means guarantee that we would quickly transition to a peaceful and loving society, but it could certainly encourage us to take others' needs into account more often when deciding what to do.[16]

The moralist hastens to add that we should not expect this strategy to be foolproof. She certainly does not mean to suggest that morality would never be put to harmful use if most of us grew to be more empathetic and epistemically responsible.[17] But we do not need this strategy to be foolproof to justify preserving our moral practices; it is not necessary to establish that these practices have no costs. We need only provide grounds for thinking that the cost–benefit analysis favors their continued use. So long as our moral practices confer distinctive benefits, and the relevant costs can be minimized (to a suitable degree), we would seem to do better to hold onto them.

Abolitionists have given us no reason for thinking that such harm-minimizing efforts would be unsuccessful. Indeed, they never seriously consider the possibility of minimizing these harms (at least, not to my knowledge). This is surprising. Abolitionists acknowledge that moral practice confers distinctive benefits. One might have expected them to have sought a means by which these benefits could be retained and the relevant harms avoided prior to recommending that we scrap the moral edifice altogether.

To summarize, abolitionists have plausibly established that morality can support war as well as peace, breed fanaticism as well as fellow feeling, and drive violence as well as positive social change. But they have not thereby established abolitionism. These arguments merely suggest that morality is something to be used with greater caution—not that it is something that shouldn't be used at all.

Conclusion

I have argued that abolitionists do not succeed in their ambitions. Morality may have helped along conflict and oppression, but this hardly supports doing away with morality. Indeed, history suggests that we have very good reasons to preserve our moral practices, for moral commitment may well be among our most effective tools for countering oppression and other social ills. None of this is to suggest that abolitionists are completely off the mark. Morality's harmful potential is concerning. But we can plausibly control for these harms. When people are furnished with better standards of evidence and are encouraged to take others' needs more seriously, harmful agendas are less likely to gain a foothold, and so moral justifications are less likely to be offered in support of them. This provides those who propose to preserve moral discourse in some form with reason to extend their focus beyond moral practice. Empathy and epistemic vigilance ought to be exercised alongside it.

Acknowledgments

I am very grateful to Edward Elliott, Benjamin Fraser, and Richard Joyce for feedback on earlier drafts of this chapter.

Notes

1 Moral error theory is no longer, as Stephen Finlay (2008) fondly describes it, merely an "antipodean view." It has earned sponsors not only in Mackie (1977), Hinckfuss (1987), Joyce (2001), and Pigden (2007), but also Garner (1990), Burgess (2007), Marks (2013), Olson (2014), and Sobel (this volume), among others.

2 Many abolitionists take moral error theory to lend support to their proposal (see Burgess 2007: 438; Garner 2007: 500). But abolitionism need not stand or fall with moral error theory. Quite a few abolitionists think that the significant practical costs of moral practice are *sufficient* to justify doing away with it (e.g., Hinckfuss 1987: §1.5). Some have been so bold as to suggest that even moral realists have good reason to do away with moral discourse (Ingram 2015).

3 Hereafter, I omit the "non-morally" qualification, and will intend for talk of goodness and badness to be interpreted, respectively, as talk of non-moral goodness or badness.

4 I thank Ben Fraser for the example.

5 My claim here is that religious conviction has the potential to breed intolerance—not that it always does. Indeed, studies suggest that the positive correlation between religious affiliation and intolerance is more robust for those with an "extrinsic religious orientation" (who use religion to further their other ends) than for those with an "intrinsic religious orientation" (who internalize the values of their faith) (see Allport & Ross 1967). Batson and Ventis (1982) propose that another orientation which involves searching for answers to existential questions—what they call "quest"—is associated with greater tolerance and sensitivity toward others.

6 I draw upon Cohen's (2004: 69) understanding of intolerance here.

7 I acknowledge that cleanly distinguishing non-moral ideals from moral ones is difficult, and it is not a task that I can hope to undertake here. I also recognize that on certain ways of carving things up, Samba ideology may very well qualify as moral. But the general point does not stand or fall with what we choose to say about this particular case. So long as people's non-moral values and ideals have demonstrated harmful potential—something which, I believe, quite a number of cases canvassed here show—it would seem unfair to lay all the blame at the feet of morality.

8 This is not to suggest that such matters were taken for granted *by all*. Coalitions of willing dissenters have certainly not been lost in the annals of history, and I shall have more to say about them in section 3.1. However—and to relay an observation that Goodrick-Clarke (1993: ix) credits to Konrad Adenauer—it is unlikely that Nazism could have gained the momentum that it did had it not "found, in broad strata of the population, soil prepared for its sowing of poison . . . Broad strata of the people, of the peasants, middle classes, workers and intellectuals did not have the right intellectual attitude."

9 I am not here endorsing the claim that all moral disagreements come down to disagreements over non-moral matters (see Brink 1984: 116–117; Boyd 1988: 213); I am endorsing only the more modest claim that people's (specific) moral beliefs tend to be shaped by their non-moral beliefs.

10 Though in fairness to Garner (1994), he acknowledges the contribution of religion as well.

11 The AFH wouldn't *necessarily* support abolitionism in this case, since the benefits of engaging in moral practice may still outweigh the costs. But it would at least give us good *prima facie* reason for thinking that the costs are much too high. And it seems that good *prima facie* reasons are all that can be hoped for in this context. Indeed, some have suggested that we ought to be agnostic as to whether morality does more harm than good (see, for example, Moeller 2009.)

12 Lenman anticipates this line of reply when he writes that "vile things are done in the name of moral ideals. But that is not a good objection to morality any more than the existence of bad music is a good reason to dislike music . . . Rather it is an objection to bad morals and to the stupid, twisted and pathological forms that moral motivation, like any kind of motivation, can sometimes take. It may sometimes favour reform but it hardly favours abolition" (2013: 397). Joyce (2001: 181) touches upon this issue as well: "My response to Hinckfuss's claim that moral beliefs have wrought such dramatic damage is that this just shows that people have had the wrong moral beliefs."

13 See Joyce (2001, 2006) for a number of convincing arguments in support of this claim.

14 I borrow here from Mill's justification for freedom of expression ([1859] 1977).

15 Some abolitionists (e.g., Garner 2007: 501; Hinckfuss 1987: §4.5) have suggested as much—though they do so in the context of arguing that we could make do without morality. It is surprising that they do not consider the implications of cultivating these capacities while preserving moral practice.

16 There is good evidence that empathy (or, at least many of the empathetic emotions) encourages prosocial behavior. See Eisenberg (2014).
17 Indeed, empathy may not be quite enough to promote other-regarding attitudes toward *everyone*. The empathetic emotions are vulnerable to a number of well-known biases; it is typically easier to empathize with those in the "here-and-now" (Hoffman 2015: 94, 81) or with those who are similar to us (Ugazio, Majdanžić, & Lamm 2015: 169–170). For this reason, empathy may very well function best when supplemented with moral judgments (along with reasonable empirical beliefs).

References

Allport, G. & Kramer, B. 1946. "Some roots of prejudice." *Journal of Psychology* 22: 9–39.
Allport, G. & Ross, J. 1967. "Personal religious orientation and prejudice." *Journal of Personality and Social Psychology* 5: 432–443.
Altemeyer, B. & Hunsberger, B. 1992. "Authoritarianism, religious fundamentalism, quest, and prejudice." *International Journal for the Psychology of Religion* 2: 113–133.
Bales, K. 1999. *Disposable People: New Slavery in the Global Economy*. Berkeley: University of California Press.
Batson, C. & Ventis, W. 1982. *The Religious Experience: A Social-Psychological Perspective*. New York: Oxford University Press.
Boyd, R. 1988. "How to be a moral realist." In G. Sayre-McCord (ed.), *Essays on Moral Realism*. Ithaca: Cornell University Press. 181–228.
Brink, D. 1984. "Moral realism and the sceptical arguments from disagreement and queerness." *Australasian Journal of Philosophy* 62: 111–125.
Burgess, J. 2007. "Against ethics." *Ethical Theory and Moral Practice* 10: 427–439.
Cohen, A. 2004. "What toleration is." *Ethics* 115: 68–95.
Eisenberg, N. 2014. "Empathy-related responding and its relations to socioemotional development." *Asia-Pacific Journal of Research in Early Childhood Education* 8: 1–17.
Enoch, D. 2011. *Taking Morality Seriously: A Defence of Robust Realism*. Oxford: Oxford University Press.
Finlay, S. 2008. "The error in the error theory." *Australasian Journal of Philosophy* 8: 347–369.
Garner, R. 1990. "On the genuine queerness of moral properties and facts." *Australasian Journal of Philosophy* 68: 137–146.
Garner, R. 1994. *Beyond Morality*. Philadelphia: Temple University Press.
Garner, R. 2007. "Abolishing morality." *Ethical Theory and Moral Practice* 10: 499–513.
Goodrick-Clarke, N. 1993. *The Occult Roots of Nazism: Secret Aryan Cults and Their Influence on Nazi Ideology*. New York: New York University Press.
Greene, J. 2002. *The Terrible, Horrible, No Good, Very Bad Truth about Morality and What to Do About it* (PhD dissertation). Department of Philosophy, Princeton University, New Jersey.
Haidt, J. 2012. *The Righteous Mind: Why Good People are Divided by Politics and Religion*. New York: Pantheon.
Hall, D., Matz, D., & Wood, W. 2010. "Why don't we practice what we preach? A meta-analytic review of religious racism." *Personality and Social Psychology Review* 14: 126–139.
Hanlon, C. 2003. "O. S. Fowler and hereditary descent." In M. Lowance Jr. (ed.), *A House Divided: The Antebellum Slavery Debates in America, 1776–1865*. Princeton: Princeton University Press.

Herdt, G. 1982. "Sambia nosebleeding rites and male proximity to women." *Ethos* 10: 189–231.

Hinckfuss, I. 1987. *The Moral Society: Its Structure and Effects*. Discussion Papers in Environmental Philosophy 16. Canberra: Philosophy Program (RSSS), Australian National University.

Hoffman, M. 2015. "Empathy, justice, and social change." In H. Maibom (ed.), *Empathy and Morality*. New York: Oxford University Press. 71–96.

Hunsberger, B. 1996. "Religious fundamentalism, right-wing authoritarianism, and hostility toward homosexuals in non-Christian religious groups." *International Journal for the Psychology of Religion* 6: 39–49.

Ingram, S. 2015. "After moral error theory, after moral realism." *Southern Journal of Philosophy* 53: 227–248.

Joyce, R. 2001. *The Myth of Morality*. Cambridge: Cambridge University Press.

Joyce, R. 2005. "Moral fictionalism." In M. Kalderon (ed.), *Fictionalism in Metaphysics*. Oxford: Oxford University Press. 287–313.

Joyce, R. 2006. *The Evolution of Morality*. Cambridge: Cambridge University Press.

Kirkpatrick, L. 1993. "Fundamentalism, Christian orthodoxy and intrinsic religious orientation as predictors of discriminatory attitudes." *Journal for the Scientific Study of Religion* 32: 256–268.

Kornblith, H. 2001. *Knowledge and Its Place in Nature*. Oxford: Oxford University Press.

Lenman, J. 2013. "Ethics without errors." *Ratio* 26: 391–409.

Lutz, M. 2014. "The 'now what' problem for error theory." *Philosophical Studies* 171: 351–371.

Mackie, J. L. 1977. *Ethics: Inventing Right and Wrong*. New York: Penguin.

Marks, J. 2013. *Ethics Without Morals: In Defence of Amorality*. New York: Routledge.

Mill, J. S. [1859] 1977. *On Liberty*. In J. Robson (ed.), *Collected Works*. Toronto: University of Toronto Press.

Moeller, H.-G. 2009. *The Moral Fool: A Case for Amorality*. New York: Columbia University Press.

Nolan, D., Restall, G. & West, C. 2005. "Moral fictionalism versus the rest." *Australasian Journal of Philosophy* 83: 307–330.

Olson, J. 2014. *Moral Error Theory: History, Critique, Defence*. Oxford: Oxford University Press.

Pigden, C. 2007. "Nihilism, Nietzsche and the doppelganger problem." *Ethical Theory and Moral Practice* 10: 441–456.

Rosen, G. 2003. "Culpability and ignorance." *Proceedings of the Aristotelian Society* 103: 61–84.

Ugazio, G., Majdanžić, J. & Lamm, K. 2015. "Are empathy and morality linked? Evidence from moral psychology, social and decision neuroscience, and philosophy." In H. Maibom (ed.), *Empathy and Morality*. New York: Oxford University Press. 155–171.

West, C. 2010. "Business as usual? The error theory, internalism, and the function of morality." In R. Joyce & S. Kirchin (eds.), *A World Without Values: Essays on John Mackie's Error Theory*. Dordrecht: Springer. 183–198.

9

MORAL FICTIONALISM

How to Have Your Cake and Eat It Too

Richard Joyce

1 Introduction

There are good reasons for thinking that moral discourse is hopelessly broken. Engaging sincerely in moral talk seems to commit speakers to properties like moral obligation, having moral rights, blameworthiness, virtue and vice, etc., and there are, on reflection, significant grounds (metaphysical, epistemological, and empirical) for doubting that the world we inhabit contains anything like these properties. Discovering this mismatch between two theses—a conceptual thesis (concerning what our moral discourse commits us to) and an ontological thesis (concerning what the world is like)—leads to the error-theoretic result that none of our moral judgments are true (see Mackie 1977; Joyce 2001; Olson 2014).[1]

Not many people accept an all-out moral error theory, though partial moral error theories are more familiar. The notion of *sin*, for example, which used to be fairly central to moral discourse (in the West, at least), has dropped from many people's normative conceptual scheme, meaning that even those who have no sympathy with radical moral skepticism may well, upon reflection, consider themselves to be error theorists about sin. Much the same might be true of *evil*. Needless to say, there are still many people who believe in sin and evil; my aim is just to draw attention to the familiarity of this kind of doubt (recognizable even to those who don't harbor the doubt) and thus to conceptualize all-out moral error theory as a familiar kind of doubt writ large: extending to all moral concepts.

An all-out moral error theory accuses widespread and customary ways of thinking and talking of a committing a massive mistake, and is to that extent a counter-intuitive position which may be safely predicted to meet with considerable heartfelt resistance. But the resistance is born not simply of the fact that people are generally opposed to admitting that they (and probably everyone they know) are wrong. It is also born of the fact that there is a certain anxiety surrounding what might *happen* if the moral error theory is true—or, at least, if it came to be widely believed to be true. Morality is the bedrock of a civilized society (the thought goes), and any theory that comes along claiming that it's all baloney is therefore dangerous and its advocates pernicious.

On the face of it, this chapter (like this whole volume) is not about arguments for and against the error-theoretic position; it is about what happens next, were that position to be adopted. But dig a little deeper and the distinction between these two questions is not so clear-cut. If resistance to the error theory is due partly to worries about what might *happen* if it were widely adopted, then addressing the "what happens next?" question becomes a prerequisite for deciding whether and/or how strenuously to resist the theory (see Lutz 2014: 370). If a persuasive case were to be made that we could adopt the error-theoretic position and civilization would not collapse—that life would go on as before, or even go on *better!*—then the opposition to the theory might diminish, or at the very least lose some of its determination.

The three positions that I shall critically assess in this chapter are abolitionism, conservationism, and fictionalism, and my general goal is to speak in favor of the last. Each of these positions is a competing answer to the question "If we were to adopt a moral error theory, then what should we do with our moral concepts?" In a nutshell, the abolitionist answers, "By and large, stop using them"; the conservationist answers, "Keep using them, including in moral beliefs"; and the fictionalist answers, "Keep using them, but not in moral beliefs." As I say, which answer is to be preferred should be of interest not just to those who are tempted by or convinced of the moral error theorist's arguments, since the answer may well inform whether to be tempted or convinced in the first place.

In section 3 I shall compare conservationism and fictionalism, and in section 4 I shall compare abolitionism and fictionalism. First, in section 2, I shall sketch out the three options in a bit more detail.

2 Abolitionism, Conservationism, and Fictionalism

If we were to adopt a moral error theory, then what should we do with our moral concepts? Clearly, the "should" cannot be interpreted as a moral "should," and, more generally, must survive unscathed the error theorist's arguments against morality. The natural thought (though it is by no means a mandatory one) is that it is to be understood in broadly Humean terms: as some kind of function of individuals' desires (desires which need not be selfish). Since we are talking about a plural "we," then the matter can be broken into two steps: what an individual should do is a function of her desires, and what a group should do is a function of what the individuals comprising the group should do. Both steps allow various options (consonant with Humeanism), but I'm happy to leave matters open here.

The important point is that whatever considerations have led the error theorist to doubt moral normativity are assumed not to apply to these Humean group norms, and a corollary of this assumption is that moral normativity essentially has a quality or qualities that Humeanism cannot satisfy. (These are contentious assumptions, to be sure, and well worth arguing over, but for current purposes it's a background supposition that those arguments have already fallen in the error theorist's favor.)

It's fair to say that, generally, when we have in the past become error theorists about something, then abolitionism is the usual response.[2] Of course, we don't entirely refrain from using words like "unicorn," "phlogiston," and "witch"—any more than the word "God" never escapes the lips of an atheist—but we do stop making assertions that commit us to the existence of these entities. The abolitionist with whom we are concerned may be interpreted as *doubly* opposed to a subject matter: she is opposed to an ontology (she doesn't believe in witches, say) and she is opposed to a language (she recommends that we by and large stop speaking of witches).[3] The assumption that the second form of opposition follows from the first may appear so obvious that arguing for the first (that is, arguing for an error theory) will seem sufficient for establishing the second. But the assumption is mistaken, and the second form of opposition requires independent argument. An ontology should be opposed if one comes to see it as probably *false* (on either empirical or *a priori* grounds), but one should oppose a use of language if one comes to see it as *inadvisable*. To reject moral language, then, the abolitionist must argue that it is inadvisable, and this requires an analysis of its costs and benefits. Not only is establishing a moral error theory insufficient for establishing abolitionism, nor is it necessary, for even someone who believes in moral facts can nevertheless decide that moral discourse is ill-advised on pragmatic grounds (see Campbell 2014; Ingram 2015).

Nobody, of course, would claim that making moral judgments is *always* harmful, and nobody would maintain that doing so is always beneficial. Making a moral judgment might be beneficial to the judge but harmful to others, or vice versa. Making a moral judgment might be useful to the judge on Monday but harmful to the judge on Friday. Whether making a moral judgment is harmful or beneficial may also be frequency-sensitive: dependent on whether others (and how many others) are also disposed to do so. Some of these complications can be put aside if it is stipulated that we are talking about a *group* (as the question posed at the start of this section presumes). But other complications remain. There is, of course, the question of which function from members' goals to group goals should be utilized in order to allow us to speak in Humean terms of "what the group should do." Yet, even if this were settled, it remains exceedingly implausible that making moral judgments will *always* be harmful to a group regardless of how it is situated, and so we shouldn't burden the abolitionist with any such far-fetched claim. Rather, the abolitionist's claim may be focused on *typical* human groups—that is, where resources are finite, where interests often come into conflict, where mutual benefits can be gained through cooperation, and so forth, and also where "typical" human psychology (cognitive skills, emotions, epistemic limits, etc.) is in play. If it turns out that the notion of "typicality" here is insupportable, then the abolitionist can always ground the claim in actuality: as a view about how costly morality is and has been for *us*. Several contributors to this volume—Garner, Hinckfuss, Marks, and Olsson Yaouzis—set out to highlight the negative impact of moral judgments, either generally or with regard to specific topics of discourse—often focusing on the costs and benefits for *us now*, though also frequently discussing historical scenarios (see also Isserow, this volume).

Recall, however, that the kind of abolitionist in whom we are interested doesn't simply claim that moral discourse and thinking is inadvisable; she is also an error theorist, arguing that moral discourse and thinking is untrue. Thus it is not really *us* on whom her cost-benefit analysis should focus, but rather some of our counterparts; that is, us *if we came to accept a moral error theory* (which, of course, we haven't, and nor are likely to in the foreseeable future). This potentially makes a significant difference, since the costs and benefits of morality for a group *that rejects error theory* may be different from the costs and benefits of morality for a group *that accepts error theory*.

At this point one could be forgiven for wondering whether the abolitionist has rather wasted her energies discussing current and historical harms caused by moral thinking, for these are all harms that befall/befell us *when morality is believed*. And surely (the thinking goes) if we were to accept a moral error theory then the option of believing morality would evaporate, and so those types of harm may no longer be pertinent.

This is where the proponent of the second option, conservationism, enters the picture. The conservationist insists that our becoming error theorists would *not* cause the option of believing in morality to evaporate. The conservationist accepts that morality is often harmful (both to the judge and/or to others), but thinks that the abolitionist has undersold the benefits it brings: on balance, the benefits outweigh the costs (for typically situated groups of humans). Yet these benefits, the conservationist observes, have historically depended on morality's being *believed*—and therefore the conservationist simply recommends that we carry on believing in morality as far as everyday decisions in everyday life go. We may *disbelieve* morality when doing metaethics (after all, the conservationist believes that the moral error theorist is correct, and when discussing metaethics will assert this), but the rest of the time—which is most of the time—the advisable course is that we should just carry on with our old moral discourse and old moral beliefs, both of which commit us (erroneously) to properties like moral obligation, having moral rights, blameworthiness, virtue and vice, etc.

It should be noticed that the world about which the conservationist conducts his cost-benefit analysis should not really be the actual world, for much the same reason as before: the costs and benefits of morality for a group *that rejects error theory entirely* (which is us now and in the past) may be different from the costs and benefits of morality for a group *that accepts error theory when doing metaethics but rejects it when engaged in everyday life*. For example, the latter group must "compartmentalize" their beliefs in a way that the former group need not, and this very practice may incur additional costs. (Indeed, as we'll see later, this is likely to be a central argument that the abolitionist will employ against the conservationist.) So conservationism, like abolitionism, relies on the truth of a counterfactual. That is not to say that the abolitionist and the conservationist have no business wrangling over the net costs and benefits of morality in the actual world—now and historically—but the debate must be handled with care: the cost-benefit analysis of morality in the actual world is relevant only to the extent that it casts light on the cost-benefit analysis of morality in another possible world.

The fictionalist, our third contender, agrees in part with the abolitionist and in part with the conservationist. With the abolitionist, the fictionalist agrees that we mustn't commit ourselves to the existence of things in which we disbelieve. She (the fictionalist) also agrees with the abolitionist that the conservationist's recommendation involves doxastic practices that are likely to lead to deleterious consequences. The conservationist is, after all, recommending that we knowingly cultivate inconsistent beliefs, which is, arguably, a recommendation of irrationality. The fictionalist and the abolitionist together recoil at such a violation of epistemic norms.

With the conservationist, the fictionalist agrees that morality is and has been, on balance, useful (for typically situated groups). The fictionalist's distinctive claim is that morality can to some extent remain useful even if it is not believed. The fictionalist looks to the way familiar fictions operate as a model for how we can usefully talk about topics without committing ourselves to the entities under discussion. Just as we can discuss Sherlock Holmes without committing ourselves to his existence, treat a stick as if it's a sword without committing ourselves to its being so, or complain that an enemy is a "spineless snake" without committing ourselves to unorthodox views on zoological taxonomy—so, too (the fictionalist maintains), our error theorist counterparts could talk about promise-keeping as morally obligatory (say) without committing themselves to the existence of moral obligations.

The fictionalist in whom we are interested does not claim that our current moral discourse is anything like a fiction; rather, she thinks that were we to realize the truth of error theory, then we should *change* our moral discourse, to make it in some sense similar to fiction, so as to remove commitment to entities in which we disbelieve.[4] But, of the infinity of possible moral fictions, *which* one should be chosen? The one in which promise-keeping is obligatory regardless of consequences? The one in which promise-keeping is valuable but overridable? In which promise-keeping is supererogatory? In which it is neutral? Frowned upon? Evil? The answer is simply that a group should choose whichever moral fiction best satisfies their Humean ends.

I have acknowledged that there are many challenges to be overcome sur-rounding this type of answer, but the point to notice here is that these are challenges that arise simply from the way we have posed the question "If we were to adopt a moral error theory, then what should we do with our moral concepts?" They arise for fictionalist, abolitionist, and conservationist alike (and, indeed, anyone else who wants to offer an answer), and so it is not a special problem for the fictionalist at this moment in the dialectic. I also acknowledge that it is possible that one might hold that Humeanism works for individual practical rationality but (for some reason) isn't feasible for groups. Very well, then; in that case we shall have to reformulate our original question so as to con-cern what an *individual* should do if he or she adopts a moral error theory. Our three contending theories can still compete as answers to that question, though we would face the additional complication of relativism: that one individual's interests might best be served by conservationism, another individual's interests might best be served by fictionalism (and one moral fiction rather than another), and so on. It may come to this, but for now let's be optimistic Humeans and assume that the original question can stand.[5]

Think of the moral fiction as an overlay on the group's actual Humean goals—an erroneous overlay that allows the group to better achieve its Humean goals. Of the types of fictional discourse that are familiar to us, perhaps the best model for the fictionalist is *metaphor*. When I believe that someone (call him "Jake") is dishonest and cowardly, then I could just describe him as such, but I also have the option of speaking figuratively: I could say "Jake is a spineless snake!" If you ask me whether I really believe that Jake is a spineless snake, then, caught up in my annoyance, I'm likely to answer "Yes!" But if you press me in the right way—"So, wait, you believe that there are *literally* invertebrate reptiles, and that this apparent human, Jake, is *literally* one of them??"—then I'm likely to back off: "No, of course I don't really think *that*, but you're missing the point!" There are facts about Jake that I want to convey—his dishonesty and cowardice—and by saying something that is literally false I draw attention to those facts more evoca-tively and dramatically, which might serve my goals better than straight talk.

Let's vary the example slightly, and suppose that I described Jake as "an *immoral* spineless snake." The fictionalist pictures a world where what goes for "spineless snake" goes for "immoral." In this world, if you ask me whether I really believe in immorality—where immorality involves (let's suppose) things that mustn't be done regardless of one's goals (i.e., non-Humean norms)—then at some point I'll back off: "No, of course I don't really think *that*, but you're missing the point!" There are facts about Jake that I will want to convey—this time concerning his frustrating of the group's Humean goals—and by saying something that is liter-ally false I draw attention to those facts more evocatively and dramatically, which might serve my goals (or the group's goals) better than straight talk.[6]

I will return to this fictionalist model of metaphor repeatedly in the following critical discussion of these three theoretical options.

3 Fictionalism vs. Conservationism

In order to assess the debate between the fictionalist and the conservationist, we first need a working hypothesis (at the very least) of the benefits that morality has brought. Limitations of space restrict me to focusing on just one plausible way that moral thinking is generally useful: by strengthening our motivation to act. Judging an act to be "something that must be done whether one likes it or not" (i.e., as required in non-Humean terms) may strengthen one's resolve to perform it; in certain contexts, it may even be motivationally superior to the thought "this action would satisfy my desires." After all (the thinking goes), the latter judgment seems to invite inner negotiation: "But how much do I really desire such-and-such?"—allowing for all-too-familiar rationalizations that ultimately amount to self-sabotage. By contrast, thinking "I just *must* do it" works to shut down inner debate (though by no means guaranteeing that the action in question will be performed).

Of course, having psychological mechanisms that strengthen motivation isn't necessarily useful *per se*—it depends on which motivations are being strengthened! Where such mechanisms might be most useful is when they promote faint and intangible desires that are at risk of being overwhelmed by more immediate and concrete desires (on the assumption that the satisfaction of the former desires really is more useful). An obvious commonplace example of this pattern is where desires for the benefits of living in a cooperative society are at risk of being overwhelmed by short-sighted selfish temptations. And this, it seems to me, is a quite plausible and intuitive sketch of one basic way in which moral thinking is generally useful: it acts as a bulwark against nearsighted self-centeredness, strengthening our motivation to act cooperatively by providing no-nonsense (non-Humean) imperatives in favor of doing so. With this hypothesis in hand, we can turn to the debate between the conservationist and the fictionalist.

The conservationist worries that merely "make-believing" that morality is true is likely to strip it of its usefulness. The conservationist allows that the moral thought "I must cooperate, whether I like it or not" may well be useful in the hypothesized manner, but surely only when it is an item of *belief.* The conservationist sees the fictionalist as striving to avoid falling into the habit of moral belief by practicing "cognitive self-surveillance" and having to occasionally remind herself of the truth of error theory "in order to prevent slipping into holding real moral beliefs and making genuine moral assertions" (Eriksson & Olson, this volume).[7]

> But this reveals a deep practical tension in moral fictionalism, for it also seems that in order for moral precommitments to be effective in bolstering self-control, beliefs to the effect that morality is fiction need to be suppressed or silenced.
>
> *(Olson 2011: 197)*

In place of this tension, the conservationist recommends that we give up the fight and surrender ourselves to moral *belief*. That way, there is no need for constant "self-surveillance" and no risk that moral judgment will lose the motivation-strengthening qualities that it enjoyed before we became error theorists. It may be true that the person simultaneously believes in the moral error theory, but this metaethical belief can be utterly suppressed in everyday contexts, the conservationist thinks, and that's all to the good as far as the usefulness of morality goes. By contrast, there is something problematic in the idea of the fictionalist "utterly suppressing" her skeptical metaethical beliefs, for then the suspicion arises that she will in fact have slipped into moral *belief*, thus betraying her fictionalism.[8]

Reflection on how familiar metaphors work should reveal, I believe, that these anti-fictionalist worries are misplaced. When I call Jake "a spineless snake," surely I do not need to practice any self-surveillance to ensure that I avoid inadvertently slipping into believing that he literally is an invertebrate reptile.

Or consider the metaphor "I love you with all my heart." The association of the heart with love goes back historically to a time when it was believed that the heart is the seat of human emotion (as Aristotle thought); so perhaps in the time of the ancient Greeks the sentence could be intended literally. But now we know better, and when one uses the phrase there remains no temptation whatsoever to inadvertently believe that one's love really is the product of cardiac activity. Everyone now knows that the speaker of the phrase is employing a falsehood to convey an important truth. The speaker could, of course, eschew the falsehood and talk in literal terms, but there may be all sorts of pragmatic reasons for preferring not to. Declaring love is one context where speaking in precise and unembroidered language is especially likely to be ill-advised.

Consider a third example: of someone accusing me of being a pig at dinner, to which I indignantly respond "I was *not* a pig at dinner!" In this case, the sentence I've uttered is actually *true* (for at dinner I was not, nor have I ever been, a pig), and yet the sentence still employs a metaphor. But even here, where I've uttered something that is literally true, no one (least of all me) is likely to interpret me as having asserted the obvious fact that I was not, during dinnertime, temporarily a member of the genus *Sus*. I have *not* asserted this fact (although it is a fact, and, had I wanted to, I could have used the very same sentence to assert it); rather, I've used the sentence to convey some different information, concerning my not violating the demands of etiquette at dinner.

In short, we already have entrenched and well-developed skills at saying and thinking false things in order to convey important truths (or, in the third example, saying an obviously true thing in order to convey a very different and less obvious truth), and the conservationist underestimates our capacity to do this smoothly and without confusion.

The other component of the conservationist's doubt about fictionalism is the worry about how an act of make-believe could be "effective in bolstering self-control" unless the knowledge that it is a fiction is "suppressed or silenced." But I think again that the example of metaphor fairly easily answers this doubt. Consider once more the earnest declaration: "I love you with all my heart." This utterance, and the associated thoughts, can be emotionally moving and deeply motivating in ways that are of enormous importance to the speaker and hearer. The utterance can have this significance even though both speaker and hearer know that the sentence is false. Pressed in the right way—"So, you really think that love arises from cardiac activity??"—they will both back off from the claim (though probably with the annoyed observation that the questioner is missing the point). The utterance of the false sentence can have this practical significance because it's not just a free-floating falsehood uttered for the hell of it: there are *real* truths of great importance standing behind it. And, indeed, uttering this false sentence may well convey those truths *more effectively* than trying to do so using straight talk.

This is a model that the fictionalist can usefully employ. On the assumption that no moral claims are true, we can picture a world where in certain contexts their utterance might nevertheless usefully convey information about real truths of great importance (concerning Humean values). And, indeed, uttering these false sentences may well convey those truths more effectively than trying to do so using straight talk. Yet there need be no risk of sliding into really *believing* any moral claims—any more than one who declares "I love you with all my heart" risks sliding into believing an Aristotelian view of the physiology of emotions. Thus it seems to me that the hypothesis that we set out with—of how morality is useful as a device for bolstering one's resolve to act cooperatively—is one that remains plausible even when the attitude taken toward morality alters from belief to something more akin to make-believe.[9]

The question arises whether conservationism and fictionalism are really substantively distinct positions (see Jaquet & Naar 2016: 204). Both the conservationist and the fictionalist recommend that speakers declare their belief in the moral error theory when they're in a metaethical frame of mind (accepting, for instance, "It is not the case that promise-keeping is morally obligatory"), while also both recommending that the rest of the time (which is most of the time) they go along with ordinary moral judgments (e.g., "Promise-keeping is morally obligatory"). The difference is that the conservationist maintains that the latter are beliefs and assertions, while the fictionalist maintains that they are something that falls short of belief and assertion. But (one might be tempted to think) the fictionalist doesn't want the mental state in question to fall *much short* of belief, for she recommends its adoption on the grounds that it provides many of the practical benefits of genuine moral belief. Indeed, the fictionalist would prefer it if the user of the moral fiction is not even aware that it is a fiction (at the time of use). This, however, raises the possibility that the fictionalist really is just discussing a state of *belief* but avoiding that label. So perhaps the disagreement between the fictionalist and the conservationist is not ultimately a metaethical one at all, but rather one about the nature of belief (and speech acts).

It is a mistake, however, to interpret the fictionalist as recommending a state that falls short of belief *but only just* (to the point that it might not fall short at all). When I claim that Jake is a "spineless snake," do I *almost believe* that he really is an invertebrate reptile? No—I come nowhere near believing this! And yet, for all that, I may well be virtually unaware that I'm engaged in a piece of make-believe. Consider this conversation:

A: I hear that you called Jake a spineless snake.
B: Yes, I did.
A: Do you really believe that?
B: Absolutely. He's often acted in a dishonest and cowardly fashion.
A: Mary said that she thinks that Jake *isn't* a spineless snake.
B: Well, she's wrong; she doesn't know him like I do. I've known Jake to behave in ways that prove that he's a complete snake, and I've also seen him reveal himself to be totally spineless.
A: So you believe that some reptiles are invertebrates?
B. Oh . . . I see what you've done there.

I'll leave it to the reader to re-run that conversation on the fictionalist's behalf, substituting the phrase "Jake acted immorally."

There is a sense in which the fictionalist can allow that the speaker believes that Jake acted immorally, just as we can ordinarily allow that the speaker believes that Jake is a spineless snake. But this sense is a kind of shorthand for something else. When we say that the speaker sincerely believes that Jake is a spineless snake, what we mean is that he or she sincerely believes that Jake is dishonest and cowardly; we are interpreting the metaphor. But there should be no temptation to conflate these two senses of belief ascription; it is quite evident that they are distinct, for there is also very obviously a point of view—one quickly adopted—according to which the speaker *does not for a moment* believe that Jake is a spineless snake. (By comparison, regarding the "real" belief ascription—that the person believes that Jake is dishonest and cowardly—there is no matching point of view according to which the person doesn't for a moment believe it.) The fictionalist envisages a world where the same thing goes for moral discourse.

4 Fictionalism vs. Abolitionism

The abolitionist maintains that moral discourse should go the way of talk of dragons, phlogiston, witches, and Zeus. In most of these historical cases, the abolitionist will have faced no opposition from fictionalists or conservationists. Upon discovering that phlogiston doesn't exist, for example, the proposals that we carry on talking as if phlogiston does exist, or carry on believing that it does in everyday contexts, would have little to recommend them. The reason is pretty clear: the benefits of believing in and talking about phlogiston depend almost entirely on the assumption that in doing so we are accurately describing the way the world really is; once it is discovered that the world is not that way, we incur no significant cost and lose no significant benefit if we just drop the talk.[10] Moral discourse is different. Here the costs and benefits are considerable, and it is far from obvious that they rely on moral judgments being true, so unorthodox avenues like fictionalism and conservationism emerge as possibilities worthy of consideration.

Abolitionists could support their theory by arguing that conservationism and fictionalism would involve our incurring extra harms just in virtue of the weird kind of psychological states they recommend. The abolitionist Richard Garner imagines the error theorist trying to carry on with morality:

> Since moral judgments, we are now assuming, are false, what we say is sure to conflict with reality at many points, and then we will need to resort to evasion, obfuscation, or sophistry just to maintain our fiction. It is hard to estimate the damage this can do. If we continue to insist on the truth of our fiction, if we defend it as strongly as a convinced moralist would, then we are courting doxastic disaster, Orwellian epistemology, and perhaps a nervous breakdown.
>
> *(Garner 2010: 227)*

Garner's target in this passage is what he calls "assertive moral fictionalism"—but it appears that the theory he means to attack is none other than what we are here calling "conservationism" (the label of which wasn't around in 2010). If this is right, then I am fairly sympathetic with Garner's objection. Note that his concerns are quite general—presumably applying to *any* conservationist recommendation regarding not just morality but any similarly prevalent and customary (though erroneous) discourse (see Garner 1993).

It is much less clear, however, that Garner's objection, or any like it, bites against the kind of fictionalism under discussion here. Worries that fictionalism might require a kind of damaging dissonance of mental states seem predicated on the misunderstanding that fictionalism is pretty similar to conservationism—that it recommends that people come perilously close to having contradictory beliefs. But this need be no truer of fictionalists than it is true of someone who utters "Jake is a spineless snake." Does the latter person run the risk of both believing that Jake is a reptile while believing that Jake is not a reptile? Does declaring "I love you with all my heart" require "evasion, obfuscation, or sophistry"? Does one court doxastic disaster or a nervous breakdown by protesting "I was *not* a pig at dinner!"? Clearly not.

One might complain that even if fictionalism doesn't involve people coming close to having contradictory beliefs, it nevertheless does encourage a damaging kind of psychological dissonance, for it recommends that a person believes that it is not the case that promise-keeping is obligatory (for example) while cultivating the emotions and motivations consistent with promise-keeping's being obligatory.

In order to see that this complaint is misplaced, remember that there is more in play in the fictionalist's psyche than just (i) the disbelief that X is obligatory and (ii) the emotions (etc.) in favor of performing X. There is also (iii) the belief that X is a good idea on non-moral (Humean) grounds. There is no dissonance here. It is (again!) like someone's disbelieving that Jake is a snake but nevertheless avoiding him. What justifies the avoidance behavior is the belief that Jake is dishonest and cowardly. To bring this analogy better into line with the fictionalist proposal, let's imagine that this person might suffer some weakness of will and feel the occasional foolish temptation enter into cooperative ventures with Jake. (Perhaps Jake is a bit of a smooth-talker.) The emotions associated with avoidance are still the appropriate ones to have, but (let's suppose) merely rehearsing dry beliefs about Jake's past bad behavior sometimes don't quite arouse those emotions. What the person finds works better is conjuring up a juicy metaphor: "Jake is such a *spineless snake!*" This metaphor has vividness and focuses attention in a way that straight talk cannot (or cannot so well). This is, arguably, the principal general reason that metaphor has such a central place in our language and thoughts. It is not an idle foible of language or the province predominantly of poets; it is ubiquitous and constantly earns its keep.[11]

Thus, I do not think that the abolitionist has much hope of discrediting fictionalism *in general terms*: showing that the type of psychological profile recommended by the fictionalist is likely to have damaging consequences. Each of us already has that type of psychological profile. Rather, the abolitionist must take on the *moral* fictionalist in particular: arguing that making a fiction of morality would be pragmatically worse than just abolishing it. And the abolitionist certainly thinks she has the resources for pressing such an argument, for she thinks that morality is on balance harmful when the object of belief, so is likely to remain harmful when the object of make-believe. Garner writes: "The bad effects of believing in moral facts are as likely to result from the pretence as from the belief" (2010: 230). Indeed, it is likely to be the very qualities touted as *benefits* by the fictionalist (and conservationist) that the abolitionist is inclined to place in the column labeled "costs." All parties can accept that one of the effects of moralized thinking is the strengthening of motivation, but where the fictionalist and conservationist thereby see a useful tool for combating weakness of will (*inter alia*), the abolitionist sees something that inflames disagreements and encourages disputants to dig in their heels and refuse to compromise.

I suspect that when all parties sit down and consider the matter calmly, they will agree on what really seems a fairly obvious truth: that morality is sometimes beneficial and sometimes harmful. And they will also, I suspect, be open to the suggestion that keeping the benefits while reducing the harms may involve neither the wholesale embrace of morality nor its wholesale elimination, but something altogether messier. In this vein, Jessica Isserow (this volume) promotes an "epistemic vigilance" based on the assumption "not only that that there are tangible benefits of moral practice, but that we can conceivably reap these benefits while controlling for the costs." Along similar lines, Björn Eriksson and Jonas Olson (this volume) endorse "negotiationism," according to which we "should normally be on the lookout for adverse effects of potential moralizing, and be prepared to retract and go for demoralization if possible." (Even Garner allows that circumstances might arise where moralizing is called for.)

I endorse these proposals that we should treat the baby and the bathwater separately if we can, but I remain more sympathetic to fictionalism remaining in the mix than do Isserow, Eriksson, or Olson. At the risk of being repetitive, let me once more suggest that we think about metaphor. Metaphors can be beneficial, but can also be harmful. Calling Jake a "spineless snake" may well usefully motivate me and others to shun him through its being more dramatic and evocative than simply referring to his personality traits and/or behavioral dispositions, but it could also be harmful: it could blind us to Jake's attempts at self-improvement, for example, or it could be self-destructive for Jake to habitually label himself in this manner, or it could be simply too vague for certain conversational purposes. There are, after all, certain familiar contexts where the use of metaphor seems misplaced and is discouraged: for example, in writing up scientific experiments and in official legalistic settings. This is not to say that the very practice of metaphor is banned from these contexts—I have no doubt that a glance at real examples of scientific and legalistic language will in fact reveal a plethora of metaphor. But figurative language for key elements will be frowned upon. An anthropologist investigating cross-cultural limerence, for example, may refer to a subject's "intense emotions of interpersonal connection" (say), but not his "loving another with all his heart." Jake's reliability as a witness in a court case may be cast into doubt due to his track record of "dishonesty," but not his history of being "a snake."

Part of why metaphor is discouraged in these settings is, I suppose, that it evokes emotion when participants are endeavoring to remain reflective and dispassionate. Yet it is also highly plausible that it is, *inter alia*, its very capacity to evoke emotion that makes metaphor so valuable in other contexts. Another reason that metaphor is discouraged in these formal settings is, I suppose, that it is too vague and open to interpretation when participants are endeavoring to speak with precision of empirically tractable subjects. I would like to suggest that this is another quality that makes metaphor so valuable in other contexts: sometimes we don't *want* to speak in a determinate way; sometimes it suits our communicative purposes much better to make vague gestures, even when talking about matters of extreme importance.

In the case of metaphor, it appears that we generally do a pretty good job of shifting back and forth between metaphor-discouraging contexts and metaphor-encouraging contexts: we do it smoothly without much internal anxiety or interpersonal confusion. This is promising news for those proposing "epistemic vigilance" or "negotiationism." But it's important to note that the example of metaphor shows that we move smoothly between embracing and dropping *a fictive attitude* toward something that we believe to be false, not that we move smoothly between embracing and dropping *a belief* toward something that we believe to be false. For example, in some contexts I will use the metaphor "Jake is a spineless snake," while in other contexts I will acknowledge that it is more suitable for me to drop the metaphor and instead speak literally and more carefully about Jake's personality and behavioral dispositions. We can describe this as moving in and out of a fiction, and metaphor shows it to be a commonplace practice. But it is not the case that in some contexts I will believe and assert that Jake is *literally* a spineless snake, while in other contexts I will drop the belief and assertion and instead speak more carefully about Jake's personality and behavioral dispositions.

In other words, if the abolitionist is partially right in maintaining that we should drop the moral overlay in certain contexts, but is also partially wrong because the moral overlay can usefully remain in other contexts, *and* if we look to our use of metaphor as a potential model of how something like this is already a familiar practice, then a mixture of abolitionism *and fictionalism* looks more promising than a mixture of abolitionism and conservationism.

5 Conclusion

The conclusion just reached, that there is something to be said for a mix of abolitionism and fictionalism, may seem like rather a back-down for the fictionalist—as if she has had to water down the ambitions of her original theory. But I do not believe that this is correct, for I don't think that any "un-watered-down" version of fictionalism has ever been seriously proposed—certainly not by me. To the extent that moral fictionalism is a *recommendation*, it has always presupposed the existence of non-moral values, norms, and reasons that survive the error-theoretic arguments, so it has always presupposed that whatever the moral fiction recommends as morally obligatory (say) will—assuming one has chosen the right moral fiction—be strongly recommended on non-moral grounds as well. A common (but misplaced) worry about moral fictionalism is that it is difficult to see how something that one believes to be a "mere fiction" can possibly motivate serious decision-making on weighty matters. The worry is misplaced because it overlooks the serious and weighty *non-moral* considerations that are expected to lie behind the moral overlay.

The fictionalist need not claim that making a fiction of morality is *always* recommended, regardless of how a group or individual is situated, and nor need she claim that, for groups and individuals for which it *is* recommended, the moral fiction must be maintained constantly and come what may. All that the fictionalist claims is that, for typical groups of humans situated pretty much as we are, but who become moral error theorists, the practice of maintaining morality as a fiction will be, much of the time, a good idea. (And the vagueness of "much of the time" doesn't bother me in the slightest.) If it turns out that there exist serious or formal contexts where the moral fiction is best dropped and matters explicitly dealt with in literal Humean terms, that's no skin off the fictionalist's nose.

Notes

1 Whether we conclude that they are all false, or neither true nor false (as Howard Sobel thinks, this volume) is a nice distinction that, perhaps, doesn't matter terribly much. Another nice distinction to be put aside on this occasion is whether the failure of moral discourse is a contingent or necessary one.

2 In my 2001 book I used the term "abolitionism" (Joyce 2001), but subsequently tended to prefer the label "eliminativism" for this theory (see Joyce 2013, 2017). I harbor a small worry that "abolitionism" carries some historical baggage that could skew the debate (after all, in the 18th and 19th centuries the abolitionists were the *good guys*, right?). But the tide seems to be turning toward the label "abolitionism," and I shan't put up a fight.

3 In fact, the abolitionist may be interpreted as *triply* opposed: she is also opposed to a way of *thinking*. For the sake of brevity, on this occasion I'm happy to fudge together language and thought. (The term "moral judgment" is quite useful in this regard.)

4 In other words, the fictionalist under discussion in this chapter is the *revolutionary* fictionalist. Someone who thinks, by contrast, that our current moral discourse is already somewhat like a fiction is the *hermeneutic* fictionalist. For advocacy of the latter view, see Kalderon (2005). For further discussion, see Joyce (2017).

5 In fact, of course, we already face the complication of relativism, since what one group ought to do in this respect may differ substantially from what another group should do. I don't think we should fear this relativism. The abolitionist, conservationist, and fictionalist are all in the business of offering advice, and good advice rarely, if ever, holds universally. Consider the excellent advice "Eat your greens."

6 My original example here involved calling Jake "an immoral dickhead"—but then I worried that the ensuing explanation (of what would be involved in someone's being literally "a dickhead") might be distracting.

7 Terence Cuneo and Sean Christy make a similar point: "To operate in this way requires not only that the folk reliably keep critical and ordinary contexts distinct, but also that they exercise remarkable discipline and imagination when in ordinary contexts, governing their belief-forming faculties in such a way that they do not produce moral beliefs. Perhaps this could be accomplished in some way. But we imagine that for many this will prove psychologically very difficult" (Cuneo & Christy 2011: 98).

8 I use the label "fictionalist" to denote both a person who advocates fictionalism and a person of whom fictionalism provides an (allegedly) accurate psychological description. Troubled by this ambiguity, Cuneo and Christy (2011) introduce the term "fictioneer" for the latter. But I find the ambiguity innocuous.

9 I am making here a substantive assumption that using metaphor involves make-believe—something about which there is some debate. See Joyce (2019) for discussion and references. No arguments in the current chapter depend on the matter being settled one way or the other; my occasional references to "make-believe" are all dispensable.

10 An exception might be "Zeus." There are cases to be mounted for both religious fictionalism and religious conservationism, and at some historical time and place this could have gone for Zeus and his coterie. Ovid's fictionalistesque recommendation from *The Art of Love* springs to mind: "It is expedient there should be gods, and as it is expedient let us deem that gods exist" (trans. J. H. Mozley [Loeb Classical Library, 1969: 57]).

11 After writing this sentence, I realized that I had unconsciously paraphrased a passage from the anthropologist Bronisław Malinowski (which years ago I quoted elsewhere) writing on the role of *myths* in human cultures. He writes of myth that "it is not an idle tale, but a hard-worked active force; it is not an intellectual explanation or an artistic imagery, but a pragmatic charter" (1926: 23). The connection between metaphor and myth is a very apt one to highlight.

References

Campbell, E. 2014. "Breakdown of moral judgement." *Ethics* 124: 447–480.

Cuneo, T. & Christy, S. 2011. "The myth of moral fictionalism." In M. Brady (ed.), *New Waves in Metaethics*. New York: Palgrave Macmillan. 85–102.

Garner, R. 1993. "Are convenient fictions harmful to your health?" *Philosophy East and West* 43: 87–106.

Garner, R. 2010. "Abolishing morality." In R. Joyce & S. Kirchin (eds.), *A World Without Values: Essays on John Mackie's Moral Error Theory*. Dordrecht: Springer. 217–233.

Ingram, S. 2015. "After moral error theory, after moral realism." *Southern Journal of Philosophy* 53: 227–248.

Jaquet, F. & Naar, H. 2016. "Moral beliefs for the error theorist?" *Ethical Theory and Moral Practice* 19: 193–207.

Joyce, R. 2001. *The Myth of Morality*. Cambridge: Cambridge University Press.

Joyce, R. 2013. "Psychological fictionalism and the threat of fictionalist suicide." *Monist* 96: 517–538.

Joyce, R. 2017. "Fictionalism in metaethics." In D. Plunkett & T. McPherson (eds.), *Routledge Handbook of Metaethics*. New York: Routledge. 72–86.

Joyce, R. 2019. "Fictionalism: Morality and metaphor." In F. Kroon & B. Armour-Garb (eds.), *Philosophical Fictionalism*. Oxford: Oxford University Press.

Kalderon, M. 2005. *Moral Fictionalism*. Oxford: Oxford University Press.

Lutz, M. 2014. "The 'now what' problem for error theory." *Philosophical Studies* 171: 351–371.

Mackie, J. L. 1977. *Ethics: Inventing Right and Wrong*. New York: Penguin.

Malinowski, B. 1926. *Myth in Primitive Psychology*. London: Kegan Paul.

Olson, J. 2011. "Getting real about moral fictionalism." In R. Shafer-Landau (ed.), *Oxford Studies in Metaethics, Vol. 6*. New York: Oxford University Press. 182–204.

Olson, J. 2014. *Moral Error Theory: History, Critique, Defence*. Oxford: Oxford University Press.

PART IV

Moral Skepticism: Case Studies

10

MORALITY AND OPPRESSION

Nicolas Olsson Yaouzis

1 Introduction

Assume that we discover that our beliefs about justice contribute to maintaining what seems to be an oppressive status quo. Assume further that we discover that this contributes to explaining the popularity of these beliefs. Does this mean that we should give them up?

There are good reasons to believe that it does not follow from these facts alone. After all, a proponent of mainstream political philosophy can argue that professional moral and political philosophers at prestigious departments tend to be the closest we have to moral experts. They have received extensive training that allows them to recognize the nature of justice. So, when John Rawls, for example, tells us that justice entails that the difference principle is satisfied, we have good reasons to believe that it is true. However, suppose that there are no moral facts. Then political philosophers cannot be considered experts at identifying such non-existent facts and consequently the "expertise defense" fails. This chapter will accept this supposition and examine the implications for radical political philosophy.

Many radical critics of mainstream political philosophy are, however, careful to point out that they do not want to commit themselves to moral nihilism. They are worried that if they were to accept that there are no moral facts, they would be committed to accepting that it is, for example, false that men and women morally ought to be treated with equal respect. Furthermore, they are worried that without moral facts it would be impossible, for example, to convince others to treat men and women with equal respect.

One of the main points of this chapter is to show that radical critics should not be too concerned about having to concede that it is false that men and women ought to be treated with equal respect. After all, if moral error theory is correct, then it is equally false that it is morally permissible to treat women with less respect than men. Regarding the second worry, it is argued that it is more efficient to convince people by appealing to their beliefs and desires than to appeal to alleged objective moral facts. It is also argued that because moral terms are often used to obscure group interests, historically disadvantaged groups have good reasons to abolish the use of moral terms from political discourse.

The plan of the chapter is as follows. Section 2 provides a rational reconstruction of Charles Mills's (2005) explanation of the popularity of Rawlsian political philosophy. In section 3 the expertise defense is introduced and the epistemic relevance of Mills's explanation is questioned. Section 4 shows that if there are no moral facts, then the expertise defense of mainstream political philosophy is undermined. In section 4.1, some consequences of moral error theory are described, and sections 4.1.2 and 4.1.3 discuss how activists can and should argue against perceived injustices if there are no moral facts. Section 5 concludes the chapter.

2 Charles Mills on Contemporary Political Philosophy

There are many historical examples of philosophers who have objected to their contemporaries' moral beliefs on the ground that these beliefs contributed to maintaining what they viewed as an oppressive status quo. Jean-Jacques Rousseau ([1755] 1985), Karl Marx ([1932] 1998), and Friedrich Nietzsche ([1887] 1996) are but a few. In this chapter, however, I shall take an essay by contemporary political philosopher Charles Mills (2005) as my point of departure.

Mills asks why people who belong to historically disadvantaged groups should care about John Rawls's (1971) theory of justice. After all, the theory does not address issues that members of such groups are typically interested in. Take, for example, issues concerning race and racial injustices in the United States. Mills (2009) reports that if all mentions of race and racism in Rawls's major works are added up, they fit on six pages. This is surprising considering that *A Theory of Justice* was written in the 1960s while the American Civil Rights movement relentlessly called attention to racial injustices in the US.

In response to this, it is often pointed out that Rawls did not address real-world problems because he did ideal theory, and that ideal theory is "the only basis for the systematic grasp of these more pressing [real-world] problems" (Rawls 1971: 8). In other words, Rawls and those working in this tradition believe that we need an ideal theory of justice before we can turn our attention to more pressing problems, such as racial segregation, mass incarceration, and racial profiling. The problem with this response, according to Mills (2005: 179), is that mainstream political philosophers have shown little interest in moving on to real-world problems, such as race and racism. For example, Mills notes that only one essay, in a five-volume collection of 85 essays from 30 years of writings on Rawls (Richardson & Weithman 1999), deals with race.

Rawlsian political philosophy also seems to be bad at addressing other issues that members of underprivileged groups are typically interested in. Iris Marion Young (1990), for example, argues that Rawls's focus on distributive justice tends to obscure important social facts. Young provides a list of injustices that Rawls's theory of justice is ill-equipped to account for: exploitation, marginalization, powerlessness, cultural imperialism, and violence. For example, powerlessness is an injustice suffered by blue-collar workers in virtue of having no real control over their life. Unlike white-collar workers and professionals, blue-collar workers often have no influence over their working conditions, are constantly monitored by managers, and generally do not have much say over public policy. Because Rawls's theory of justice cannot be used straightforwardly to account for the injustice of powerlessness, it will be difficult for those who suffer from powerlessness to describe their experience as an injustice within a Rawlsian framework. By making it difficult to use the theory to articulate experiences of injustice, Rawlsian political philosophy contributes to preventing challenges to the status quo.[1] Raymond Geuss (2008: 90) sums up this criticism of Rawls: "to the extent, then, to which Rawls draws attention *away* from the phenomenon of power and the way in which it influences our lives and the way we see the world, his theory is itself ideological."

A brief explanation of why Rawlsian political philosophy remains popular despite failing to account for important social facts can be extracted from Mills (2005: 170–172). The explanation postulates the existence of a selection mechanism that ensures that Rawlsian ideas are overrepresented among political philosophers at American universities. The explanation consists of three steps.

First, Mills assumes that each year a cohort of students signs up for Political Philosophy 101. Some of the students go on to take a BA, MA, and finally a PhD in political philosophy. Some of those who take a PhD will go on to join the faculty. Some of those who sign up for Political Philosophy 101 are from a working-class background, some are non-male, some are non-white, but most of them are middle- to upper-class white males.

The second assumption is that members of historically subordinated groups are deeply skeptical of the type of ideal theory proposed by Rawls. They "generally see its glittering ideals as remote and unhelpful, and are attracted to non-ideal theory" (Mills 2017: 77). Mills illustrates this with a passage from Frederick Douglass's 1852 speech, "What to the slave is the 4th of July?":

> I am not included within the pale of this glorious anniversary! Your high independence only reveals the immeasurable distance between us. The blessings in which you, this day, rejoice, are not enjoyed in common.— The rich inheritance of justice, liberty, prosperity and independence, bequeathed by your fathers, is shared by you, not by me. The sunlight that brought life and healing to you, has brought stripes and death to me. This Fourth [of] July is *yours*, not *mine*. *You* may rejoice, *I* must mourn.[2]

Although contemporary members of historically subordinated groups might not be as far removed from the mainstream ideals as Douglass, there are still reasons to believe that students from these groups feel alienated by a theory of justice that does not take their experiences and concerns seriously. Thus, when they realize that political philosophers are mostly concerned with a theory that does not directly deal with the issues they are typically interested in, they will tend to turn to other subjects, such as sociology, political science, or economics. Indeed, there tends to be proportionally fewer members of historically subordinated groups at higher levels. For example, in the US in 2014, black students constituted 5 percent of all Bachelors and 2.5 percent of all Masters in Philosophy.[3] When members of historically subordinated groups do not go on to do PhDs in political philosophy, there is little chance of getting members of these groups into the faculty.

The third assumption is that there is an "absence of any countervailing group interest that would motivate dissatisfaction with dominant paradigms and a resulting search for better alternatives" (Mills 2005: 172). Thus, there will be few challenges to mainstream political philosophy from within the departments. Mills also points out that, as long as the challenges come from outside the philosophy departments or are not articulated by someone with philosophical authority, it is unlikely that mainstream political philosophy will take much notice. Indeed, if you did not work at Harvard, Princeton, or Oxford, it was unlikely that your name or comments would end up in any of the major 20th-century works on political philosophy. In *A Theory of Justice*, Rawls acknowledges Robert Nozick and Amartya Sen; in *Anarchy, State and Utopia*, Nozick acknowledges Rawls and Ronald Dworkin; Dworkin's 1981 papers on equality (1981a, 1981b) refer almost solely to Rawls, Nozick, and Sen—and all of them acknowledge the help of Derek Parfit. In other words, if there are no, say, black political philosophers at the prestigious philosophy departments, then it is unlikely that the "white-centrism" of mainstream political philosophy will ever be challenged.

If these assumptions are correct, then Rawlsian political philosophy will remain popular for the foreseeable future. Since Rawlsian political philosophy tends to obscure social issues that members of underprivileged groups are typically interested in, this explanation also shows how these issues will remain obscured at philosophy departments. Last, to the extent that (prestigious) philosophy departments influence the way politicians and decision-makers think about justice, the above model contributes to explaining that, and how, these issues remain obscured in the public debate.

What has been said so far can be summed up with the two following claims: (1) Rawlsian political philosophy contributes to preventing challenges to the status quo, and (2) Rawlsian political philosophy remains popular in part because it prevents challenges to the status quo.[4]

3 "So What?" A Challenge to Epistemic Relevance

Assume that it is true that members of historically disadvantaged groups turn away from political philosophy because it does not address their main concerns or reflect their central experiences. A proponent of Rawlsian political philosophy could respond by questioning the epistemic relevance of this insight. After all, it does not follow that Rawlsian political philosophy remains popular *because* it alienates members of these groups. To see this, consider the following thought experiment (adapted from White 2010):

> Adam throws a party and everyone is invited. When you arrive at the door Adam asks you whether you believe that there are naturally occurring penguins north of the Galapagos. You truthfully answer "no" and are let in to meet the other guests. When you mingle, you discover that everyone shares your belief that there are no naturally occurring penguins north of the Galapagos. Later you find out that Adam had a gun in his pocket and planned to kill anyone who believed that there are naturally occurring penguins north of the Galapagos. Should you lower your confidence in your belief?

The point of this morbid thought experiment is to show that Adam's policy does not cause you to believe that there are no penguins north of the Galapagos. After all, Adam's policy ensures that the party is populated only with people who believe that there are no naturally occurring penguins north of the Galapagos. Therefore, Adam's policy does not undermine whatever justification you might have for your belief. Similarly, even if there is a causal mechanism that sees to it that only Rawlsian political philosophers become part of a faculty, this does not undermine the beliefs of the faculty members.

However, if Mills is right, then there are good reasons to believe that members of historically disadvantaged groups make different judgments about justice than middle- to upper-class white male philosophers. The disagreement between poor, non-white, and non-male laypersons, on the one hand, and mainly middle- to upper-class white male philosophers, on the other hand, may be taken as evidence that their respective judgments reflect group interests and do not track moral truths.[5]

To fend off this objection, Rawlsian political philosophers may employ the so-called *expertise defense*. The idea is that a professional philosopher can be compared to a chess grandmaster. A chess grandmaster has no reason to give up her belief about what to do in a game of chess when she discovers that there is a layperson who disagrees with her. Similarly, a professional political philosopher with extensive training at reasoning and generating reliable judgments about abstract concepts, such as justice, has no reason to give up her judgment about justice if she discovers that laypersons disagree with her.

The epistemological gist of the argument is that laypersons and experts use different methods to form their judgments. Laypersons typically use unreliable methods, whereas philosophers use reliable "expert methods." Because philosophers are much better at tracking philosophical truths than laypersons, they do not have to take the layperson's judgments into account when they evaluate their theories about justice.[6] Note also that, as long as the philosopher's judgment is retained by a reliable method, it does not matter that she originally came to accept the belief because it served her group interests. In other words, the expertise defense is compatible with the philosopher first coming to accept Rawls's conception of justice on completely irrational grounds as long as she retains it on rational grounds.

One objection to the expertise defense consists of questioning what professional political philosophers are experts about. Are they experts at analyzing *conceptions* of justice, or are they experts at identifying what justice actually is?[7] Extensive training may have made professional philosophers much better than laypersons at analyzing conceptions of justice, but their training may not have made them much better than laypersons at identifying what justice actually is.

Think of a philosopher who specializes in 18th-century chemistry. After a thorough reading of the 18th-century books on science, she provides a good analysis of the concept of *phlogiston*. Her conceptualization of phlogiston as *xyz* is accurate in the sense that it captures what 18th-century scientists had in mind when they spoke and wrote about phlogiston. However, by having analyzed the concept of phlogiston, it does not follow that the philosopher has identified any phlogiston. After all, there is nothing in the real world that the concept of *phlogiston* picks out.

It may be pointed out that, whereas there is no such thing as phlogiston, many political philosophers agree that there are such things as just and unjust states of affairs. In fact, for example, when Nozick (1974) objects to Rawls's theory of justice he does not think that Rawls fails to analyze their shared conception of justice, but rather that Rawls is wrong about what characterizes just states of affairs. Furthermore, it can be argued that if anyone can form reliable intuitions about what justice is, then it must be political philosophers. After all, unlike most laypersons, political philosophers spend much of their time examining different theories of justice, and forming intuitions about whether real and imagined social orders are just or unjust. This allows them to reach a *reflective equilibrium* between general principles and particular judgments.[8] So, when a political philosopher judges that justice requires that the *difference principle* is satisfied, for example, this should be taken as evidence that in a just state of affairs the difference principle is indeed satisfied. If this is correct, then there are good reasons to believe that Rawlsian political philosophy remains popular because it has correctly identified the requirements of justice, and not because it prevents challenges to the status quo.

4 Nihilism as Political Radicalism

Is the political philosopher's relationship to justice different from the 18th-century scientist's relationship to phlogiston? According to a metaethical position called *moral error theory*, the answer is "no." A political philosopher who describes Sweden as just is in the same position as an 18th-century scientist who claims that there is phlogiston in a piece of wood. Both express false beliefs. The property of being just is not instantiated by Sweden (or any other society, for that matter) and the property of being phlogiston isn't instantiated by anything.

Generally, moral error theory consists of a semantic and an ontological claim: The semantic claim is that moral judgments purport to state moral facts, and the ontological claim is that there are no moral facts.[9] Hence, according to moral error theory, all moral judgments are false.

J. L. Mackie (1977) presents several arguments for moral error theory, one of which—the argument from relativity—actually has some similarities to Mills's argument against mainstream political philosophy. Mackie (1977: 36) notes "the difference in moral beliefs between different groups and classes within a complex community," then argues that the best explanation of these differences is that people tend to project their own feelings of approval and disapproval to actions. So, a person who believes that stealing is wrong does so because she disapproves of stealing and has projected her disapproval of stealing to acts of stealing, and not because she has perceived that stealing has the property of begin morally wrong. Mackie argues that because the actual variations in moral beliefs are best explained as projections of feelings of approval or disapproval, there is no need to postulate the existence of moral facts.

Mackie illustrates the phenomenon with our approval of monogamy: "people approve of monogamy because they participate in a monogamous way of life rather than they participate in a monogamous way of life because they approve of monogamy" (1977: 36). This fits with Mills's criticism of mainstream political philosophy. White middle- to upper-class men approve of certain ways of life because they live these sorts of lives; they disapprove of other ways of life because such ways of life threaten their ways of life. For example, because they live lives that require that formal rights are respected, they believe that justice requires that these formal rights are respected. On the other hand, a person who belongs to a historically disadvantaged group might disagree because respect of formal rights is not as fundamental to her way of life.

Suppose that moral error theory is correct and that there are no moral facts. This means that contemporary political philosophers' study of justice *is* analogous to 18th-century chemists' study of phlogiston. So, even if philosophers are experts at forming judgments about our (or others') conceptions of justice, moral error theory entails that there is no such thing as justice for political philosophers to be experts about. Accepting moral error theory should cause the blinders to drop.

There is no illusion that the judgments of political philosophers track moral facts. So, if Mills is correct, then there are good reasons to believe that their judgments track the group interests of middle- to upper-class white men.

4.1 Consequences of Accepting Moral Error Theory

It might seem that moral error theory comes with a hefty price tag. Although Mills does not explicitly discuss moral error theory or nihilism, he expresses some related worries when he says that moral relativism

> makes it difficult to affirm that, objectively, women and people of color are indeed oppressed—not merely that they believe they're oppressed. In addition, the mainstream apparatus (for example, of justice and rights) then becomes a necessarily alien tool in the oppressor's arsenal, rather than a weapon to be used and turned against him. One can no longer demand gender or racial justice.
>
> *(2005: 174)*

The passage can also be interpreted as expressing three, somewhat different, worries regarding moral error theory. First, moral error theory entails that it is *false* that women and people of color are oppressed. Second, accepting moral error theory makes it *difficult to affirm* that women and people of color are oppressed. Third, without moral concepts such as "justice" and "rights," it is *difficult to convince* others to get rid of gender and racial inequalities. I'll address the worries one at a time.

4.1.1 Does Moral Error Theory Entail That Women Are Not Oppressed?

The short answer to this question is "yes." If *oppression* is a moral concept, then "Women are oppressed" is true only if there is a corresponding truth-making moral fact. However, according to moral error theory there is no such fact, and therefore it is false that women are oppressed. The same is true of other first-order moral claims such as:

1. *Justice* requires that reparations be paid to the descendants of the victims of the transatlantic slave trade.
2. Men and women morally *ought* to be treated with equal respect.
3. It is morally *wrong* to send refugees back to Afghanistan.

At first sight, it might seem revolting to accept a theory with such implications. After all, normally we assume that if it is not the case that something is wrong, then it is permissible; and according to moral error theory it is not the case that it is wrong to send refugees back to Afghanistan; therefore, it seems to be permissible to send refugees back to Afghanistan. However, it is important to remember that, according to moral error theory, the negation of the above propositions does not entail that the following propositions are true:

4. Justice allows that reparations not be paid to the victims of the transatlantic slave trade.
5. It is morally permissible to not treat men and women with equal respect.
6. It is morally permissible to send refugees back to Afghanistan.

According to moral error theory, *all* first-order moral propositions (including 4–6) are false. Propositions 1–6 are all false because there are no moral facts to make them true.

Jonas Olson (2014) explains why, contrary to popular belief, the negation of 2 does not entail 5. He argues that the implications from "not wrong" to "permissible" are not conceptual, but rather, he suggests, "they are instances of generalized conversational implicatures" (2014: 15). Normally when we claim that something is not wrong we speak from within a moral standard. In most moral standards, an action that is not wrong is permissible. However, according to Olson, such implicatures can be canceled by an error theorist simply by signaling that she isn't speaking from within a moral standard. In fact, by rejecting the moral standard according to which "not wrong" implies "permissible," moral error theory is compatible with the claim that it is not the case that it is permissible to not treat men and women with equal respect. In other words, although moral error theory entails that it is false that women are oppressed, it does not entail that it is permissible to oppress women.

4.1.2 Does Moral Error Theory Make It Difficult to Affirm That Women Are Oppressed?

Remember that Mills (2005: 174) claimed that accepting relativism "makes it difficult to affirm that, objectively, women and people of color are oppressed—not merely that they believe that they're oppressed." Similarly, it is true that a moral error theorist cannot coherently deny the existence of moral reasons *and* hold that there are moral reasons to, say, support reparations to the descendants of the victims of the transatlantic slave trade. However, why would this be a problem? Here is a possible argument. If moral error theory is accepted then it is impossible to coherently affirm that, say, women are oppressed. If it is impossible to coherently affirm that a group is oppressed, then it is impossible to get rid of this oppression. So, if moral error theory is accepted, it is impossible to get rid of, say, the oppression of women.

The first and second premises of the argument will be dealt with in this and the next section. In this section it will be shown that accepting moral error theory does not make it impossible to coherently affirm that, say, women are oppressed.

However, once this has been shown it will be argued that there are prudential reasons for historically disadvantaged groups to abolish moral discourse and
thought. In the next section it will be argued that moral discourse isn't necessary
to convince people to get rid of extreme inequalities.

First, note that there is nothing incoherent in explicitly denying the existence
of irreducible moral reasons and still saying things like "There are compelling
moral reasons to support reparations to the descendants of the victims of the transatlantic slave trade." Accepting moral error theory entails accepting that there are
no irreducibly moral reasons, but it does not entail that all moral terms and concepts should (in a prudential sense) be abolished from speech and thought.

Some moral error theorists, such as Ian Hinckfuss (1987, excerpted in this
volume), advocate moral *abolitionism*. According to abolitionism, ordinary moral
thought and discourse should simply be abolished: we should stop using the moral
versions of "ought," "reason," "justice," "rights," "oppression," and other moral
terms and concepts in our discourse and thought. Instead of saying "Women and
men ought to be treated with equal respect," I should say, for example, "Most
women would like it if they were treated with equal respect as men."

However, most moral error theorists do not accept abolitionism. According
to one suggestion, so-called *fictionalism* advocated by Joyce (2006; see also Joyce,
this volume), moral error theorists should *pretend-believe* and *pretend-assert* moral
propositions, while they sincerely believe (and sometimes assert) that there are
no true moral propositions. Moral propositions should be treated in the same
way as fictional propositions are treated. For example, I can believe that it is true
according to the fiction that Sherlock Holmes lived at 221B Baker Street, while
I, at the same time, deny that there is a master detective who goes by the name
of "Sherlock Holmes." Similarly, I can believe and assert that it is true according to the moral fiction that there are moral reasons to support reparations to the
descendants of the transatlantic slave trade, while I, at the same time, deny that
there are any moral reasons.

According to another suggestion, so-called *conservationism* advocated by Olson
(2014; see also Eriksson & Olson, this volume), moral error theorists should
go about believing and asserting moral propositions as they have always done.
Although a moral error theorist believes that what she is saying or thinking is
false, she recognizes that her moral assertions pragmatically convey imperatives.
For example, I may believe that my assertion is false when I say "Women and
men ought to be treated with equal respect," but intend to use it to pragmatically
convey the imperative "Treat men and women with equal respect!"

So, although they disagree about the details, most error theorists agree that
there is no need to abolish ordinary moral thought and discourse. Thus, it is
possible to accept moral error theory and, in some sense, maintain that women
and people of color are oppressed. However, what reasons are there to prefer
fictionalism or conservationism to abolitionism? What is at stake in this debate is
whether abolitionism, conservationism, or fictionalism best serves "our" interests.

Hinckfuss, for example, argues in favor of abolitionism because he believes that ordinary moral thought and discourse have a tendency to promote elitism, author-itarianism, conflict, and war. Olson, however, objects that it is unclear whether ordinary moral discourse and thought promotes or prevents elitism. According to Olson, a general desire for praise and a disposition to admire the powerful often seems to be responsible for elitism, which, in turn, is often condemned in moral terms. More generally, fictionalists and conservationists like Mackie, Joyce, and Olson reject abolitionism because they think that moral thought and discourse are useful in coordinating attitudes and in regulating interpersonal relations.[10] Mackie (1977: 43) says that "[w]e need morality to regulate interpersonal relations, to control some of the ways in which people behave toward one another, often in opposition to contrary inclinations." Joyce (2006: 208) writes:

> The moralization of our practical lives contributes to the satisfaction of our long-term interests and makes for more effective collective negotiation by supplying license for punishment, justification for likes and dislikes, and bonding individuals in a shared framework of decision-making.

Finally, Olson (2014: 181) claims:

> We need to be able to trust agreements and to rely on other people's promises. The idea that it is morally wrong to violate agreements and break promises is an extraordinary useful tool to ensure that agreements are respected and promises kept.

It is worth considering some differences between Mackie's, Joyce's, and Olson's projects on the one hand, and my project, on the other hand. Traditionally, moral error theorists paint a relatively rosy picture of the origins of morality. Supported by evolutionary models, it is argued that both the capacity to form moral beliefs and much of their content has evolved to facilitate coordination and cooperation. For example, the reason we believe that it is wrong to lie is that having the ability to form a belief that lying is wrong has facilitated coordination and cooperation for our ancestors.

In this chapter, however, I've provided a less rosy view of the persistence of our political philosophical beliefs. Based on Mills's observations, I argued that the popularity of mainstream political theories is best explained in terms of the interests of the elite. The explanation is in terms of differentiated chance for "survival" for students in academic political philosophy. Because lecturers tend to be white middle- to upper-class males, they tend to lecture on theories that reflect their interests and experiences. Students who tend to accept such theories (i.e., that are white middle- to upper-class males) tend to have a greater chance of survival in academic political philosophy than students who reject or feel uncomfortable with such theories. Thus, the students who eventually go on to become lecturers in political philosophy tend to also be white middle- to upper-class males. Consequently, theories that reflect the interests and experiences of the dominant group will be perpetuated.

Note that this explanation is structurally similar to the evolutionary explanations provided by error theorists. The difference is that for Mackie, Joyce, and Olson the popularity of a moral belief is explained by the benefits conferred to our ancestors, whereas the popularity of a political belief is here explained in terms of the benefits conferred to some privileged group. Although all of us probably benefit from the moral beliefs that have been selected because they benefited our ancestors, it is less clear that all of us benefit from the political beliefs that have been selected because they benefit some elite. To the extent that these beliefs obscure inequalities, members of historically disadvantaged groups have prudential reasons to reject these political beliefs.

Of course, this does not by itself show that members of historically disadvantaged groups should embrace abolitionism rather than fictionalism or conservationism. However, when a member of a historically disadvantaged group employs moralized discourse in the political domain (without clearly signaling acceptance of error theory), she conversationally implicates a commitment to metaethical realism. This is problematic insofar as she communicates that it is worthwhile to search for a theory of justice. After all, in communicating that it is worthwhile to look for a theory of justice she legitimizes the ideology-producing work of mainstream political philosophers. Because this form of ideology-production is not in the best interests of historically disadvantaged groups, they have strong prudential reasons to accept abolitionism in the political domain.

Finally, note that because different groups may have different interests, it is possible that members of one group have reason to become abolitionists, whereas members of another group have reasons to become fictionalists or conservationists about moral discourse and thought. Furthermore, it is possible that one group has reasons to take up one attitude in one domain and another attitude in another domain. For example, a moral error theorist can have a strong reason to be a conservationist about moral thought and discourse in the "personal" domain and accept utterances and thoughts of the sort "It's morally wrong to tell a lie" and "I morally ought to keep promises." However, the same group of moral error theorists may also realize that, in the political domain, when we discuss what policies to adopt, moral terms obscure the influence of group interests on policy suggestions; therefore, she may have reason to abolish moral discourse and thought from the political realm.[11]

4.1.3 Does Abolitionism Make It Difficult to Convince People to Get Rid of Oppression?

Remember that Mills's third worry is that if relativism is accepted, the "mainstream apparatus (for example, of justice and rights) then becomes a necessarily alien tool in the oppressor's arsenal, rather than a weapon to be used and turned against him." Translated to this context: if members of historically disadvantaged groups accept abolitionism in the political domain, it will become difficult to convince others to turn against what is perceived to be oppressive social orders. For example, if people came to accept abolitionism, it would be difficult to convince them to accept, say, a policy to pay reparations to the descendants of the victims of the transatlantic slave trade.

First, note that although moral error theory entails that there are no *moral* reasons, it does not entail that there are no other kinds of reasons. For example, Olson (2014) points out that there is a reductive meaning of "reason" that does not entail irreducible normativity. I have a *prudential* reason for attending the department's political philosophy seminar rather than go out for ice cream because I'm interested in learning more about political philosophy, and the best way to accomplish this is to attend the seminar. Similarly, someone can have a prudential reason to support a policy to pay reparations to the descendants of victims of the transatlantic slave trade if they think that this will further their interests.

This will not alleviate Mills's worry. Even if the descendants of the transatlantic slave trade have prudential reasons to support such a policy, it seems (at first glance) unlikely that most members of other groups have prudential reasons to support it.

However, I think that there is cause for optimism. After all, humans feel sympathy for each other. We grieve at others' sorrow and rejoice at their pleasure. We also tend to become upset at people who cause suffering and applaud people who make others happy. To use David Hume's words ([1740] 1985: 436): "When we observe a person in misfortunes, we are affected with pity and love; but the author of their misfortunes becomes the object of our strongest hatred, and is the more detested in proportion to the degree of our compassion." So, when a person hears about, say, the plight of an Afghan refugee soon to be deported, it is natural for the observer to feel affection and pity for the refugee, while at the same time hatred and antipathy toward the persons responsible for the decision to deport the refugee. Affection for the refugee and antipathy for the persons responsible for the decision often tend to give rise to a desire for change. Therefore, an activist can appeal to these desires, rather than to non-existing moral facts, to convince politicians and fellow citizens to not deport Afghan refugees.

However, this picture of human psychology might seem too optimistic. While Hume was confident of our tendency to feel sympathy for each other, he was also well aware that we tend to care more for these who are like us and less for these who are unlike us: "An Englishman in Italy is a friend: A European in China; and perhaps a man wou'd be belov'd as such, were we to meet him in the moon" (Hume [1740] 1985: 534). If we are to use Hume as an authority on human motivation, it might seem as though white Americans, say, are primed to care more about other white Americans than about black Americans.[12]

To make matters worse, psychologists have discovered that people have a tendency to view themselves as being morally good rather than morally bad even if it forces them to adopt new beliefs.[13] Consider Bertrand, a privileged middle-class white man in contemporary USA. Bertrand has a strong con-attitude toward undeserved social and economic inequalities. Suppose Ada confronts Bertrand with evidence about the severe social and economic inequalities between black and white Americans and suggests that because of Bertrand's con-attitude to undeserved inequality he should accept a redistributive policy even if it would make him worse off. However, according to psychologists, such as Claude Steele (1999), it is common for people who find themselves in this type of situation to change their beliefs so that they can retain their privilege while avoiding the conclusion that they are acting wrongly. For example, Bertrand can avoid the conclusion by adopting a belief that black Americans somehow deserve to be worse off than white Americans. This could be rationalized by the belief that differences in IQ[14] (rather than contemporary and historical inequalities) explain why black Americans have a much lower life expectancy, are poorer, and are more incarcerated than white Americans. Indeed, if people, including white Americans, tend to suffer from this type of in-group and self-serving bias, then it will be difficult to convince them to give up their privilege to help historically disadvantaged groups.

An abolitionist cannot condemn Bertrand's in-group bias on *moral* grounds. At best, she can point to prudential reasons for Bertrand to get rid of his racist in-group bias. For example, if Bertrand wants to have coherent beliefs and his racist belief is incompatible with some of his other beliefs, then the abolitionist can advise him to get rid of the racist belief. However, if Bertrand's bias does not come into conflict with his other beliefs and desires, or if he has no desire to have coherent beliefs, then the abolitionist cannot really provide Bertrand with any good reason at all.

Ultimately, it is an empirical question whether it is possible to convince people to give up their privilege. Pessimists claim that we cannot feel enough sympathy for members of other groups to motivate us to give up our own privileges to help them. Optimists, on the other hand, hold that although it may be difficult to convince people to give up their privileges, it is in principle possible.[15]

One reason to side with optimists is that middle-to-upper-class white men like Bertrand have become much more sensitive to the plight of the poor, non-whites, and non-men during the course of the 20th century. Not too long ago, "She's a woman" or "He's black" were considered acceptable explanations of why a person was not admitted to a university; today, most white middle- to upper-class men would view such explanations as utterly unacceptable.[16] One way of explaining this shift is in terms of changed beliefs about what it means to be a woman or non-white. If it is generally believed that women and blacks lack the cognitive capacities necessary to attend university, it is also acceptable to answer the question "Why can't John go to university" with "Because he's black."

Fortunately, the long and hard work of feminists and civil rights activists has changed the perception of women and non-whites' cognitive abilities so that today such answers are unacceptable.

To sum up the last two sections. Moral discourse and thought contribute to legitimizing the production of ideology that perpetuates a social order that is not in the best interests of historically disadvantaged groups. There are reasons to be optimistic about the possibility of convincing people to give up their privilege without moral discourse. Therefore, historically disadvantaged groups have prudential reasons to abolish moral discourse and thought from the political domain.

5 Conclusion

In this chapter I have argued that mainstream Rawlsian political philosophy contributes to preventing challenges to the status quo. I have also argued that it is likely that Rawlsian political philosophy remains popular in part because it contributes to preventing challenges to the status quo. I considered the objection that Rawlsian political philosophy remains popular because it has actually identified the nature of justice. However, I then suggested that, if moral error theory is correct, then there is nothing for Rawlsian political philosophy to identify. Consequently, there are good reasons to believe that Rawlsian political philosophy remains popular because it prevents challenges to the status quo. Finally, I discussed the consequences of accepting moral error theory for political philosophers and activists interested in challenging the status quo. I argued that Mills's worries were exaggerated and that accepting moral error theory does not make political activism futile. Finally, I suggested that in the light of Mills's claims about why Rawlsian political philosophy remains popular, there are reasons to prefer abolitionism to fictionalism and conservationism, at least in the political domain.

Acknowledgments

Work on this chapter was supported by the Swedish Research Council for Health, Working Life and Welfare (FORTE). I would like to thank the participants at the higher seminar at the Department of Philosophy at Stockholm University for their comments when an early draft of this chapter was presented. I'm also very grateful to Conrad Bakka, Åsa Burman, Björn Eriksson, Richard Joyce, and Jonas Olson for their valuable comments.

Notes

1 See also Susan Moller Okin's (1991) criticism of Rawls's inability to account for gender inequalities.
2 http://teachingamericanhistory.org/library/document/what-to-the-slave-is-the-fourth-of-july/, accessed September 25, 2017

3 https://humanitiesindicators.org/content/indicatordoc.aspx?i=266, accessed September 28, 2017.
4 Incidentally, this is how some philosophers characterize *false consciousness* or *ideologies*. See, for example, G. A. Cohen (1978); Michael Rosen (1996).
5 Compare Weinberg, Nichols, and Stich's (2001) argument against the reliability of philosophical judgments about knowledge based on the discovery that there are cross-cultural differences.
6 See, for example, Williamson 2004; Plantinga 1999.
7 See, for example, Stephen Stich and Kevin Tobia's (2016) discussion about the role of intuitions for philosophy.
8 See, for example, Rawls 1971: 48–51.
9 See Mackie 1977, Joyce 2001, and Olson 2014.
10 See also Nolan, Restall, & West 2005.
11 Abolishing moral terms from the political domain is in line with the *political realism* suggested by, for example, Bernard Williams (2005) and Raymond Geuss (2008).
12 In modern social psychology lingo, this phenomenon is called *in-group bias*. For a recent study, see Rand et al. 2009.
13 See, for example, Steele 1999 on self-affirmation theory.
14 See, for example, Hernstein & Murray 1994.
15 See also Lorna Finlayson (2015) concerning pessimism and optimism in political theory.
16 Compare Williams (2005: 11) on how some things "make sense" as justifications in one historical context but not in another. See also Jason Stanley (2015) who discusses a similar point under the heading of *reasonableness*.

References

Cohen, G. A. 1978. *Karl Marx's Theory of History: A Defence*. Oxford: Oxford University Press.

Dworkin, R. 1981a. "What is equality? Part 1: Equality of welfare." *Philosophy & Public Affairs* 10: 185–246.

Dworkin, R. 1981b. "What is equality? Part 2: Equality of resources." *Philosophy & Public Affairs* 10: 283–345.

Finlayson, L. 2015. "With radicals like these, who needs conservatives? Doom, gloom, and realism in political theory." *European Journal of Political Theory* 16: 264–282.

Geuss, R. 2008. *Philosophy and Real Politics*. Princeton: Princeton University Press.

Hernstein, R. & Murray, C. 1994. *The Bell Curve*. New York: Free Press.

Hinckfuss, I. 1987. *The Moral Society: Its Structure and Effects*. Discussion Papers in Environmental Philosophy 16. Canberra: Philosophy Program (RSSS), Australian National University.

Hume, D. [1740] 1985. *A Treatise of Human Nature*. London: Penguin Classics.

Joyce, R. 2001. *The Myth of Morality*. Cambridge: Cambridge University Press.

Joyce, R. 2006. *The Evolution of Morality*. Cambridge, MA.: MIT Press.

Mackie, J. L. 1977. *Ethics: Inventing Right and Wrong*. New York: Penguin.

Marx, K. [1932] 1998. *The German Ideology*. Amherst, NY: Prometheus Books.

Mills, C. W. 2005. "'Ideal theory' as ideology." *Hypatia* 20: 165–184.

Mills, C. W. 2009. "Rawls on race/race in Rawls." *Southern Journal of Philosophy* 47: 161–184.

Mills, C. W. 2017. *Black Rights/White Wrongs: The Critique of Racial Liberalism*. Oxford: Oxford University Press.

Nietzsche, F. [1887] 1996. *On the Genealogy of Morals*. Oxford: Oxford University Press.

Nolan, D., Restall, G., & West, C. 2005 "Moral fictionalism versus the rest." *Australasian Journal of Philosophy* 83: 307–330.

Nozick, R. 1974. *Anarchy, State, and Utopia*. New York: Basic Books.

Okin, S. M. 1991. *Justice, Gender, and the Family*. New York: Basic Books.

Olson, J. 2014. *Moral Error Theory: History, Critique, Defence*. Oxford: Oxford University Press.

Plantinga, A. 1999. "Pluralism: A defense of religious exclusivism." In K. Meeker & P. Quinn (eds.), *The Philosophical Challenge of Religious Diversity*. New York: Oxford University Press. 172–192.

Rand, D., Pfeiffer, T., Dreber, A., Sheketoff, R., Wernerfelt, N., & Benkler, Y. 2009. "Dynamic remodeling of in-group bias during the 2008 presidential election" *PNAS* 106: 6187–6191.

Rawls, J. 1971. *A Theory of Justice*. Cambridge, MA: Harvard University Press.

Richardson, H. & Weithman, P. (eds.). 1999. *Philosophy of Rawls: A Collection of Essays*. London: Routledge.

Rosen, M. 1996. *On Voluntary Servitude: False Consciousness and the Theory of Ideology*. Cambridge: Polity.

Rousseau, J.-J. [1755] 1985. *A Discourse on Inequality*. New York: Penguin Books.

Stanley, J. 2015. *How Propaganda Works*. Princeton: Princeton University Press.

Steele, C. M. 1999. "The psychology of self-affirmation: Sustaining the integrity of the self." In R. Baumeister (ed.), *Key Readings in Social Psychology: The Self in Social Psychology*. New York: Psychology Press. 372–390.

Stich, S. & Tobia, K. 2016. "Experimental philosophy and the philosophical tradition." In J. Sytsma & W. Buckwalter (eds.), *A Companion to Experimental Philosophy*. Oxford: Wiley Blackwell. 3–21.

Weinberg, J., Nichols, S. & Stich, S. 2001. "Normativity and epistemic intuitions." *Philosophical Topics* 29: 429–460.

White, R. 2010. "You just believe that because . . . " *Philosophical Perspectives* 24: 573–615.

Williams, B. 2005. *In the Beginning Was the Deed: Realism and Moralism in Political Argument*. Princeton: Princeton University Press.

Williamson, T. 2004. "Philosophical 'intuitions' and scepticism about judgement." *Dialectica* 58: 109–153.

Young, I. M. 1990. *Justice and the Politics of Difference*. Princeton: Princeton University Press.

11

SHOULD FEMINISTS BE MORAL ERROR THEORISTS?

Caroline West

1 Introduction

I am a feminist. I am also a moral error theorist: I find the arguments for the view that there are no moral values, as ordinarily conceived, intellectually compelling. But for some time I have been troubled by a nagging sense that these two commitments may not entirely be compatible. This chapter is an attempt to engage this question head-on.

Should feminists be moral error theorists? More specifically, should those of us antecedently committed to helping to bring about social reforms that protect and promote women's interests ("feminist activists") try to internalize the error theory in ourselves and go around advocating this theory publicly with the aim of persuading others to believe that nothing is morally right or wrong (good or bad, forbidden or obligatory, etc.)? Or does an activist feminism need—or, at least, benefit from—the prevailing idea of an "objectively prescriptive" moral reality, however illusory?

Obviously, if we are moral error theorists, we cannot consistently conceive the goals of feminism in terms of righting present wrongs—for moral error theory denies the existence of moral rights and wrongs, as ordinarily conceived. Instead, there are certain non-moral states of affairs (e.g., equal pay for equal work) that most of us who call ourselves "feminists" are committed to trying to bring about. The question is then to what extent achieving these goals depends on widespread—but mistaken—belief in a realm of "objectively prescriptive" moral facts, recognition of which is supposed to provide agents with a reason to act (or to refrain from acting) regardless of their antecedent desires?

The answer to these questions turns largely on what is likely to happen if belief in the error theory were to become widespread. Would central feminist goals—such as equal representation, equal pay for equal work, security from sexual violence, etc.—be more, or less, likely to be achieved if we all came sincerely to believe that nothing is morally right or wrong, good or bad, etc.? Would exposing morality for the myth that it is (by the lights of the error theorist) help to end sexism; or would it slow, halt, or even reverse, such hard-won progress as has been made towards a more sexually egalitarian society?

To date, error theorists have had little to say about the likely consequences specifically for *women* as a group should the error theory succeed in gaining widespread currency. More generally, though, some have suggested that the notion of objective moral truth may operate to benefit certain social groups, while disadvantaging others. For instance, there is a tradition that sees the institution of realist morality functioning primarily as an instrument of oppression, operating as a convenient smokescreen for entrenching and promoting the interests of a ruling elite at the expense of the masses. In *The Communist Manifesto*, Marx famously lists morality along with law and religion as "bourgeois prejudices, behind which lurk in ambush just as many bourgeois interests" ([1848] 2012: 83). Ian Hinckfuss echoes Marx's view, claiming that morality fosters, rather than limits, the exploitation of the "poor and the weak by the rich and powerful" (Hinckfuss 1987: 20–21). Hinckfuss observes that, when one is a privileged member of a moral elite, "it is easy to believe that what one wishes for oneself is morally permissible, and how one wants others to behave is morally obligatory" (1987: 27). In a similar vein, Stephen Ingram writes:

> If your group is in the business of subjugating some other group, one effective way to help sustain that subjugation is to convince everyone that your group is more competent at moral judgement . . . Plausibly, such methods have been used throughout history to help sustain social hierarchies.
>
> *(2015: 238–239)*

Some feminists—most notably, certain strands of postmodern feminism—share a broader version of this suspicion. According to this tradition, the idea of "truth" in general, and hence the notion of moral truth, is oppressive to women; women as a group would be (pragmatically) better off without it (see Bryson 2016).

In this chapter, I make a case for almost the opposite view. I do not deny that moral concepts have sometimes been deployed to motivate and rationalize sexual oppression. Emmeline Pankhurst, a leading suffragette, herself makes the point that men have tried to co-opt morality to support the subjugation of women. (She also notes that men who invoke morality to oppose the enfranchisement of women are conveniently—and indefensibly—selective in their application of moral concepts.) In her autobiography, she writes:

> Men make the moral code and they expect women to accept it. They have decided that it is entirely right and proper for men to fight for their liberties and their rights, but that it is not right and proper for women to fight for theirs.
>
> *(1914: 268)*

It is hard to deny that, when combined with other human failings, such as ignorance, greed, and lack of empathy, morality can be used to serve, rather than to counteract, social oppression. But harmful though the system of morality may be in combination with these other failings, the alternative of a world widely acknowledged to be devoid of moral values is likely to be much, much worse—especially, I will argue, for women and members of other marginalized groups. It is therefore useful for feminists to continue to deploy traditional moral concepts such as *right* and *wrong* in some way, regardless of whether these concepts are instantiated. Properly directed, the institution of morality has an important—perhaps even indispensable—role to play in motivating and sustaining the kind of social changes required to protect and promote women's interests—or so I will argue.

My arguments turn on the widely acknowledged fact that moral beliefs have special connections with motivation and behavior. I will argue that preserving these connections is helpful—perhaps even necessary—for achieving feminist social reform—especially in the absence of other forms of reliable institutional support for such reform. It is doubtful that any non-moral substitute, such as fellow feeling or self-interested rationality (or both), would fully, or even adequately, fill the breach left by morality in motivating progressive social change. Perhaps in a world where there exist enough other institutional incentives for bringing about sexually egalitarian reforms (e.g., legally enforceable pay equity policies, representation quotas), first-order moral convictions about the necessity of making such reforms would be superfluous. Sadly, we do not (yet) live in such a world; to realize feminist aspirations in this world, I will argue, the institution of morality is vital.

If so, one important upshot is that committed feminists would be well advised to steer clear of at least one brand of error theory: moral abolitionism. The abolitionist recommends that the institution of morality be summarily dispensed with: we should all stop using moral language, thinking moral thoughts, and deploying moral concepts when deliberating about what to do. A major conclusion of this chapter is that abolitionists are dangerously misguided to be so confident that the world would be a (non-morally) better—i.e., peaceful and happier—place for all, if we stopped believing in objective moral values. Evidence from evolutionary biology and social psychology suggests that, if anything, the reverse is more likely to occur: without the powerful check on narrowly self-interested motives and behavior provided by the institution of morality, we are likely to end up much closer to a Hobbesian state of nature than we presently are—and certainly a very long way from peace on earth. This is likely to be bad for many people, but especially for those less privileged members of our society.

It is worth noting that the advice to feminists to eschew moral abolitionism holds quite generally, and independently of what you may happen to think about the plausibility of the error theory. For you do not need to be an error theorist to think that the institution of realist morality is net harmful, and to recommend its abolition on the grounds that, when push comes to shove, promoting human welfare is more important than preserving some true beliefs. Obviously, however, the instrumental value of moral practice seems to put the feminist error theorist in a particularly uncomfortable bind. The utility of moral practice means that feminists who believe in the existence of moral facts enjoy a double victory: not only are moral claims true, they are also useful. For the feminist error theorist, however, there is no such happy coincidence; we must choose between intellectual honesty, on the one hand, and the successful pursuit of many of our most heartfelt personal and political commitments, on the other—or so it may seem.

To show that feminists (pragmatically) should not be moral abolitionists is not sufficient to show that feminists should not be error theorists, for abolitionism is just one possible response to the recognition that there are no moral values, as ordinarily conceived. Four other options have been proposed: propagandism, fictionalism, conservationism, and revisionism. In conclusion, I briefly sketch these options, and consider which, if any, should be recommended, insofar as we are concerned to protect and promote the interests of women.

2 Three Functions of Morality

Why think that the institution of realist morality is of great instrumental value—not disvalue—to feminists? After all, as previously mentioned, history appears to show that morality has often been used in ways that are contrary to women's interests. However, while moral concepts have been invoked by some people to defend the subordination of women to men as right and just, we should not conclude from this fact that morality bears all or even much of the responsibility for the oppression of women.

We should begin by noting that morality has not motivated and rationalized patriarchy on its own. It has had some powerful helpers, including social custom, religion, vested interests, and ignorance. It is hard to know exactly how much of the causal responsibility for past and present sexual oppression is owing to people's sincere belief in the justice of women's subordination to men, and how much is down to tradition, self-interest, general ignorance about women's character and capabilities, and the like. Much of morality's apparently sorry track record is plausibly due to the unsavory content of particular first-order moral systems that have wielded currency at various times, rather than to the general idea of morality that includes (among other things) the idea of a class of actions that we have categorical reason to perform (or to refrain from performing), regardless of whether it serves our own interests to do so.

Second, it is a very selective view of history that ignores the role of morality in *counteracting* women's oppression. Moral convictions have played a central role in many reformist social and political movements, motivating activists to make significant personal sacrifices in order to challenge oppressive social and political arrangements. The idea of morality also functions to discourage those in power from abusing their position of power in ways that they could, and probably otherwise would. Ideas such as that women have a moral right to be treated with equal concern and respect, that current social arrangements are unjust, that sexual discrimination is wrong, that men ought not be differentially advantaged, and so on, have played an important role in motivating feminist activists, and in persuading those in power to extend some of the rights and privileges once reserved exclusively for white property-owning men. In what follows, I outline three important functions of morality—motivating feminist activism, discouraging sexism, and persuasion—and explain why they matter for feminism.

To clarify, I will not here be defending the strongest possible view about the importance of morality for feminist politics—viz., the view that the institution of realist morality is strictly *necessary* for the realization of central feminist goals—although I do not discount the possibility that something close to this claim may well be true for creatures psychologically like us. This strong claim rests on a counterfactual that is difficult to confirm empirically. There is, however, considerable evidence to support a weaker claim; namely, that widespread belief in morality makes it considerably more likely that we will achieve central feminist goals more readily.[1] (Conversely, abolishing the institution of morality is very likely to make it much more difficult, if not impossible, to achieve important feminist aims.) If so, there seems to be a strong pragmatic feminist argument not to believe the error theory (at least, in any full-blooded, action-guiding sense of "believe") and not to act in ways that encourage others to believe it. How feminists should respond to this realization—whether by attempting to "hush up" the truth of the error theory ("propagandism"), or else by engaging in moral make-belief, or by recommending the adoption of a surrogate "schmorality," or by some other means—is an important further question. I briefly discuss this question in conclusion.

Moral concepts (*right, wrong, good, bad*, etc.) plausibly function to promote altruism and to discourage narrowly self-interested behavior. This is important for helping to promote feminist goals, for moral thinking can facilitate feminist activism and discourage those in power from acting in ways that disadvantage women, even (or especially) when they can get away with it. I will discuss these in turn before turning to the crucial role moral concepts play in persuading others to alter their attitudes and behaviors.

2.1 Motivating Activism

Moral concepts help to motivate and sustain feminist activism. As feminist activists past and present can testify, challenging established sexist attitudes and norms typically exacts a high personal toll. Consider, for example, the experience of the suffragettes, who had to make enormous sacrifices in order to secure the vote for women. Pilloried as "sickening fools"[2] (among many less pleasant epithets), these "female hooligans"[3] were systematically harassed, threatened, beaten, force-fed, and even imprisoned. Needless to say, this was a very high price to pay—especially for middle-class activists and their families, who could otherwise expect to enjoy an easy life of material and social privilege.[4]

While early suffragettes had to wear wide-brimmed hats to fend off rotten eggs thrown by angry crowds, today's feminist activists must contend with equal if not greater amounts of hostility and intimidation. Jessica Valenti's experience is typical of the price feminists continue to pay even today for speaking out for women's rights. Valenti is a prominent journalist and founder of the blog Feministing.com. Since writing her first feminist piece, Valenti has been the victim of almost constant trolling and harassment, ranging from gross personal abuse to death threats. "You can't get called a c--- day in, day out for 10 years and not have that make a really serious impact on your psyche," writes Valenti, who says that she thinks about quitting "all the time."[5] She is sustained, she says, by deep moral commitment to equality of the sexes, and by the hope that by speaking out she will make a difference.

As cases like these illustrate, challenging sexism is not in anyone's narrow self-interest: the personal costs of "speaking out" are high, the pay-offs are uncertain, and any benefits of rocking the boat are likely to accrue to someone else. This is true not just for prominent feminists like Valenti, who may pay an especially high price for voicing their convictions, but also for less high-profile individuals who take a stand against everyday sexism in the home and workplace by, for example, reporting sexual and domestic violence, workplace harassment, or by calling out disrespectful and misogynistic "banter." In general, taking a stand against sexism is costly—which may explain why less than half of those who witness sexism and discrimination against women report saying or doing anything to challenge it, even when they want to (Pennay & Powell 2012).

Considerations of narrow self-interest therefore direct against taking an activist stance in the first place, let alone remaining committed to the cause as the personal costs of activism start to grow. Fellow feeling, when present, is unlikely often to be sufficient motivation on its own to take up the cause of sexual equality in a pro-active way, or to sustain it longer-term in the face of these kinds of costs.

On the other hand, the belief that promoting sexual equality is a moral imperative is well suited to motivate feminist activism, and to sustain it in the face of the high personal price that must often be paid. One of the roles that morality plays is to get each person sometimes to resist acting in their narrow self-interest—for instance, to challenge sexist attitudes, policies and behavior, even when it would be to their advantage to remain quiet or complicit. As Jessica Isserow writes:

> When people judge that women have a *moral right* to be treated with equal concern, or consider their society *unjust*, they take themselves to have a reason to work against these oppressive social structures. And they take themselves to have such a reason independently of whether these arrangements happen to be to their benefit. Moral requirements are invested with

> categorical authority; they present themselves as inescapable demands. One
> cannot evade their force by citing an immediate interest in non-compliance.
>
> *(Isserow 2017: 117)*

When people conceive of oppressive social structures as the sorts of things that good, rational agents must oppose, whether you want to or not, their motivation to work against them is likely to be stronger; they are less likely to throw in the towel in the face of opposition. As Richard Joyce (2001) notes, one important role that moral beliefs play in our psychology is that they "silence calculation," preventing us from undertaking recurrent cost-benefit analyses that may undermine our resolve or weaken our commitment to achieving long-term goals.

2.2 Discouraging Sexist Behavior

The role of morality in counteracting narrowly self-interested motives is important for overcoming entrenched sexism in a second way. Apart from motivating activism, it functions to discourage sexist attitudes and behavior. For example, at the level of individual behavior, the belief that sexual harassment is wrong—something that you simply must not do, no matter how great the temptation—may help to deter individual men from making unwelcome sexual advances—even (or especially) when, on a particular occasion, the chances of getting away with such behavior without paying the price are high. On an individual level, the belief that such behavior is categorically wrong (as opposed, say, to simply impolite or imprudent) provides would-be perpetrators with an additional bulwark against temptation (Joyce 2001). When widely shared, the belief that sexual harassment is morally unacceptable makes it possible to bring to bear on such behavior the full range of social sanctions that attach to moral infringements, ranging from shame and public disgrace to imprisonment. Mere rudeness or imprudence, on the other hand, though criticizable, does not attract the same forceful array of social disincentives and institutional sanctions that attach to moral misbehavior.[6]

These claims about the importance of the institution of morality for counteracting narrowly self-interested behavior are not based on mere armchair speculation. A popular hypothesis among evolutionary biologists, anthropologists, and sociologists is that moral beliefs are adaptations—both natural and cultural—selected to promote prosocial behavior and counteract the natural human tendency toward narrow self-interest (see Joyce 2006; Kitcher 2011; Tomasello 2016). Exactly what the mechanisms are by which the system of morality operates to counteract narrow self-interest is an important and complex issue. One hypothesis is that it does so partly by providing individuals with a psychologically powerful rationale for having altruistic desires and behaving altruistically. When an action is conceived as right, this is supposed (correctly or erroneously) to give you a reason to do it, and hence for being motivated to do it, other things being equal, whether you want to or not, regardless of whether it is in your own narrow self-interest to perform this act. If our system of morality in some way incorporates an assumption about the rationality of moral behavior, then one of the ways in which coming to believe the error theory may undermine altruism is by stripping away this underlying rationale for being altruistically motivated.

Some disturbing support for this hypothesis comes from studies in social psychology about the effects of studying economics on students' attitudes and behavior.[7] In business economics classes, students learn that the leading theory of rationality (by the lights of economists) is the theory of *homo economicus*, which holds that the rational agent acts so as to maximize their own narrow self-interest. According to this theory of rationality, there are no non-self-interested reasons for action. Learning this alleged truth about rationality, and/or having it reinforced, appears to make students become more self-interested—exactly as you would expect, if agents' motivations are sensitive to their beliefs about rationality. It is worth briefly reviewing some of this evidence.

Economics students are more likely to deceive others for personal gain than students from other majors (see Frank & Schulze 2000). The "Greed is good" credo is not restricted to Gordon Gekko (Oliver Stone film, *Wall Street*); it is a maxim internalized by students who have completed three or more university-level Economics courses: such students disproportionately regard greed as "correct," "generally good," and "moral" (see Wang, Malhotra, & Murnighan 2011). Economics professors give less money to charity than others, and more than twice as many give nothing (Frank, Gilovich, & Regan 1993). Economics students display less concern for fairness than students from other majors, and are much less likely to contribute to the common good. Repeated experiments show that economics students prioritize their self-interest over the common good (Marwell & Ames 1981; Carter & Irons 1991)—they were not prepared to make sacrifices for the overall benefit of the group. One group of researchers concluded that the very concept of *fairness* was "somewhat alien" for economics students (Marwell & Ames 1981: 309).

There is evidence that narrowly self-interested individuals are drawn to study economics in the first place (Frey & Meier 2007); however, there is also a causal effect at work—studying economics appears to make already self-interested individuals considerably more self-interested. Studies show, among other things, a drop in altruistic values among economics majors (Gandal, Roccas, Sagiv, & Wrzesniewski 2005). On starting their degree economics students were the same as their non-economics peers when it came to valuing helpfulness, honesty, and loyalty; yet by third year there was clear disparity—the economics students no longer valued such virtues to the same degree as their non-economics peers. Furthermore, after taking business economics, students become more selfish and have more pessimistic expectations of others (Frank et al. 1993). These findings have led some professors to express qualms about teaching business economics.[8]

Economics students are not officially moral error theorists. Nonetheless, these findings lend empirical support to the hypothesis that beliefs about rationality play a role in sustaining altruistic preferences and behavior in many, if not all, agents: coming to believe that there are no non-self-interested reasons for action makes individuals more selfish. Since moral error theory likewise teaches that one need have no reason to fail to be self-interested, there is ground for thinking that learning moral error theory is likely to produce similar effects to internalizing the economic theory of rationality. Of course, upon coming to believe the moral error theory, individuals may still have altruistic preferences and, insofar as you happen to have these preferences, you still have reason to satisfy them. What both the economic theory of rationality and the moral error theory teach you, however, is that you need have no reason to have such altruistic preferences. The evidence about the effects of studying business economics supports the hypothesis that having the belief that there are reasons in favor of having altruistic preferences plays a role in preserving such preferences (Braddon-Mitchell 2006). If so, we would expect to see a decrease in the number and strength of altruistic desires among some, if not all, of those converted to the error theory, just as we see a decrease in such preferences among students who internalize the ideology of *homo economicus*. One probable consequence of such widespread re-enculturation would be that those who are disadvantaged by sexist social arrangements, and so who stand as a group to benefit from feminist reform, will come to be less individually motivated to bear the personal costs of pursuing these reforms. Another likely result would be that those who currently benefit from such arrangements will be less likely to act against their own interests by challenging them.

The actual effects of widespread belief in the moral error theory may in fact be even worse than these studies indicate. The studies look at the effects of internalizing the theory of self-interest in the broader context of a moral society, where most other individuals believe in right and wrong, and where there exists a well-established system of incentives for moral behavior: praise for behavior that is widely judged to be morally good, and blame, disapprobation, and punishment for conduct society deems to be immoral. Since most of us desire the good opinion of others (and of ourselves), this system of social punishments and rewards has a significant influence on how we behave: it makes us more likely to behave in ways that will be regarded as morally good and hence praiseworthy, and less likely to behave in ways that will be seen as culpably wrong. However, in a society where nobody (or hardly anybody) believes in moral goodness or culpable wrongness, the self-interest effect is likely to be further compounded by the group polarization effect.[9] Moral error theorists living in a society of like-minded error theorists are therefore likely to become even more narrowly self-interested still.

2.3 Persuasion

We also use moral discourse to attempt to persuade others to alter their attitudes and behavior. According to some, the primary function of ethical talk is to "preach"—that is, to spread our desires by persuading our society to enshrine them in the form of general rules of conduct from which deviation will be punished, if not by law, then by social sanctions such as blame and shame (McDermott 1978). This may not be an especially appealing picture of moral discourse, but it is hard to deny that at least one of the functions of ethical discourse is to change the attitudes of our audience in certain ways and, through this, their behavior. We hope that by persuading our interlocutors to believe that women deserve the same pay rates as men, we will bring about a corresponding change in their behavior: they will come to be motivated to do, and hence hopefully be led actually to do, what they come to believe to be right (and, conversely, to refrain from performing those actions they believe to be wrong)—or, at least, to feel that they *should* be so motivated. Our aim in seeking to persuade others that a policy that permits unequal pay is wrong is to get them to disapprove of unequal pay, to stop supporting politicians and policies that support or allow it, perhaps to criticize other people for supporting policies that permit it, and also for failing to criticize others who fail to criticize these sorts of policies, and so on—all in virtue of having successfully been persuaded that unequal pay is morally wrong.

Moral concepts provide an especially effective tool for altering people's attitudes and behavior because they are generally supposed to have a very tight connection with motivation, at least in well-motivated and rational agents.[10] Thus, if you succeed in persuading someone that a particular action or policy is morally required, then they will feel considerable normative and psychological pressure to pursue or support it: as previously discussed, insofar as they succeed in doing what they believe to be right, they will feel the pleasure of satisfaction or pride; insofar as they fail to do so, they will experience unpleasant pangs of guilt or remorse. Further, if you succeed in convincing not just one person but many other people that some action or policy is morally just or required, then this widespread conviction will invoke the powerful social system of incentives that goes with moral belief: widespread public praise for this policy and for those who support it, along with praise for those who criticize those who fail to support it, and so forth. On the other hand, while the thought that some action (including supporting some particular policy) is the polite thing to do, or is in one's rational self-interest, may provide some normative and psychological pressure toward doing it, these considerations do not typically license the same wide and powerful array of social and institutional sanctions and supports that deeply and widely shared moral convictions do.

The moral abolitionist argues that we should dispense with the idea that policies such as equal pay for equal work are morally required as a matter of justice or some such (see Garner 2010). According to the abolitionist, humankind as a whole will be net better off if we abolish all ideas of morality from our hearts and minds. Perhaps so (although I somewhat doubt it). But will things be better for *women* as a group if we abolish morality? Will feminists be more or less able to alter people's attitudes on matters crucial to women's interests if we give up the "moral overlay"?

If we follow moral abolitionists' advice, then, instead of telling people about their moral obligations, feminists pragmatically should just tell them how feminists would like them to treat women, and explain why. For instance, feminists should just tell employers that women would like to be paid the same as their male counterparts because women are just as good at the job as the men are. Perhaps they should also mention that many female employees are angry and upset at being paid less than men. And then we should cross our fingers and hope that there are some employers who care. One does not have to be especially cynical to think that this strategy is unlikely to be very successful at getting employers to alter their remuneration policies. Most employers, I hazard, are already well aware of the fact that women would like to be paid the same as men for the same work. But they are predominantly self-interested: they would rather not pay women more than they presently do, unless the costs to them of failing to do so come to outweigh the benefits. The institution of morality provides a powerful lever of influence to counteract corporate (and other forms of) self-interest: if we can say that employers are morally obliged to pay people at the same rate for the same work regardless of their sex, then we can say that they have a reason to do so, whether they want to or not, and that they are rationally defective for failing to do so, regardless of whether this serves the interests of the company and its shareholders, and we can bring to bear the full range of social sanctions and incentives discussed previously. It is hard to believe that this moralizing strategy will not be considerably more effective than the abolitionists' strategy in effecting social change.[11]

3 The Options Remaining: Propagandism, Fictionalism, Conservationism, and Revisionism

If, as I have argued, morality is instrumentally important for achieving central feminist goals, then there is a strong pragmatic feminist argument not to dispense with it; feminists (pragmatically) should not be moral abolitionists. What, then, should we do, if we are feminists and we are intellectually persuaded that there are no moral values, as ordinarily conceived?

This depends partly on whether we are imagining a situation in which the truth of the error theory is already a matter of common knowledge or not. Let us focus on what feminist activists should do in the actual world, where, at present, the error theory is well and truly a minority view, believed only by a handful of professional philosophers and a few precocious undergraduates. In this scenario, there are four options: propagandism, fictionalism, conservationism, and revisionism. The so-called propagandist holds that the truth of the error theory should not be publicized, for doing so would result in more harm than good (Cuneo & Christy 2011). The moral fictionalist maintains that we can preserve many of the practical benefits of morality, whilst avoiding bad faith, by preserving moral language in the form of a useful fiction (Joyce 2001; Nolan, Restall, & West 2005).

The moral conservationist recommends that we can better preserve the benefits of morality by continuing with our current error-ridden moral discourse, believing it in some contexts but not others (Olson 2014; Isserow 2017). The revisionist recommends that we can best preserve the practical benefits of morality by revising our conception of right and wrong in some or other pragmatically desirable way (Köhler & Ridge 2013; Lutz 2014). Which of these options should a committed feminist error theorist favor?

The answer obviously depends crucially on which (if any) of these options is likely best to preserve the aforementioned benefits of morality in terms of counteracting narrowly self-interested motives and behavior and providing a framework for persuasion. It also depends on which conception(s) it is psychologically feasible for us to internalize, for there is no point in recommending that we internalize a conception that we are psychologically unable to deploy, however beneficial it would be if we could. These are large, contested, and ultimately empirical questions, and I will not attempt to provide a definitive answer here. None of the available options is without drawbacks. In what follows, I outline some of the principal concerns about each of the available options, without attempting to settle definitively the question of which option is likely to be least costly for women as a group.

Let's begin by considering the moral fictionalist option. The main issue here is to what extent adopting a fictionalist attitude toward morality will be effective in securing the benefits of genuine, full-blooded moral belief. This may vary depending on exactly what brand of fictionalism we are considering. So-called "preface" fictionalists, such as Joyce (2001), recommend that we all start "make-believing," rather than believing, moral propositions. A significant concern about preface fictionalism is that make-belief in women's rights may not in fact be able to play enough of the distinctive role that genuine belief in women's rights plays in counteracting sexism and motivating positive social change. For example, someone who make-believes that the principle of equal pay for equal work is a moral imperative may be more inclined to take some actions to support it than someone who has ceased to deploy moral concepts altogether, but they are likely to be less inclined to fight for this principle as long or as strongly as someone who literally believes it, especially as the personal stakes get high. Likewise, someone who make-believes that sexual harassment is morally wrong (or who believes that it is wrong according to some or other moral fiction) seems likely to give into temptation more readily than someone who genuinely believes that such behavior is morally forbidden. Similar concerns may apply to other brands of fictionalism: insofar as the fictionalist attitude toward morality differs from literal belief, it is unlikely to secure the full benefits of genuine moral belief. Some moral fictionalists (e.g., Joyce 2001: 214) have openly acknowledged that moral make-belief, while better than nothing, is likely to be less effective than genuine moral belief at combating weakness of will and motivating prosocial behavior. The question is whether any of the other available options can do better.

Will the revisionist fare better in securing the benefits of morality for women? This will depend somewhat on the details of the particular revision that is being recommended: there are multiple different ways in which our existing moral concepts could be revised, and some revisions are likely to be better than others in terms of securing the benefits of the existing system of morality. There is, however, a general worry about revisionism: whichever *schmoral* conception that the revisionist recommends we deploy will have to be one that is purged of the problematic feature of morality—namely, its supposed "categorical authority" or "objective prescriptivity." But many of the beneficial roles that morality plays, especially the distinctive action-guiding force of moral judgments, seem inextricably linked to this problematic feature (West 2010). It is therefore highly questionable whether any system of *schmorality* will be able to play (enough of) the distinctive role of morality in motivating activism, persuading people to alter their attitudes toward women and women's issues, and counteracting narrowly self-interested sexist behavior. This makes revisionism, like fictionalism, a risky proposition for committed feminists to recommend.

On the face of it, conservationism may seem better placed than either fictionalism or revisionism to secure the practical benefits of existing moral practice, since it recommends that we continue to believe (in a full-blooded, action-guiding sense of "believe") in objectively prescriptive moral facts, just as we always have. The main distinction between the conservationist and the moral realist is supposed to lie in what each will be disposed to say in "critical contexts" (e.g., the philosophy classroom) when asked questions such as "Is sexually harassing women really morally wrong?" To this question, in this context, the realist, but not the conservationist, will answer "Yes." For all practical intents and purposes outside the philosophy room, however, the moral conservationist will be psychologically and behaviorally indistinguishable from the moral realist—for example, they will continue to assert that sexually harassing women is wrong, and also to experience outrage at such behavior, and also to condemn those who engage in it, along with those who fail to condemn those who engage in it, and so on. Leaving aside definitional issues about whether mere verbal-cum-intellectual assent in the philosophy room is sufficient to count in any sense as "belief," there also remains an empirical psychological question as to what extent one's intellectual "disbelief" in morality is likely to sap one's practical belief in morality. It is hard to accept that a reflective conservationist would not experience some psychological tension and leakage from critical to practical contexts that would test and potentially diminish their level of personal commitment to feminist goals, especially when engaged in critical reflection on social policy questions (when belief in the error theory is likely to be engaged), or when the pursuit of feminist goals demands significant personal sacrifices.

The final option is "propagandism."[12] The propagandist holds that the truth of the error theory should not be publicized, for doing so would result in more harm than good. Propagandism is not a particularly popular view—not least because its success is thought to require "systematic intellectual dishonesty, deception and elitism" (Köhler & Ridge 2013: 438). These worries are real, but possibly overstated. Truth and honesty are important values: other things being equal, we should honor them when we can. But—as many people agree—if the consequences of truth-telling on a particular occasion are sufficiently bad, then concealing the truth may be the best thing to do on that occasion, all things considered. If, as previously argued, the consequences for women of publicizing the error theory would be very bad—if, for instance, widespread belief in the error theory would halt social progress and threaten many of the hard-won gains of the women's movement—then concealing the truth of the moral error theory may be justified, all things considered.[13] (Truth is often concealed for considerably less important reasons than these.) Given how psychologically difficult it is for most error theorists to believe (in a full-blooded, action-guiding sense of "believe") the error theory outside of the philosophy classroom, concealing the moral error theory is unlikely to have the consequence of rendering us all "epistemological wrecks," as Richard Garner (1993: 96) fears.[14]

In fact, however, concealment is probably unnecessary, for the error theory is unlikely to spread very widely, even if it is publicized. Hard though many committed error theorists find it to believe, most people do not find the arguments for the error theory very compelling. (For instance, despite having been presented with all the arguments in class and readings, most philosophy students are not converted to the error theory by the end of their metaethics courses—even when the arguments are presented most sympathetically.) If the danger were real that the error theory would spread, then the case for propagandism would be strong. But insofar as the danger in fact seems small, propagandism is for all practical purposes irrelevant.

Conclusion

It is important for all of us—including, but not limited to, those of us who are moral error theorists—to recognize the vital role that the institution of morality has to play in protecting and promoting the interests of women. For feminists who are moral realists, this is a happy result; the work to be done consists in enlightening and encouraging us to enact the sexually liberatory policies and behaviors that morality demands. For feminist moral error theorists, however, important further conceptual and empirical work still remains to be done. We must determine which conception is most likely to secure most fully the benefits of the system of morality for women—and then promote it.

Acknowledgments

Thanks to Richard Joyce, Moira Gatens, Robert Bezimienny, David Braddon-Mitchell, and members of the Department of Philosophy at the University of Sydney for many helpful comments and suggestions.

Notes

1 It is probably of little consequence if a few people believe the error theory, but it would be pragmatically best for women as a group if this belief does not become too common.
2 This phrase was used in hate mail sent to "Miss Pankhurst and her crew" in 1909 (as seen in an exhibition on the suffragette movement at the Museum of London, 2018).
3 So called by Arthur Conan Doyle (quoted in *The Times*, April 29, 1913: 10).
4 Working-class activists often had less to lose. Consequently, although many working-class activists were also in fact motivated by moral convictions, this conviction may not have needed to play the same role in counteracting self-interest as it did for middle-class suffragettes.
5 "Feminists in a digital age pay a steep psychological price," www.chicagotribune.com/news/opinion/commentary/chi-feminists-internet-psychological-price-20150221-story.html
6 Hinkfuss (this volume) lists "guilt" as one objectionable feature of our present system of morality. I agree that guilt is unpleasant to experience, and that a system of morality that makes people feel guilty for harmless acts (e.g., masturbation) is pragmatically undesirable. On the other hand, it is surely desirable for people to feel guilt for acts such sexually harassing women, insofar as it deters them from performing acts of this type.
7 Thanks to David Braddon-Mitchell for drawing my attention to these findings.
8 See http://evonomics.com/more-evidence-that-learning-economics-makes-you-selfish/
9 Extensive research confirms that interaction with people who share one's views on a certain topic tends to amplify one's view—turning a moderate belief into a more extreme one. See Isenberg 1986.
10 This connection might be a constitutive, conceptual connection, as internalists claim, or alternatively a robust external, empirical connection, as externalists claim. I do not take a stand on this issue here.
11 At least, insofar as our society and interlocutors buy into the idea of morality. It is an important further question to what extent moralizing will continue to be effective in a world where the error theory is widely believed, and whether there is any way to preserve the benefits of moralizing short of full-blooded moral belief.
12 This somewhat pejorative label is due to Joyce (2001).
13 For a sympathetic discussion of moral propagandism, see Cuneo and Christy (2011).
14 Braddon-Mitchell (2006) defends a kind of propagandism that does not involve the theorist in false belief.

References

Braddon-Mitchell, D. 2006. "Believing falsely makes it so." *Mind* 115: 833–866.

Bryson, V. 2016. *Feminist Political Theory*. London: Macmillan.

Carter, J. & Irons, M. 1991. "Are economists different, and if so, why?" *Journal of Economic Perspectives* 1991: 171–177.

Cuneo, T. & Christy, S. 2011. "The myth of moral fictionalism." In M. Brady (ed.), *New Waves in Metaethics*. London: Palgrave Macmillan. 85–102.

Frank, B. & Schulze, G. 2000. "Does economics make citizens corrupt?" *Journal of Economic Behavior and Organization* 43: 101–113.

Frank, R., Gilovich, T., & Regan, D. 1993. "Does studying economics inhibit cooperation?" *Journal of Economic Perspectives* 7: 159–171.

Frey, B. & Meier, S. 2007. "Are political economists selfish and indoctrinated? Evidence from a natural experiment." *Economic Inquiry* 41: 448–462.

Gandal, N., Roccas, S., Sagiv, L., & Wrzesniewski, A. 2005. "Personal value priorities of economists." *Human Relations* 58: 1227–1252.

Garner, R. 1993. "Are convenient fictions harmful to your health?" *Philosophy East and West* 43: 87–106.

Garner, R. 2010. "Abolishing morality." In R. Joyce & S. Kirchin (eds.), *A World Without Values: Essays on John Mackie's Moral Error Theory*. Dordrecht: Springer. 217–233.

Hinckfuss, I. 1987. *The Moral Society: Its Structure and Effects*. Discussion Papers in Environmental Philosophy 16. Canberra: Philosophy Program (RSSS), Australian National University.

Ingram, S. 2015. "After moral error theory, after moral realism." *Southern Journal of Philosophy* 53: 227–248.

Isenberg, D. 1986. "Group polarization: A critical review and meta-analysis." *Journal of Personality and Social Psychology* 50: 1141–1151.

Isserow, J. 2017. *What to Do When Life Doesn't Play Along: Life after Moral Error Theory* (PhD dissertation). Australian National University, Canberra.

Joyce, R. 2001. *The Myth of Morality*. Cambridge: Cambridge University Press.

Joyce, R. 2006. *The Evolution of Morality*. Cambridge, MA: MIT Press.

Kitcher, P. 2011. *The Ethical Project*. Cambridge, MA: Harvard University Press.

Köhler, S. & Ridge, M. 2013. "Revolutionary expressivism." *Ratio* 26: 428–449.

Lutz, M. 2014. "The 'now what' problem for error theory." *Philosophical Studies* 171: 351–371.

McDermott, M. 1978. "How to preach." *Canadian Journal of Philosophy* 8: 633–652.

Marwell, G. & Ames, R. 1981. "Economists free ride, does anyone else?" *Journal of Public Economics* 15: 295–310.

Marx, K. & Engels, F. [1848] 2012. *The Communist Manifesto*. New York: Verso.

Nolan, D., Restall, G., & West, C. 2005. "Moral fictionalism versus the rest." *Australasian Journal of Philosophy* 83: 307–330.

Olson, J. 2014. *Moral Error Theory: History, Critique, Defence*. Oxford: Oxford University Press.

Pankhurst, E. 1914. *My Own Story*. London: Eveleigh Nash.

Pennay, D. & Powell, A. 2012. *The Role of Bystander Knowledge, Attitudes and Behaviours in Preventing Violence Against Women: A Full Technical Report*. The Social Research Centre, Melbourne.

Tomasello, M. 2016. *A Natural History of Human Morality*. Cambridge, MA: Harvard University Press.

Wang, L., Malhotra, D. & Murnighan, J. 2011. "Economics education and greed." *Academy of Management Learning and Education* 1: 643–660.

West, C. 2010. "Business as usual? The error theory, internalism and the function of morality." In R. Joyce & S. Kirchin (eds.), *A World Without Values: Essays on John Mackie's Moral Error Theory*. Dordrecht: Springer. 183–198.

12

THE EFFECTS OF MORALITY ON ACTING AGAINST CLIMATE CHANGE

Thomas Pölzler

Suppose you are a moral error theorist, i.e., you believe that no moral judgment is true (see, e.g., Mackie 1977; Joyce 2001, 2013, 2015; Lillehammer 2004; Pigden 2007).[1] What, then, ought you to do with regard to our common practice of making such judgments?

At first sight, the answer to this question seems straightforward. If one denies that any moral judgment is true, then one obviously ought to stop making such judgments. Instead of believing actions to be morally wrong, for example, one should only be opposed to them, dislike them, or be willing to punish those who engage in them. Many error theorists have indeed recommended such an "abolitionist" stance (Hinckfuss 1987; Garner 1994, 2007, this volume; Burgess 2007: 438; Marks 2013). However, as even acknowledged by these abolitionists themselves, it is by no means obvious—and hence requires argument—that adopting moral error theory forces one to give up on moral judgments.

Assuming the truth of error theory, one cannot possibly have *moral* reasons to stop making such judgments. The question of how to go on is, rather, exclusively prudential in nature, i.e., it depends on which course of action is most conducive to our individual or collective interests (see Joyce 2001: 177; Garner 2007: 507; Ingram 2015: 228). Many error theorists have recently argued that our ordinary moral practice serves our interests pretty well. In particular, "conservationists" claim that error theorists ought to make moral judgments in the same way as non-error theorists do (e.g., Olson 2014; Eriksson & Olson, this volume; Isserow, this volume); and "fictionalists" recommend that error theorists at least *pretend* to make such judgments, i.e., that they treat morality as a "useful fiction" (Joyce 2001, 2005, this volume; Nolan, Restall, & West 2005).

Let us grant that conservationism and fictionalism are logically and psychologically coherent.[2] The appropriateness of the above three error theoretic recommendations (abolitionism, conservationism, and fictionalism), then, mainly depends on two issues: (1) on the nature of our interests, and (2) on whether making or not making moral judgments is more conducive to these interests. In this chapter I will be concerned with the second of these issues. So far this issue—the question of the usefulness of moral judgments—has typically been addressed in very general terms. Richard Garner, for example, tries to show that "there are more problems with morality [i.e., morality as a general social practice] than moralists and moral fictionalists usually admit" (2007: 511). And, according to Richard Joyce, "morality [again, morality in general] can continue to furnish significant benefit" (2001: 205).

To my mind, the validity of such general reflections about the usefulness of moral judgments is doubtful. Moral judgments are omnipresent and multifaceted. They can be about actions, persons, or states of affairs; they can involve thin moral concepts (such as "right" or "bad") or thick ones (such as "honest" or "just"); they can be about issues as diverse as care, fairness, liberty, loyalty, authority, or sanctity; they can be accompanied by realist or antirealist metaethical experiences; they can be caused by slow, voluntary, and effortful reasoning or quick, automatic, and effortless affective reactions; they can be made in private or in professional contexts; and so on (e.g., Greene, Sommerville, Nystrom, Darley, & Cohen 2001; Haidt 2012; Sinnott-Armstrong & Wheatley 2012; Wright, Grandjean, & McWhite 2013; Wright, McWhite, & Grandjean 2014). Given this great number and variety of moral judgments, it seems that error theory's practical implications are better investigated by (scientifically informed) in-depth case studies than by considerations about the usefulness of all of these judgments taken together.

In this chapter I provide such an in-depth case study with regard to a particularly important matter: climate change. Climate ethicists to some extent agree that (many) individuals in industrialized countries are morally obliged to act against climate change. For example, these individuals are said to have a responsibility to limit their amount of consumption, to use public transportation instead of cars, to switch to a (largely) meat-free diet (see, e.g., Schwenkenbecher 2014; Peeters, De Smet, Diependaele, & Sterckx 2015), or at the very least to vote for political parties that can be expected to promote climate-friendly legislation (Sinnott-Armstrong 2005; Maltais 2013). My main hypothesis in this chapter is that the judgment that people in industrialized countries are obliged to act against climate change is neither harmful (as abolitionism suggests) nor beneficial (as conservationism and fictionalism suggest).[3] The judgment, rather, does not have any significant effect on those who accept it at all.

My argument for the above hypothesis involves two main steps. In section 1, I outline general conditions for when a moral judgment has any effect on those who accept it. In section 2, I then show that the judgment that people in industrialized countries are morally obliged to act against climate change does not fulfill these conditions to any significant extent.[4] This already completes my case for the ineffectiveness of the above judgment. Considering the threat that climate change poses to so many human and non-human beings as well as ecosystems, however, it would clearly be disappointing to end on such a pessimistic note. In section 3, I therefore sketch several strategies for increasing people's non-moral motivation to act against climate change.

1 The Effectiveness of Moral Judgments

Moral judgments can affect our lives in many different ways; it would be impossible for a chapter such as this to cover all of them. Fortunately, doing so is not even necessary. My aim here is to contribute to the debate between abolitionists, conservationists, and fictionalists. Proponents of each of these positions have (plausibly) emphasized different ways in which moral judgments might matter to those who make them. In what follows I will thus draw on these well-established views.

Very roughly, abolitionists, conservationists, and fictionalists assume that moral judgments mainly tend to be effective in two ways: (1) by immediately prompting corresponding actions, and (2) by affecting our thoughts and utterances (which may then motivate further action). Let me explain these two possible forms of effectiveness in more detail.

a) Immediate Effects on Action

Moral judgments often immediately lead persons to act according to them. Someone who judges that it would be morally wrong to sleep with his sister, for example, may for that very reason refrain from actually sleeping with her.[5] But under what conditions do moral judgments have such an immediate behavioral effect?

The answer to this question to some extent depends on moral judgments' conceptual relation to motivation. In this chapter I assume an "internalist" account of this relation. This is not only due to internalism's plausibility (e.g., Hare 1952; Smith 1994; Blackburn 2000; Gibbard 2003), but also to dialectical reasons. Moral judgments turn out significantly more behaviorally effective according to motivational internalism than according to the opposing "externalist" account. Assuming internalism thus helps to forestall an obvious objection against my arguments in this chapter: namely, the objection that the judgment that we are morally obliged to act against climate change turns out ineffective only on externalist grounds (and not assuming internalism).

Motivational internalists believe that for a person to make a moral judgment entails that s/he has a motive to act in conformity with this judgment.[6] Suppose one conceives of this motive as overriding, i.e., as stronger than any conflicting motive. Then the relation between moral judgments and corresponding actions could be determined on purely conceptual grounds. As a matter of conceptual necessity, any moral judgment would immediately lead to corresponding action. But even internalists themselves widely acknowledge that this view is far too strong. Although moral judgments under normal circumstances[7] entail motives for corresponding action, persons may fail to act upon these motives. In particular, they may fail to do so for either or both of two contingent reasons: (1) these moral motives are (very) weak, or (2) the persons' conflicting non-moral motives are (very) strong (see Birnbacher 2009; Zangwill 2015; but see McDowell 1978).

It is difficult to come up with meaningful generalizations about the strength of people's *non-moral* motives. These motives just vary too much, both from person to person and from issue to issue. That said, recent findings in empirical moral psychology at least allow for predictions about the strength of people's *moral* motives.

On a plausible "dual process model," as most famously advocated by Joshua Greene et al. (2001, Greene, Nystrom, Engell, Darley, & Cohen 2004), moral judgments can result from two different kinds of mental processes: (1) slow, voluntary, and effortful reasoning, and (2) quick, automatic, and effortless affective reactions,[8] also referred to as "moral intuitions" (Haidt 2001). Judgments arising from the reasoning system and judgments arising from the affective system have been found to differ in various respects. Most importantly for our purposes, "hot" (i.e., affectively grounded) judgments typically involve much stronger motives to act according to them than "cold" (i.e., reasoned) judgments (Haidt 2001: 824; Haidt & Kesebir 2010: 806; Lerner, Li, Valdesolo, & Kassam 2015). For example, while few people are moved by their judgment that copyright infringement is morally impermissible, judgments about the wrongness of incest typically exert a very strong behavioral influence.

We may thus conclude that, other things being equal, moral judgments are more likely to immediately lead to corresponding actions if they result from moral intuitions rather than from reasoning.

b) Effects on Thought and Talk

Besides immediately prompting corresponding actions, people's moral judgments can variously affect the ways in which they think and speak as well (which may then motivate further action). Abolitionists, conservationists, and fictionalists are notoriously divided about the nature and relative significance of these indirect effects. Here I will focus on those three kinds of effects which—rightly, to my mind—have so far received most attention.

First, as pointed out by conservationists and fictionalists, (particular) moral judgments might matter because avoiding them is *difficult*, in the sense of requiring conscious cognitive effort, (e.g., Lutz 2014: 357; Nolan et al. 2005). The sources of this difficulty can vary. Sometimes a person cannot help but make a particular moral judgment because s/he has held this judgment for many years, and is thus driven to it by the sheer force of habit. Humans may also have innate tendencies to judge particular actions to be morally right, wrong, good, bad, etc.—i.e., tendencies that develop in (almost) any environment, irrespective of a person's socialization, culture, beliefs, and so forth (see Lycan 1986: n. 29; Ruse 1998). Finally, particular moral judgments can also be difficult to avoid because they are constitutive elements of a person's self or character (think, for example, of people who are vegetarians or who oppose abortion).

Second, as also pointed out by conservationists and fictionalists, (particular) moral judgments might have an effect on how we think and speak in virtue of their avoidance being *inconvenient*. Sometimes moral concepts allow us to state certain non-moral facts particularly economically (Lutz 2014: 357–358; Nolan et al. 2005). For example, if a political theorist claims of a certain social policy that it is "just," his colleagues may unequivocally interpret him as expressing various complicated beliefs about the consequences of this policy on persons' basic liberties, on the well-being of the least well-off among them, and on equality of opportunity. Moreover, avoiding particular moral judgments may also be inconvenient in that it may be regarded as "awkward and suspicious" (Lutz 2014: 358). Suppose a person publically refuses to agree that ISIS fighters are morally depraved. Chances are that this person will be confronted with some serious questions.[9]

Finally, abolitionists have often claimed that moral judgements affect persons' thoughts and utterances by making them *less tolerant towards disagreeing others*. Garner, for example, writes: "Morality inflames disputes . . . If we hope to resolve conflicts by arriving at a compromise, our task will be easier if moral disagreements are seen as partial conflicts of interest 'without the embroidery of rights and moral justification'" (2007: 502; see also Hinckfuss 1987, excerpted in this volume; Marks 2013: 45). While recent psychological research supports this hypothesis (e.g., Haidt, Rosenberg, & Hom 2003; Skitka, Bauman, & Sargis 2005; Wright, Cullum, & Schwab 2008; Wright 2012), it is important to note that it does not do so invariably. Persons' tolerance for disagreeing others rather seems to decrease as a function of their metaethical interpretations of moral judgements. If one interprets a moral judgement according to moral realism, i.e., as true in an objective (mind-independent) sense, this judgement indeed tends to make one less open towards diverging moral views. Judgements which are regarded as subjectively true or as expression of desires, by contrast, do not have a comparably strong effect (Wright et al. 2014: 37, 46; see also Goodwin & Darley 2008; Skitka et al. 2005, Skitka & Morgan 2014).

2 The Effectiveness of Judging Oneself Morally Obliged to Act Against Climate Change

In order for a moral judgment to be able to have beneficial or harmful effects it obviously must have any effects at all. In section 1, I introduced and explained two main ways in which moral judgments might be effective. Such judgments tend to prompt immediate corresponding actions, I argued, if they are caused by affective reactions; and they tend to influence our thought and talk if they are difficult to avoid, inconvenient to avoid, or decrease our tolerance for disagreeing others. After these preliminaries, we can now come to our actual object of interest: namely, the judgment that one is morally obliged to act against climate change. In this section I will suggest that for most people in industrialized countries this judgment does not fulfill any of the above conditions to a significant extent. The judgment must therefore be regarded as ineffective.

a) Immediate Effects on Acting Against Climate Change

To begin with, for people in industrialized countries, the judgment that one is morally obliged to act against climate change does not tend to be caused by affective reactions, and thus does not immediately prompt them to take such action.[10]

Converging evidence from psychology and neighboring sciences suggests that harmful actions trigger affective reactions to the extent to which these actions exhibit the following three features: (1) the harm is inflicted intentionally, i.e., the agent *wants* to harm the victim(s) (see Greene et al. 2001: 2107, 2004: 389; Cushman 2008; Guglielmo, Monroe, & Malle 2009); (2) the victim(s) is(/are) perceived as socially similar ("one of us"), which at the very least requires that they can be identified as determinate persons (see Tajfel, Billig, Bundy, & Flament 1971; Greene et al. 2001: 2107, 2004: 389); and (3) the action can be processed in a cognitively effortless way, i.e., it is simple (as opposed to complex), concrete (as opposed to abstract), and non-probabilistic (as opposed to probabilistic) (see Weber 2006; Markowitz & Sharif 2012: 243–244).

It is easy to see that the problem of climate change lacks all three of the above intuition-triggering features.

First, nobody who emits greenhouse gases intends to do so. These emissions just happen to be causally implied by many ordinary (otherwise often innocent) actions that people perform—actions such as picking up one's children from school, buying a new smartphone, or eating a burger (Jamieson 2010; Markowitz & Shariff 2012: 244).

Second, the victims of emission-generating activities are predominantly very dissimilar from people currently living in industrialized countries. Most of these victims live in developing countries (where people are less able to protect themselves from environmental threats, the frequency and intensity of extreme meteorological events is particularly high, etc.). Many of them will also only live in the (distant) future (where the effects of climate change will be more grave than they are today). Moreover, due to the attribution problem stated below, and our limited knowledge of the future, for at least some of the victims of climate change we cannot tell what they are or will be like at all (Gardiner 2011; IPCC 2014).

Third, climate change is also a highly complex, abstract, and probabilistic problem. Greenhouse gases become effective only years or decades after they have been emitted, and stay in the atmosphere for very long times, dispersing according to highly complex patterns. People generally tend to represent future events as rather abstract. Nobody personally experiences greenhouse gases, and many people currently living in industrialized countries have not yet been sufficiently noticeably exposed to their environmental consequences either. Scientists can provide only statistical data about whether particular droughts, floods, storms, and other harmful events are attributable to climate change. They cannot also tell precisely who is causally responsible to what extent for climate change (e.g., Jamieson 1992: 149, 2010: 436; Weber 2006: 108; Markowitz & Shariff 2012: 243–244; Van der Linden, Maibach, & Leiserowitz 2015: 759).

Finally, humans' lack of affective reactions towards climate change makes good sense from an evolutionary perspective as well. Many of our moral intuitions have been shaped by natural selection (e.g., Ruse 1998; Haidt 2001: 826). This happened thousands, maybe even hundreds of thousands, of years ago. At this time global and future-affecting environmental problems had not yet come into existence. For example, our distant ancestors could not affect the fate of people living in faraway places or in the distant future, they had unlimited access to land and other resources, and they could reproduce without giving any thought to overpopulation. Responding affectively to global and future-affecting environmental problems therefore could not have possibly increased our ancestors' biological fitness—which means that it could not become promoted by evolved psychological mechanisms (Jamieson 1992: 148).

Let me conclude our investigation of morality's immediate effect on acting against climate change by a quote from Daniel Gilbert, which vividly depicts the problem that I just pointed out:[11]

> [G]lobal warming doesn't . . . violate our moral sensibilities. It doesn't cause our blood to boil (at least not figuratively) because it doesn't force us to entertain thoughts that we find indecent, impious or repulsive. When people feel insulted or disgusted, they generally do something about it, such as whacking each other over the head, or voting. Moral emotions are the brain's call to action. Although all human societies have moral rules about food and sex, none has a moral rule about atmospheric chemistry. And so we are outraged about every breach of protocol except Kyoto. Yes, global warming is bad, but it doesn't make us feel nauseated or angry or disgraced, and thus we don't feel compelled to rail against it as we do against other momentous threats to our species, such as flag burning. The fact is that if climate change were caused by gay sex, or by the practice of eating kittens, millions of protesters would be massing in the streets.
>
> *(Gilbert 2006)*

b) Effects on Climate-Related Thought and Talk

Judging ourselves morally obliged to act against climate change fails to immediately prompt corresponding action. In addition, I believe that this judgment does not significantly affect the thoughts and utterances of people in industrialized countries either—or, at least, not in the three ways explained in section 1b.

First, people in industrialized countries can easily avoid judging that they are morally obliged to act against climate change. This claim is most obviously supported by the observation that many people simply do not make this judgment. In two recent psychological studies by Ezra Markowitz (2012), for example, as many as 58 percent (study 1) and 49 percent (study 2) of subjects indicated that they did not regard climate change as an "ethical or moral issue" (2012: 485). Moreover, even some of those who did regard it as a moral issue might not have accepted that they ought to consume less, use public transportation, eat less meat, etc. They may have rather moralized climate change in the (bizarre) sense of judging *not* acting against it to be obligatory (because, say, climate change policies would dampen economic growth or would imply government regulation and thus "lead into communism"; see, e.g., Rochlin 2009; Devine 2011).

That we can easily avoid judging ourselves morally obliged to act against climate change is also suggested by various other factors. To begin with, public concern about and discussion of climate change is still only developing (Pew Research Center 2014). Few people will therefore have yet acquired a strong habit of judging that they are morally obliged to act against climate change. Recall also that judgments about global and future-affecting environmental problems are unlikely to have promoted our ancestors' biological fitness. As these judgments are not necessary byproducts of other adaptive traits either, they likely lack any innate basis. Finally, with the exception of some particularly environmentally conscious persons, the judgment that we are morally obliged to act against climate change also does not tend to be part of our identity or character (not least because this judgment lacks the affective import that is typically necessary for acquiring such an identity- or character-constituting status).

Second, for most people in industrialized countries, the judgment that one is morally obliged to act against climate change is not inconvenient to avoid, either. One reason for believing so is simply that, as suggested above, ordinary people still only rarely think and talk about their climate-related moral obligations. But even where a proclivity to engage in such thought and discourse arises, this proclivity tends to be easy to resist. For one thing, the non-moral facts implied by moral judgments about climate change action typically do not require lengthy explanation. (Instead of justifying such action in terms of intergenerational "injustice," for example, one may as well point out that, while currently living persons accrue most of the benefits associated with emission-generating behaviors, future persons will suffer most of the corresponding costs.) For another thing, refusing to judge that one is morally obliged to act against climate change will hardly get one into social trouble, either (unless one's family or friends include a disproportionately high number of environmentalists).

Finally, the judgment that one is morally obliged to act against climate change is also unlikely to considerably decrease one's tolerance towards those who deny this judgment. Earlier I argued that if coupled with antirealist metaethical interpretations, moral judgments do not go a long way in decreasing tolerance. Scientific research about how people in industrialized countries regard the metaethical status of the judgment that they ought to act against climate change is admittedly indirect, sparse, and controversial (see, e.g., Beebe 2015; Pölzler 2016b). However, there is at least some reason to believe that antirealism about this judgment is quite common. First, people generally tend to regard judgments about unintentional harms or harms suffered by socially dissimilar or unidentifiable persons as subjective or as expressions of desires (Pölzler 2016a: 100; see Goodwin & Darley 2008; Wright et al. 2013, 2014). Second, people also tend to view moral judgments as less objective if they perceive these judgments to be controversial (Goodwin & Darley 2012)—and many people (sadly) still perceive the judgment that people in industrialized countries are obliged to act against climate change as controversial (see Markowitz 2012).

3 Increasing People's Non-Moral Motivation to Act Against Climate Change

Sections 1 and 2 showed that the judgment that we are morally obliged to act against climate change does not significantly affect the lives of people in industrialized countries. In particular, neither does it immediately lead these people to actually take action, nor does it influence their thought and talk in three of the most common and significant ways. This result is clearly bad news in regards to preventing the global catastrophe that we are approaching. After all, people's relevant non-moral motives typically do not weigh in favor of action, either (APA 2010; Pölzler 2015: 209–210). Due to the spatial, temporal, and social distance of the victims of climate change, for example, people do not naturally develop prosocial attitudes such as friendship or solidarity towards them (Birnbacher 2009: 282). They also generally shy away from the uncomfortable changes to their ways of life that acting against climate change would entail.

Some scholars have recently suggested that the effectiveness of moral judgments about climate change may be increased beyond its current low level—say, by getting people to focus on their characters rather than the consequences of their actions (see Jamieson 2007), or by grounding these judgments in nonliberal values such as loyalty, authority, and sanctity (Markowitz & Shariff 2012). Strategies such as these may indeed contribute to easing climate change inaction. However, even if employed extensively, their effect is likely fairly limited. Judgments about one's moral obligations regarding climate change tend to lack effectiveness mainly because they do not arise from moral intuitions (see sections 1 and 2); and whether humans intuitively register something as a moral problem is to some extent beyond our conscious control. For one thing, many moral intuitions are adaptations to past environments, and thus often have some innate basis.[12] For another thing, where innate intuitions can be culturally shaped or complemented, this plasticity is largely confined to certain critical periods in childhood and adolescence (see, e.g., Haidt 2001: 827–828; Hauser 2006).[13]

To my mind, it is more effective to tackle climate change inaction by increasing people's non-moral motivation to take action. In this final section I will accordingly present four promising strategies of this kind: (1) educating people about climate change, (2) not linking climate change to negative emotions, (3) linking climate change to positive emotions, and (4) communicating climate change in simple and concrete ways. I particularly recommend strategies 3 and 4. This is because, given these strategies' aim of rendering climate change an affective issue, they may not only increase people's non-moral motivation to take action, but may also have the side effect of increasing moral motivation (within the limits pointed out above).

a) Educate People About Climate Change

Just as in the case of morality, the most important explanation for why so many people lack non-moral motivation to act against climate change concerns their affective mental states (see sections 3b, 3c, and 3d). But there are also several cognitive barriers to action. A significant proportion of people still deny that climate change is caused by anthropogenic greenhouse gas emissions, or that it is even real (Pew Research Center 2014). Ignorance about the specific processes that cause or constitute climate change (action) is widespread, too. For example, some people mistakenly confuse weather with climate, believe that reductions in the emissions of CO_2 would almost immediately cause global temperature decreases, or are unable to assess the climate-related effects of their own actions (e.g., Sterman & Sweeney 2002; Reynolds, Bostrom, Read, & Morgan 2010). Finally, many people also tend to exaggerate the uncertainty of scientific hypotheses about climate change, which tends to promote both self-oriented behavior and wishful thinking (APA 2010: 65; Markowitz & Shariff 2012: 244). The most obvious antidote to all of these cognitive barriers to climate change action is *education*. States, organizations, and individuals need to inform the public about the scientific consensus about climate change (see IPCC 2014)—and, as the following sub-sections will show, they need to do so in particular ways (avoiding negative but promoting positive emotions, and keeping things simple and concrete).

b) Do Not Link Climate Change to Negative Emotions

People's non-moral motivation significantly depends on their emotions. So far messages about climate change have mostly tended to evoke negative emotions such as guilt, shame, or fear. (Think about phrases such as "Time is running out" or "Humans are ruining the planet.") It is doubtful whether these emotions are motivationally effective. Humans generally attempt to avoid negative emotions, in particular emotions which imply that they are bad persons or have done something wrong. To sustain a positive self-conception, their guilt, shame, and fear have accordingly led people to doubt the significance and certainty of climate change, downplay their own causal responsibility for it, and judge that they cannot significantly contribute to alleviating the problem anyway (see Stoll-Kleemann, O'Riordan, & Jaeger 2001; Markowitz & Shariff 2012: 244–245). An analogous "guilty bias" has been identified on a societal level as well. According to Keri Norgaard (2009: 26–33, 2011), Western societies try to suppress negative emotions in relation to climate change by engaging in what she calls "implicatory denial." People are often well aware of the reality of the problem, of their contributions, and of their moral obligations. However, their societies are governed by norms of conversation and politeness which forbid them from addressing climate change in public, and by emotional norms (like the norms of remaining in control, or being tough) which make them reluctant to even think about the issue.

c) Link Climate Change to Positive Emotions

People are much more likely to develop non-moral motivation for taking action when climate change is linked to positive, rather than negative, emotions. Some researchers have suggested that such motivation may be increased by raising hopes about keeping climate change under control, by evoking pride for individual or collective efforts which have already been taken, or by showing people the gratitude of beneficiaries of their climate-friendly actions (Norgaard 2009: 46; Markowitz & Shariff 2012: 245). Another powerful emotion that may be employed in promoting climate change action is love. As a first step, people may be encouraged and taught to extend their love for partners, children, friends, etc. to people in developing countries and/or in the (distant) future. In the end it may even be made to encompass non-human nature. While it is psychologically difficult to develop such a universal love for nature, several strategies may facilitate this development. For example, one might try to appreciate nature's beauty; to understand how humans depend on it and the different elements of ecosystems are connected to each other; and to cultivate awareness for the fact that non-human species evolved through the very same processes of mutation, genetic drift, and natural selection that brought forth *Homo sapiens* (see, e.g., Seamon 1984; Leopold 1986; Briggs 2009).

d) Communicate Climate Change (Action) in Simple and Concrete Ways

Climate change's affective non-salience obstructs people's non-moral as well as their moral motivation. In section 2a, we learned that this non-salience is partly due to the problem's complexity and abstractness. My final suggestion for increasing people's motivation to take action, therefore, is to frame climate change in simpler and more concrete ways. For example, one might tell the stories of hypothesized future victims of climate change or present pictures of these victims, so that they no longer remain anonymous and easy to ignore;[14] one might give individuals more specific instructions as to how they can mitigate or adapt to climate change (e.g., "Cut the standby power of your TV set!" instead of "Save energy!"); one might explain the precise effects of these particular measures (e.g., "By cutting standby power, your household can reduce carbon dioxide emissions by 500 pounds a year, and can save up to $1,000"); and one might draw attention to the effects that increasing greenhouse gas concentrations have already had and will have on people's immediate environment (see Markowitz & Shariff 2012: 246; Van der Linden et al. 2015: 759–760). An advanced model of how to motivate specifically intergenerational consideration, exhibiting these virtues of simplicity and concreteness and also incorporating our above lessons about positive emotions, is represented by John Passmore's idea of a "chain of love" (1980). In the context of climate change, this idea implies that climate change action should be framed as an act of caring for our own children and grandchildren. Given people's particularly close relationship to these individuals, seeing climate change action in this way may raise their emotional engagement, and hence their motivation to take action.

4 Conclusion

This chapter has addressed the question of whether moral error theorists have prudential reasons for making moral judgments. It did so in an unusual way. Instead of considering the usefulness of all of our moral judgments taken together, the chapter investigated the effects only of one particular such judgment; namely, the judgment that individuals in industrialized countries are morally obliged to act against climate change. In the face of the great number and variety of moral judgments, in-depth case studies such as this seem to be our best bet for advancing the abolitionism/conservationism/fictionalism debate.[15] I thus hope for many similar studies to come, providing us with so much data that one day we can reliably assess the usefulness of the practice of making moral judgments in general.

Abolitionists, conservationists, and fictionalists sometimes create the impression that any moral judgment is either harmful or beneficial. The main finding of my chapter is that, at least for the judgment that people in industrialized countries are morally obliged to act against climate change, this assumption is false. Whether a person makes this judgment or not does not tend to have significant effects on his/her life. My arguments also provide reason to believe that this diagnosis generalizes. After all, moral judgments about copyright infringement, passive euthanasia, and various other actions share at least some of the features that we found render such judgments ineffective. So might it be that morality in the end makes no difference to our lives at all (as argued, for example, by Zimmerman 1962)? And, hence, might it simply not matter for moral error theorists whether they make moral judgments?

This conclusion would clearly overshoot the mark. Many moral judgments lack the above effectiveness-decreasing features, and accordingly do affect people's actions, thoughts, and talk. The influence of these judgments may even be more far-reaching than is commonly acknowledged. Recent empirical studies suggest, for example, that people's moral evaluations can influence their ascriptions of intentionality, causality, and various other non-moral properties (see Knobe 2003, 2006; Knobe & Fraser 2008)—they influence our whole way of seeing the world. Like so many other features of moral judgments, their effectiveness thus rather seems to vary. While some of these judgments have a big influence on our lives, others do not matter much or at all. But, still, this is a result that abolitionists, conservationists, and fictionalists should keep in mind when they set out to assess whether morality is harmful or beneficial.

Notes

1 Most error theorists have restricted the above claim to "simple," "atomic," or "positive" moral judgments (but see, e.g., Loeb 2007).
2 Some metaethicists have recently rejected conservationism and/or fictionalism on grounds of their *not* being logically or psychologically coherent (e.g., Joyce 2001: 178–179; Garner 2007: 512; Suikkanen 2013: 171 Lutz 2014: 354–355; Olson 2014: 187–188).
3 Needless to say, abolitionism does not logically entail that the above moral judgment is harmful, nor do conservationism/fictionalism entail that the judgment is beneficial. All three positions are concerned with the usefulness of moral judgments in general. They thus allow that the particular moral judgment that people in industrialized countries are obliged to act against climate change does not fit their analysis.
4 Sections 1a and 2a of this chapter elaborate findings reported in Pölzler (2015).
5 Conservationists and fictionalists operate under the assumption that morality typically promotes our (egoistic or altruistic) interests. Accordingly, they have often characterized our moral judgments as a "bulwark against weakness of will" (Joyce 2006: 208); a device for motivating ourselves to achieve what we want to achieve.
6 If error theorists are right that moral judgments are constituted by beliefs, then these judgments cannot be intrinsically motivating in the sense that they are necessarily *constituted* by motivating mental states. Beliefs, after all, are not motivating mental states. This may lead one to regard error theory as logically incompatible with motivational internalism. However, motivational internalism is most commonly understood in a non-constitutional sense (Tresan 2006; see also Björklund, Björnsson, Eriksson, Ragnar, & Strandberg 2012: 129–130). In order for it to come out true, moral judgments must only be necessarily *accompanied* by motivating mental states. And moral judgments *qua* beliefs can, of course, be necessarily accompanied by such states; for example, they can be necessarily caused by them. Conversely, as demonstrated by Joyce (2007: 74–75), error theory (even fictionalist error theory) is, of course, logically compatible with motivational externalism as well.
7 Motivational internalists typically acknowledge that under certain rare conditions— such as apathy, depression, or emotional exhaustion—moral judgments do not entail corresponding motivation at all (see Smith 1994: 120–121).
8 For the sake of brevity, I will henceforth refer to these morally quick, automatic, and effortless affective reactions either as "affective reactions" or as "moral intuitions."
9 Of course, this kind of effect presupposes that abolitionists are a minority. But we can safely assume that currently this condition is fulfilled. Apart maybe from psychopaths,

who do so unintentionally, only few people refrain from judging at least some actions morally right, wrong, good, bad, etc.

10 This non-affectiveness does not only lead to the judgment being ineffective; it also leads to many persons not making this judgment in the first place, i.e., failing to see climate change as a moral problem.

11 This passage is taken from Jamieson (2010: 438).

12 Of course, the relationship between being an adaptation and being innate (in the sense of developing irrespectively of environmental input) is, in fact, less straightforward than the above claim suggests. Some adaptations do require environmental input to become manifest. Calluses, for example, evolved because they protect deeper layers of the skin. They are thus adaptations. Nevertheless, they only develop in the face of friction (see Schmitt & Pilcher 2004: 644).

13 Compare how humans are badly equipped to acquire new languages after certain critical periods in childhood.

14 Of course, one must be wary of evoking too much guilt in presenting the victims of climate change in the above ways (see the second strategy).

15 That is, of course, apart from examinations of the logical and psychological coherence of these recommendations.

References

American Psychological Association (APA). 2010. *Psychology and global climate change: Addressing a multi-faceted phenomenon and set of challenges.* Available at www.apa.org/science/about/publications/climate-change-booklet.pdf

Beebe, J. 2015. "The empirical study of folk metaethics." *Etyka* 15: 11–28.

Birnbacher, D. 2009. "What motivates us to care for the (distant) future?" In A. Gosseries & L. Meyer (eds.), *Intergenerational Justice.* Oxford: Oxford University Press. 273–300.

Björklund, F., Björnsson, G., Eriksson, J., Ragnar, F., & Strandberg, C. 2012. "Recent work on motivational internalism." *Analysis* 72: 124–137.

Blackburn, S. 2000. *Ruling Passions: A Theory of Practical Reasoning.* Oxford: Oxford University Press.

Briggs, R. 2009. "The greening of heart and mind: A love story." *Environmental Ethics* 31: 155–168.

Burgess, J. 2007. "Against ethics." *Ethical Theory and Moral Practice* 10: 427–439.

Cushman, F. 2008. "Crime and punishment: Distinguishing the roles of causal and intentional analyses in moral judgment." *Cognition* 108: 353–380.

Devine, M. 2011. "Green agenda has parallels with excesses of communism." *Herald Sun,* July 28. Available at www.heraldsun.com.au/opinion/green-agenda-has-parallels-with-excesses-of-communism/story-e6frfhqf-1226103023674

Gardiner, S. 2011. *A Perfect Moral Storm: The Ethical Tragedy of Climate Change.* Oxford: Oxford University Press.

Garner, R. 1994. *Beyond Morality.* Philadelphia: Temple University Press.

Garner, R. 2007. "Abolishing morality." *Ethical Theory and Moral Practice* 10: 499–513.

Gibbard, A. 2003. *Thinking How to Live.* Cambridge, MA: Harvard University Press.

Gilbert, D. 2006. "If only gay sex caused global warming." *Los Angeles Times* 2 July 2006. Available at http://articles.latimes.com/2006/jul/02/opinion/op-gilbert2

Goodwin, G. & Darley, J. 2008. "The psychology of meta-ethics: Exploring objectivism." *Cognition* 106: 1339–1366.

Goodwin, G. & Darley, J. 2012. "Why are some moral beliefs seen as more objective than others?" *Journal of Experimental Social Psychology* 48: 250–256.

Greene, J., Nystrom, L., Engell, A., Darley, J., & Cohen, J. 2004. "The neural bases of cognitive conflict and control in moral judgment." *Neuron* 44: 389–400.

Greene, J., Sommerville, B., Nystrom, L., Darley, J., & Cohen, J. 2001. "An fMRI investigation of emotional engagement in moral judgment." *Science* 293: 2105–2108.

Guglielmo, S., Monroe, A., & Malle, B. 2009. "At the heart of morality lies folk psychology." *Inquiry* 52: 449–466.

Haidt, J. 2001. "The emotional dog and its rational tail: A social intuitionist approach to moral judgment." *Psychological Review* 108: 814–834.

Haidt, J. 2012. *The Righteous Mind: Why Good People Are Divided by Politics and Religion.* New York: Pantheon.

Haidt, J. & Kesebir, S. 2010. "Morality." In S. Fiske, D. Gilbert, & L. Gardner (eds.), *Handbook of Social Psychology.* Hobeken, NJ: Wiley. 797–832.

Haidt, J., Rosenberg, E., & Hom, H. 2003. "Differentiating diversities: Moral diversity is not like other kinds." *Journal of Applied Social Psychology* 33: 1–36.

Hare, R. 1952. *The Language of Morals.* Oxford: Oxford University Press.

Hauser, M. 2006. *Moral Minds. How Nature Designed Our Universal Sense of Right and Wrong.* New York: HarperCollins.

Hinckfuss, I. 1987. *The Moral Society: Its Structure and Effects.* Discussion Papers in Environmental Philosophy 16. Canberra: Philosophy Program (RSSS), Australian National University.

Ingram, S. 2015. "After moral error theory, after moral realism." *Southern Journal of Philosophy* 53: 227–248.

Intergovernmental Panel on Climate Change (IPCC). 2014. "Summary for policymakers." In *Climate Change 2014: Synthesis Report. Contribution of Working Groups I, II and III to the Fifth Assessment Report of the Intergovernmental Panel on Climate Change.* Geneva: IPCC.

Jamieson, D. 1992. "Ethics, public policy and global warming." *Science, Technology, & Human Values* 17: 139–153.

Jamieson, D. 2007. "When utilitarians should be virtue theorists." *Utilitas* 19: 160–183.

Jamieson, D. 2010. "Climate change, responsibility, and justice." *Science and Engineering Ethics* 16: 431–445.

Joyce, R. 2001. *The Myth of Morality.* Cambridge: Cambridge University Press.

Joyce, R. 2005. "Moral fictionalism." In M. Kalderon (ed.), *Fictionalism in Metaphysics.* Oxford: Oxford University Press. 287–313.

Joyce, R. 2006. *The Evolution of Morality.* Cambridge, MA: MIT Press.

Joyce, R. 2007. "Morality, schmorality." In P. Bloomfield (ed.), *Morality and Self-Interest.* Oxford: Oxford University Press. 51–75.

Joyce, R. 2013. "Error theory." In H. LaFollette (ed.), *International Encyclopedia of Ethics.* Oxford: Wiley-Blackwell. 123–147.

Joyce, R. 2015. "Moral anti-realism." In E. Zalta (ed.), *The Stanford Encyclopedia of Philosophy.* Available at https://plato.stanford.edu/archives/win2016/entries/moral-anti-realism

Knobe, J. 2003. "Intentional action and side effects in ordinary language." *Analysis* 63: 190–194.

Knobe, J. 2006. "The concept of intentional action: A case study in the uses of folk psychology." *Philosophical Studies* 130: 203–231.

Knobe, J. & Fraser, B. 2008. "Causal judgment and moral judgment: Two experiments." In W. Sinnott-Armstrong (ed.), *Moral Psychology. The Cognitive Science of Morality: Intuition and Diversity.* Cambridge, MA: MIT Press. 441–447.

Leopold, A. 1986. *A Sand County Almanac.* New York: Ballantine.

Lerner, J., Li, Y., Valdesolo, P., & Kassam, K. 2015. "Emotion and decision making." *Annual Review of Psychology* 66: 799–823.

Lillehammer, H. 2004. "Moral error theory." *Proceedings of the Aristotelian Society* 104: 95–111.

Loeb, D. 2007. "Moral statements for error theorists." In *PEA Soup—A blog dedicated to philosophy, ethics, and academia.* Available at http://peasoup.typepad.com/peasoup/2007/09/moral-statement.html

Lutz, M. 2014. "The 'now what' problem for error theory." *Philosophical Studies* 171: 351–371.

Lycan, W. 1986. "Moral facts and moral knowledge." *Southern Journal of Philosophy* 24 (special issue): 79–94.

McDowell, J. 1978. "Are moral requirements hypothetical imperatives?" *Proceedings of the Aristotelian Society* 52: 13–29.

Mackie, J. L. 1977. *Ethics: Inventing Right and Wrong.* London: Penguin.

Maltais, A. 2013. "Radically non-ideal climate politics and the obligation to at least vote green." *Environmental Values* 22: 589–608.

Markowitz, E. 2012. "Is climate change an ethical issue? Examining young adults' beliefs about climate and morality." *Climatic Change* 114: 479–495.

Markowitz, E. & Shariff, A. 2012. "Climate change and moral judgment." *Nature Climate Change* 2: 243–247.

Marks, J. 2013. *Ethics Without Morals.* New York: Routledge.

Nolan, D., Restall, G., & West, C. 2005. "Moral fictionalism versus the rest." *Australasian Journal of Philosophy* 83: 307–330.

Norgaard, K. 2009. "Cognitive and behavioral challenges in responding to climate change." *World Bank Policy Research Working Paper No. 4940.* Washington, DC: World Bank.

Norgaard, K. 2011. *Living in Denial: Climate Change, Emotions and Everyday Life.* Cambridge, MA: MIT Press.

Olson, J. 2014. *Moral Error Theory: History, Critique, Defence.* Oxford: Oxford University Press.

Passmore, J. 1980. "Conservation." In E. Partridge (ed.), *Responsibilities to Future Generations.* Buffalo, NY: Prometheus Books. 45–59.

Peeters, W., De Smet, A., Diependaele, L. & Sterckx, S. 2015. *Climate Change and Individual Responsibility: Agency, Moral Disengagement and the Motivational Gap.* Basingstoke: Palgrave Macmillan.

Pew Research Center. 2014. "Polls show most Americans believe in climate change, but give it low priority." Available at www.pewresearch.org/fact-tank/2014/09/23/most-americans-believe-in-climate-change-but-give-it-low-priority

Pigden, C. 2007. "Nihilism, Nietzsche, and the doppelganger problem." *Ethical Theory and Moral Practice* 10: 441–456.

Pölzler, T. 2015. "Climate change inaction and moral nihilism." *Ethics, Policy & Environment* 18: 202–214.

Pölzler, T. 2016a. "Further problems with projectivism." *South African Journal of Philosophy* 35: 92–102.

Pölzler, T. 2016b. "Revisiting folk moral realism." *Review of Philosophy and Psychology* 8: 455–476.

Reynolds T., Bostrom, A., Read, D. & Morgan, G. 2010. "Now what do people know about global climate change? Survey studies of educated laypeople." *Risk Analysis* 30: 1520–1538.

Rochlin, D. 2009. "Is climate change a communist plot? Britain's new Joseph McCarthy." *Care2* 1 November 2009. Available at www.care2.com/causes/is-climate-change-a-communist-plot.html

Ruse, M. 1998. *Taking Darwin Seriously. A Naturalistic Approach to Philosophy.* New York: Prometheus Books.

Schmitt, D. & Pilcher, J. 2004. "Evaluating evidence of psychological adaptation. How do we know one when we see one?" *Psychological Science* 15: 643–649.

Schwenkenbecher, A. 2014. "Is there an obligation to reduce one's individual carbon footprint?" *Critical Review of International Social and Political Philosophy* 17: 1–21.

Seamon, D. 1984. "Emotional experience of the environment." *American Behavioral Scientist,* 27: 757–770.

Sinnott-Armstrong, W. 2005. "It's not my fault: Global warming and individual moral obligations." In W. Sinnott-Armstrong & R. Howarth (eds.), *Perspectives on Climate Change.* Amsterdam: Elsevier. 221–253.

Sinnott-Armstrong, W. & Wheatley, T. 2012. "The disunity of morality and why it matters to philosophy." *Monist* 95: 355–377.

Skitka, L., Bauman, C., & Sargis, E. 2005. "Moral conviction: Another contributor to attitude strength or something more?" *Journal of Personality and Social Psychology* 88: 895–917.

Skitka, L. & Morgan, S. 2014. "The social and political implications of moral conviction." *Advances in Political Psychology* 35 (special issue): 95–110.

Smith, M. 1994. *The Moral Problem.* Oxford: Blackwell.

Sterman, J. & Sweeney, L. 2002. "Cloudy skies: Assessing public understanding of global warming." *System Dynamics Review* 18: 207–240.

Stoll-Kleemann, S., O'Riordan, T., & Jaeger, C. 2001. "The psychology of denial concerning climate mitigation measures: Evidence from Swiss focus groups." *Global Environmental Change* 11: 107–117.

Suikkanen, J. 2013. "Moral error theory and the belief problem." In R. Shafer-Landau (ed.), *Oxford Studies in Metaethics, Vol. 8.* Oxford: Oxford University Press. 168–194.

Tajfel, H., Billig, M., Bundy, R., & Flament, C. 1971. "Social categorization and inter-group behaviour." *European Journal of Social Psychology* 1: 149–178.

Tresan, J. 2006. "De dicto internalist cognitivism." *Noûs* 40: 143–165.

Van der Linden, S., Maibach, E., & Leiserowitz, A. 2015. "Improving public engagement with climate change: Five 'best practice' insights from psychological science." *Perspectives on Psychological Science* 10: 758–763.

Weber, E. 2006. "Experience-based and description-based perceptions of long-term risk: Why global warming does not scare us (yet)." *Climatic Change* 77: 103–120.

Wright, J. 2012. "Children's and adolescents' tolerance for divergent beliefs: Exploring the cognitive and affective dimensions of moral conviction in our youth." *British Journal of Developmental Psychology* 30: 493–510.

Wright, J., Cullum, J., & Schwab, N. 2008. "The cognitive and affective dimensions of moral conviction: Implications for attitudinal and behavioral measures of interpersonal tolerance." *Personality and Social Psychology Bulletin* 34: 1461–1476.

Wright, J., Grandjean, P., & McWhite, C. 2013. "The meta-ethical grounding of our moral beliefs: Evidence for meta-ethical pluralism." *Philosophical Psychology* 26: 336–361.

Wright, J., McWhite, C. & Grandjean, P. 2014. "The cognitive mechanisms of intolerance: Do our meta-ethical commitments matter?" In J. Knobe, T. Lombrozo, & S. Nichols (eds.), *Oxford Studies in Experimental Philosophy, Vol. 1.* Oxford: Oxford University Press. 28–61.

Zangwill, N. 2015. "Motivational externalism: Formulation, methodology, rationality, and indifference." In G. Björnsson, C. Strandberg, R. Francén, J. Eriksson, & F. Björklund (eds.), *Motivational Internalism.* Oxford: Oxford University Press. 44–60.

Zimmerman, M. 1962. "The 'is-ought': An unnecessary dualism." *Mind* 71: 53–61.

INDEX